BAKERY

80 STEP-BY-STEP RECIPES
FOR BREAD AND VIENNOISERIES SCHOOL

LE CORDON BLEU®

BAKERY SCHOOL

80 STEP-BY-STEP RECIPES
FOR BREAD AND VIENNOISERIES

Recipe and lifestyle photographs Delphine Constantini

Step-by-step photographs Juliette Turrini

Recipe styling Mélanie Martin

GRUB STREET • LONDON

FOREWORD

Le Cordon Bleu's *Bakery School* offers you a new culinary adventure. In the same way that our students are taught, you will find different illustrated chapters to help you master the various skills required by a professional baker, such as handling the fermentation and baking of products, making a range of modern viennoiseries, and learning new professional techniques from here and elsewhere. From the traditional baguette to the roll, through regional and international creations, you will discover a world of new flavours and textures.

Le Cordon Bleu is the world's leading network of culinary arts and hospitality management institutes. With more than 125 years of experience in education, the institute offers a wide range of training courses, from introductory courses to certificates and diplomas, including university level bachelor's and master's degrees in restaurant, hotel management and tourism. Accredited in more than 20 countries, each year Le Cordon Bleu trains nearly 20,000 students from over 100 nationalities in cuisine, pastry and bread-making as well as in wine and hospitality management.

Le Cordon Bleu, with its institutes and university, has developed quality curricula to best support its students in their career choices. Le Cordon Bleu students thrive in a variety of professions such as journalists, food critics, sommeliers, wine agents, writers, food photographers, restaurant managers, nutritionists, chefs and/or entrepreneurs.

The success achieved by many of our graduates attests to the quality of our teaching, from Julia Child to Yotam Ottolenghi. Many of our alumni have been honoured with prestigious titles and awards, such as Garima Arora, Clara Puig and Cristobal Muñoz being awarded a Michelin star, and Luciana Berry and Jessica Wang being grand prize winners of Top Chef and MasterChef in 2020. Le Cordon Bleu is proud to see the professional recognition of its alumni around the world.

Le Cordon Bleu, which has always remained faithful to its philosophy of excellence, offers an exceptional educational environment in the international capitals of gastronomy. Taught by the world's leading chefs and other industry experts, Le Cordon Bleu academic staff are tenured and have worked in some of the world's finest establishments. Le Cordon Bleu programmes are recognised around the world for their high quality.

Educational innovation is part of the institute's DNA. Over the years, Le Cordon Bleu has kept abreast of changes in the world of culinary arts and hospitality, and these observations have led to new programmes to better guide its students towards a successful career. Responding to the strong interest in nutrition, well-being, vegetarian cuisine, food science, and social and environmental responsibility, the institute offers new training courses that are adapted to the changes that constantly affect the world of gastronomy.

Being an agent of change is nothing new for Le Cordon Bleu. Journalist Marthe Distel founded Le Cordon Bleu in 1895 with the pioneering vision of providing culinary training for all. Open to the non-professional public, Le Cordon Bleu offered access to the techniques used by the great masters of French cuisine with great success. Women and an international audience were welcomed, with the first Russian student being enrolled in 1897 and the first Japanese student in 1905. In 1914, Le Cordon Bleu had four schools in Paris and had succeeded in its commitment to innovation.

Today, Le Cordon Bleu's mission is to promote gastronomy. In its teaching, it instils international standards as well as respect for local tastes and customs, and puts French culinary techniques at the service of world cuisines. Among the programmes offered at the institute – some at the request of the Ministries of Education from different countries – are Peruvian, Brazilian, Mexican, Spanish, Japanese and Thai cuisines. Le Cordon Bleu also participates in numerous events celebrating culture, expertise, flavours and ingredients from around the world, working with embassies, local governments and several organisations, as well as at international trade shows and competitions.

Le Cordon Bleu regularly publishes books, many of which have received international acclaim, and some have become benchmarks in culinary education. Over 14 million books have been sold worldwide. Encouraging food lovers of all levels to get started, we are happy to accompany our readers in the discovery of new techniques towards the creation and flavour of good food.

I hope that *Bakery School* will make you love bread in all its forms and in all the stages of its creation. Making bread is an invitation to reconnect with your senses. It's the magic of fermentation, smelling the delicious aromas from loaves in the oven, touching a unique texture; it's hearing the bread crack when it's broken, but it's also the exceptional taste of warm bread. Enjoy your discoveries!

Amitiés gourmandes,

ANDRÉ COINTREAU

President of Le Cordon Bleu International

CONTENTS

Introduction 13

Le Cordon Bleu key dates 14

Le Cordon Bleu institutes throughout the world 19

FROM KNEADING TO THE OVEN 23

Bread baking: a profession, a passion,
   an openness to others 24

The ingredients for bread 27

Pre-fermentation methods 31

Fermentation 37

The basic steps of making bread 39

Imperfections in the dough 52

The equipment 54

TRADITIONAL BREADS 57

White baguette without pre-fermentation 60

Baguette using fermented dough 62

Baguette using poolish 64

'French tradition' baguette using stiff leaven 66

'French tradition' baguette (cold bulk fermentation)
   without pre-fermentation 68

'French tradition' baguette (cold bulk fermentation)
   using liquid leaven 70

Milk bread baguette 74

Milk bread baguette with white chocolate 74

T110 Stoneground bread using stiff leaven 76

Country-style bread (cold bulk fermentation) using liquid leaven 78

Nutritional bread with mixed grains 80

Whole wheat bread using stiff leaven 82

Buckwheat loaf 84

Spelt bread using liquid leaven 88

Festive rolls 90

Party bread 94

AROMATIC BREADS   98

Cider bread with apples 100

Provençal laminated bread 102

Pulse and grain bread 104

Special bread for foie gras 108

Harlequin bread 110

Short rye loaves with raisins 114

Rye bread with pink pralines 114

Beaujolais bread with Rosette de Lyon sausage 116

Gluten-free bread with grains 118

Spinach-goat's cheese bars with dried apricots, pumpkin seeds and rosemary 122

Special buffet milk bread rolls 124

REGIONAL BREADS   130

Rye loaf 132

Traditional Normandy bread 136

Lodève bread 138

Sübrot bread 140

Fougasse with olives 146

Beaucaire bread 148

Hand of Nice 152

INTERNATIONAL BREADS   157

Focaccia 158

Ciabatta 160

Ekmek..162

Pitta..164

Batbout..166

Steamed bao buns...............................168

Challah..170

Vollkornbrot.......................................174

Borodinsky bread................................176

Corn bread (broa)...............................178

SNACKS 181

Bagel with salmon and seaweed butter.....................182

Croque-monsieur with ham, buckwheat butter
and Mornay sauce.......................184

Savoury tartlets with bacon and Béchamel
sauce..184

Neapolitan pizza..................................186

Potato tourte......................................188

Pain perdu quiche Lorraine...................190

Vegetarian toast with red cabbage, carrot,
cauliflower and currants...................192

Smoked duck magret sandwich with goat's cream
cheese, pear and honey....................194

Vegetarian open sandwich with avocado,
horseradish, celery and Granny Smith apple........196

Cocktail brioche..................................198

Spent grain muffins.............................200

Orange muffins...................................200

VIENNOISERIES 203

Brioche dough.....................................204

Croissant dough..................................206

Puff pastry...212

Nanterre brioche.................................214

Parisian brioche..................................216

Bicolour folded brioche........................218

Brioche from Vendée............................222

Milk bread rolls..................................226

Raspberry Danish 226

Saint-Genix brioche 228

Kouglof 230

Babka 232

Stollen 236

Panettone 238

Caramelised pear tart with candied pecans 240

Bressane sugar and cream tart 242

Pompe aux grattons 244

Pastis landais 246

Three Kings' brioche 248

Normandy surprise 250

Raspberry choux buns 254

Choco-coco 258

Croissant 262

Pain au chocolat 266

Pain au gianduja with hazelnuts 270

Pain aux raisins 274

Rolled praline-pecan nut buns 274

Kouign-amann 276

Crisp pineapple 278

Vanilla flan 282

Chocolate dome with a caramel centre 284

Raspberry-lemon flower 288

Plaited wreath with mango and passion fruit 292

Apple Tatin baker's style 296

Almond-hazelnut mini cakes 298

Lime-meringue mini cakes 298

Three Kings' cake with frangipane 300

French apple turnover (chausson aux pommes) 304

Sacristain 308

Glossary 312

Alphabetical index of recipes 316

Acknowledgements 318

INTRODUCTION

Le Cordon Bleu is proud to present *Bakery School*, a reference book that combines Le Cordon Bleu's culinary and pedagogical expertise with the quality of Éditions Larousse publications.

In this book you will find the best of classic, modern and international bakery, including viennoiseries and some snack treats. Le Cordon Bleu Chefs from around the world present their secrets in more than 80 illustrated recipes, from the simplest to the most advanced.

From traditional breads and viennoiseries (baguette, a rye loaf from Auvergne, ciabatta, steamed bao buns, croissant, brioche, pitta) to more elaborate specialities (gluten-free bread, plaited wreath, Normandy surprise, Provençal laminated bread), you will find recipes worthy of a Le Cordon Bleu Chef that you can reproduce at home, thanks to Le Cordon Bleu's renowned teaching methods. To make the recipes easier to understand and ensure success, Le Cordon Bleu has provided basic baking techniques with illustrated step-by-step instructions.

The Chefs at Le Cordon Bleu are committed to developing exclusive recipes, as well as to providing tips on techniques and ingredients. You'll also discover ingenious ideas to help reduce waste in the kitchen.

After *Chocolate Bible* and *Pastry School*, this new publication illustrates Le Cordon Bleu's mission: to impart skills and showcase contemporary models of gastronomy, both in France and around the world.

A true bible for amateurs wishing to create original or more traditional recipes, this book is an invitation to explore the world of French and international baking and viennoiserie making, as taught at Le Cordon Bleu, and to take on new culinary challenges.

This book is your guide, all you have to do is get started.

Chef Olivier Boudot

TECHNICAL DIRECTOR – BOULANGERIE

Le Cordon Bleu
key dates

1895   A French journalist, Marthe Distel, publishes a culinary magazine in Paris called *La Cuisinière Cordon Bleu*. In October of this year, subscribers are invited to the first Le Cordon Bleu cooking lessons.

1897   Le Cordon Bleu Paris welcomes its first Russian student.

1905   Le Cordon Bleu Paris trains its first Japanese student.

1914   Le Cordon Bleu has four schools in Paris.

1927   The 16 November edition of *The Daily Mail* newspaper reports on a visit to Le Cordon Bleu Paris school: 'It is not unusual for as many as eight different nationalities to be represented in the classes.'

1933   Rosemary Hume and Dione Lucas, who both trained at Le Cordon Bleu Paris under Chef Henri-Paul Pellaprat, opens L'École du Petit Cordon Bleu school and Au Petit Cordon Bleu restaurant in London.

1942   Dione Lucas opens a Le Cordon Bleu school and restaurant in New York. She also writes the best-selling *The Cordon Bleu Cook Book* and becomes the first woman to host a television cooking show in the United States.

1948   Le Cordon Bleu is accredited by the Pentagon for the professional training of young American soldiers after their tour of duty in Europe. As a former member of the Office of Strategic Services (OSS) in the United States, Julia Child qualifies and enrols at Le Cordon Bleu Paris.

1953   Le Cordon Bleu London creates the dish for Coronation Chicken, which was served to foreign dignitaries attending the coronation banquet held for Queen Elizabeth II.

1954   The success of Billy Wilder's film *Sabrina*, starring Audrey Hepburn in the title role, adds to the growing fame of Le Cordon Bleu.

1984   The Cointreau family, descendants of the founding families of the Rémy Martin and Cointreau, take over the presidency of Le Cordon Bleu Paris, succeeding Elizabeth Brassart, who had been the director since 1945.

1988   Le Cordon Bleu Paris moves from the rue du Champ de Mars, near the Eiffel Tower, to rue Léon Delhomme in the 15th district. The school is opened by Minister Édouard Balladur.
• Le Cordon Bleu Ottawa welcomes its first students.

1991   Le Cordon Bleu Japan opens its doors in Tokyo, then in Kobe. The schools are known as 'Little France in Japan'.

1995 Le Cordon Bleu celebrates its 100th anniversary.
• For the first time the authorities of the Shanghai District in China send chefs abroad to train at Le Cordon Bleu Paris.

1996 Le Cordon Bleu begins operations in Sydney, Australia, at the request of the New South Wales government, and provides chef training in preparation for the 2000 Sydney Olympic Games. Bachelor's and master's degrees and university research are developed in Adelaide in the fields of Hospitality and Restaurant Management, Culinary Arts and Wine.

1998 Le Cordon Bleu signs an exclusive agreement with Career Education Corporation (CEC) to bring its teaching expertise to the United States and to offer Associate Degrees with a unique curriculum in Culinary Arts and Hospitality Management.

2002 Le Cordon Bleu Korea and Le Cordon Bleu Mexico open to welcome their first students.

2003 Le Cordon Bleu Peru begins operations. It flourishes and becomes the leading culinary institute in the country.

2006 Le Cordon Bleu Thailand opens in partnership with Dusit International.

2009 All Le Cordon Bleu schools participate in the release of the film *Julie & Julia*, with Meryl Streep playing the role of Julia Child, alumna of Le Cordon Bleu Paris.

2011 Le Cordon Bleu Madrid opens in partnership with the Francisco de Vitoria University.
• Le Cordon Bleu launches its first online Master of Gastronomic Tourism programme.
• Japan overtakes France as the country with the most Michelin three-star restaurants.

2012 Le Cordon Bleu Malaysia opens in partnership with Sunway University College.
• Le Cordon Bleu London moves to Bloomsbury.
• Le Cordon Bleu New Zealand opens in Wellington.

2013 Official opening of Le Cordon Bleu Istanbul.
• Le Cordon Bleu Thailand receives the award for Best Culinary School in Asia.
• An agreement is signed with the Ateneo de Manila University to open an institute in the Philippines.

2014   Le Cordon Bleu India opens and offers students bachelor's degrees in Hospitality and Restaurant Management.
• Le Cordon Bleu Lebanon and Le Cordon Bleu Hautes Études du Goût celebrate their 10th anniversary.

2015   Le Cordon Bleu's 120th anniversary is celebrated all over the world   .
• Le Cordon Bleu Shanghai welcomes its first students   .
• Le Cordon Bleu Taiwan opens in partnership with NKUHT and the Ming-Tai Institute.
• Le Cordon Bleu opens its doors in Santiago, Chile, in partnership with Finis Terrae University.

2016   After 30 years on rue Léon Delhomme, Le Cordon Bleu is back in the spotlight, opening new premises on the banks of the Seine in the 15th district, with 4,000 m² dedicated to the Culinary Arts and management in the wine, hotel and restaurant professions. Le Cordon Bleu Paris also launches two bachelor's degrees in partnership with the University of Paris Dauphine-PSL.

2018   Le Cordon Bleu Peru achieves university status.

2020   Le Cordon Bleu celebrates 125 years of teaching excellence.
• Le Cordon Bleu opens Signatures restaurant in Rio de Janeiro, in Brazil, and launches certified online graduate programmes.

2021   Le Cordon Bleu's new programmes focus on innovation and health, with degrees dedicated to nutrition, well-being, vegetarian cuisine and food science. Le Cordon Bleu also partners with renowned institutions to develop and offer a Bachelor of Integrated Food Sciences (in partnership with the University of Ottawa), a Master of Science in Culinary Innovation Management (in partnership with Birkbeck, University of London) and an MBA in International Hospitality and Culinary Leadership (in partnership with Université Paris Dauphine-PSL).

Le Cordon Bleu institutes
throughout the world

LE CORDON BLEU PARIS

13–15, quai André Citroën
75015 Paris, France

Phone: +33 (0)1 85 65 15 00
paris@cordonbleu.edu

LE CORDON BLEU LONDON

15 Bloomsbury Square
London WC1A 2LS
United Kingdom

Phone: +44 (0) 207 400 3900
london@cordonbleu.edu

LE CORDON BLEU MADRID

Francisco de Vitoria University
Ctra. Pozuelo-Majadahonda
Km. 1,800
Pozuelo de Alarcón, 28223 Madrid,
Spain

Phone: +34 91 715 10 46
madrid@cordonbleu.edu

LE CORDON BLEU INTERNATIONAL

Herengracht 28
Amsterdam, 1015 BL, Netherlands

Phone: +31,206,616,592
amsterdam@cordonbleu.edu

LE CORDON BLEU ISTANBUL

Özyeğin University
Çekmeköy Campus
Nişantepe Mevkii, Orman Sokak, No:13
Alemdağ, Çekmeköy 34794
Istanbul, Turkey

Phone: +90 216 564 9000
istanbul@cordonbleu.edu

LE CORDON BLEU LIBAN

Burj on Bay Hotel
Tabarja – Kfaryassine
Lebanon

Phone: +961 9 85 75 57
lebanon@cordonbleu.edu

LE CORDON BLEU JAPAN

Ritsumeikan University Biwako/
Kusatsu Campus
1 Chome-1-1 Nojihigashi
Kusatsu, Shiga 525–8577, Japan

Phone: + 81 3 5489 0141
tokyo@cordonbleu.edu

LE CORDON BLEU KOREA

Sookmyung Women's University
7th Fl., Social Education Bldg.
Cheongpa-ro 47gil 100, Yongsan-Ku
Seoul, 140–742 Korea

Phone: +82 2 719 6961
korea@cordonbleu.edu

LE CORDON BLEU OTTAWA

453 Laurier Avenue East
Ottawa, Ontario, K1N 6R4, Canada

Phone: +1 613 236 CHEF (2433)
Toll free: +1 888 289 6302
Restaurant line: +1 613 236 2499
ottawa@cordonbleu.edu

LE CORDON BLEU MEXICO

Anahuac University North Campus
Universidad Anáhuac South Campus
Universidad Anáhuac Querétaro Campus
Universidad Anáhuac Cancún Campus
Universidad Anáhuac Mérida Campus
Universidad Anáhuac Puebla Campus
Universidad Anáhuac Tampico Campus
Universidad Anáhuac Oaxaca Campus
Av. Universidad Anáhuac No. 46, Col.
Lomas Anahuac
Huixquilucan, Edo. The Mex. C.P. 52786,
Mexico

Phone: +52 55 5627 0210 ext. 7132 /
7813
mexico@cordonbleu.edu

LE CORDON BLEU PERU

Universidad Le Cordon Bleu Peru (ULCB)
Le Cordon Bleu Peru Institute
Le Cordon Bleu Cordontec
Av. Vasco Núñez de Balboa 530
Miraflores, Lima 18, Peru

Phone: +51 1 617 8300
peru@cordonbleu.edu

LE CORDON BLEU AUSTRALIA

Le Cordon Bleu Adelaide Campus
Le Cordon Bleu Sydney Campus
Le Cordon Bleu Melbourne Campus
Le Cordon Bleu Brisbane Campus
Days Road, Regency Park
South Australia 5010, Australia

Free call (Australia only): 1,800,064,802
Phone: +61 8 8346 3000
australia@cordonbleu.edu

LE CORDON BLEU NEW ZEALAND

52 Cuba Street
Wellington, 6011, New Zealand

Phone: +64 4 4729800
nz@cordonbleu.edu

LE CORDON BLEU MALAYSIA

Sunway University
No. 5, Jalan Universiti, Bandar Sunway
46150 Petaling Jaya, Selangor DE,
Malaysia

Phone: +603 5632 1188
malaysia@cordonbleu.edu

LE CORDON BLEU THAILAND

4, 4/5 Zen tower, 17th-19th floor
Central World
Ratchadamri Road, Pathumwan
Subdistrict,
10330 Pathumwan District, Bangkok
10330
Thailand

Phone: +66 2 237 8877
thailand@cordonbleu.edu

LE CORDON BLEU SHANGHAI

2F, Building 1, No. 1458 Pu Dong Nan
Road
Shanghai China 200122

Phone: +86 400 118 1895
shanghai@cordonbleu.edu

LE CORDON BLEU INDIA

G D Goenka University
Sohna Gurgaon Road
Sohna, Haryana
India

Phone: +91 880 099 20 22 / 23 / 24
lcb@gdgenka.ac.in

LE CORDON BLEU CHILE

Finis Terrae University
Avenida Pedro de Valdivia 1509
Providence
Santiago de Chile

Phone: +56 24 20 72 23
secretaria.artesculinarias@uft.cl

LE CORDON BLEU RIO DE JANEIRO

Rua da Passagem, 179, Botafogo
Rio de Janeiro, RJ, 22290-031
Brazil

Phone: +55 21 9940-02117
riodejaneiro@cordonbleu.edu

LE CORDON BLEU SÃO PAULO

Rua Natingui, 862 Primero andar
Vila Madalena, SP, São Paulo 05443-001
Brazil

Phone: +55 11 3185-2500
saopaulo@cordonbleu.edu

LE CORDON BLEU TAIWAN

NKUHT University
Ming-Tai Institute
4F, No. 200, Sec. 1, Keelung Road
Taipei 110, Taiwan

Phone: +886 2 7725-3600 / +886
975226418
taiwan-NKUHT@cordonbleu.edu

LE CORDON BLEU, INC.

85 Broad Street – 18th floor, New York, NY
10004 USA

Phone: +1 212 641 0331

www.cordonbleu.edu
e-mail: info@cordonbleu.edu

FROM KNEADING
TO THE OVEN

Bread baking:
a profession, a passion,
an openness to others

Bread is an essential part of the diet in many cultures around the world. Although it is always made of flour and water, different international gastronomies have developed their own version of bread, some with leaven and others without. Before it became a profession, baking skills were passed down from generation to generation so that the secrets and discoveries would live on. In addition, without the men and women who work with it on a daily basis, bread would not have the shapes and flavours that we know today.

As ancient as civilisation itself, the baker's trade is orientated towards others, characterised by the passing on of a science and processes, but also of a philosophy and a history. The sharing of preparation secrets, the variety of flours, the kneading techniques, the shaping of the different doughs are all part of the baker's vocation. Thanks to this transference, everyone in turn participates in the development of new techniques, leading to the creation of innovative recipes.

The baker's profession is manual and involves the sensorial. It is through the five senses of hearing, sight, smell, touch and taste that the artisan is in tune with the ingredients and maintains a fusional relationship with their creations. It is often said that bread varies depending on the baker. Indeed, the dough is a living material due to its composition and the essential stage of fermentation; it is sensitive to the one who handles it. For this reason, the same recipe will produce a different bread depending on the person who makes it, from the kneading, the handling of the dough and the choice of baking.

In a connected world where everything is fast-paced and we are constantly on the alert, making bread allows us to take a break and take the time to work with our hands. The preparation stages exclude any haste and require patience and listening to one's instinct for providing the greatest joy to the taste buds.

Moreover, there is a great pleasure in making bread yourself, or in a team! You become detached from the material world, you are in the present moment to build and give life to a product. This is where the baker's passion is born. The pleasure derived from kneading, shaping, watching the dough grow, and then, at the moment of baking, smelling the bread and watching it develop, gives the baker intense satisfaction and pride.

The baker must master a multitude of parameters in order to produce exceptional recipes from simple raw materials, because baking is a profession of experience. It is necessary to have made a large number of bread loaves to recognise the mistakes and to know how to make improvements for the best result.

With practice comes confidence. The more knowledge and techniques you acquire, the more you can give free rein to your creativity and develop new products, with new flavours, shapes and associations. You can convey your own sensitivity, know-how and talents, to pass on with pleasure the fruit of your work to those around you.

The ingredients
for bread

WHEAT FLOUR

Flour, an essential ingredient for bread-making, is the product obtained after milling wheat in several stages. Of the various wheat varieties, three main types are harvested and consumed: soft wheat, intermediate wheat and hard wheat. The flour we are particularly interested in comes from the soft wheat family, which contains a lot of starch and a soft gluten. These wheats, which are suited to a temperate climate, are sown in France during October and November and harvested in summer.

The composition of a wheat grain

Small in size (from 5 to 9 mm), a wheat grain has an ovoid shape with a bulging face and a flat face. The end of the grain is covered with fine hairs called the 'brush'. It consists of three parts: the bran, the germ and the endosperm.

• **Bran.** Called the 'pericarp', it covers the wheat grain and represents 13 to 15% of the total weight of the grain. The pericarp consists of several layers: the epicarp, the mesocarp and the endocarp. These are the layers that protect the grain and that will constitute, once the milling is done, the 'bran'.

• **Germ.** It represents 2% of the weight of the grain and is located at the end. It is removed during the milling process because it is rich in fat. Its presence would shorten the flour's shelf life.

• **Endosperm.** It represents 80 to 85% of the weight of the grain, and contains starch and gluten. It is the endosperm that, once ground, will become the flour.

Starch, which makes up most of the flour, is a complex carbohydrate. Without starch, there can be no fermentation. In a bread flour, it is found in two forms: whole starch, in a larger percentage, and broken starch, resulting from the milling process. The interest of the latter lies in its capacity, during the kneading, to absorb water and to burst. It is this that will be transformed first by the yeasts.

The wheat grain also contains proteins that form fine, flexible and resistant fibrils. During kneading, they hydrate, swell, refine and lengthen to form what is called the 'glutinous network'. This network of threads is fine and strong enough to retain the carbon dioxide (CO_2) produced by the yeast.

Flour types and qualities

Good-quality flour is essential in bread-making. Today, mills work closely with farmers to obtain flours from the best wheat crops, increasingly produced through sustainable farming. Several wheat varieties with different protein qualities are selected and milled together to produce a flour of consistent quality throughout the year.

Flours in France are classified according to their 'type'. The latter refers to the amount of ash or minerals remaining after incineration of a flour sample. Each type is assigned a number based on this rate. The lower the rate, the whiter the flour and the lower the type number. For example, type 45 (T45) flour is the finest, whitest and most refined, while type 150 (T150) flour is the least fine, most characterful and contains the most bran residues and wheat grain husks. Flour types can vary from country to country, and the correspondence between flours is not always easy to establish.

Note: the type number does not correspond to the gluten content of a flour, but to the ash or mineral content remaining in the flour. Gluten content is not measured in type, but in percentage. It is between 9 and 12% in French flours.

French wheat flours:

• **T45 flour.** Mainly used for yeast-based dough and pastry.

• **Fine-wheat flour (T45).** Strong flour, mainly used for yeast-based dough (viennoiseries).

• **T55 and T65 flours.** The most used flours, especially for baguettes and 'French tradition' baguettes.

• **T80 flour (fine stone-ground flour).** Mainly used for country-style bread and speciality breads.

• **T110 flour.** Semi-whole wheat flour, mainly used to make speciality breads.

• **T150 flour.** Whole wheat flour containing a lot of bran, especially used for whole wheat or bran breads. T150 integral flour is made up of the whole grain: bran, germ and endosperm.

In bread baking, T65 flour is the most used. The 'French tradition' flour is a T65 flour from carefully selected varieties of wheat. It is made in compliance with the standards of the 1993 decree on bread, which requires bakers to make their bread with flour guaranteed without additives, which enhances the taste and improves the quality of the bread.

In recent years, new flours from heirloom wheat are being increasingly used such as Rouge de Bordeaux, Touselles de Mayan. These flours, called 'heritage wheats', are richer in fibre, have less gluten and do not require long kneading. They have a major health advantage, as breads made with these flours are more digestible and have a lower glycaemic index.

THE OTHER FLOURS

• **Rye flour.** Low in gluten, it exists in T130 and T170.

• **Buckwheat flour.** It is gluten-free.

• **Maize flour.** It cannot be used alone for bread-making, as it does not contain gluten.

• **Barley flour.** Used mainly for the preparation of certain dishes (porridges, flat-breads, etc.).

• **Malt.** A bread-making additive often made from sprouted barley (but other cereals may be used). It can be added in very small quantities to a dough lacking in strength or to a dough made with a gluten-free flour, such as buckwheat flour.

• **Spent grain flour.** It is made from malt residues obtained after brewing beer. The residues are dried and then ground to produce a flour rich in protein, fibre and minerals. Like the flours

mentioned above, it can be added in small quantities to a bread flour.

• **Oat flour, spelt flour, rice flour, chestnut flour, chickpea flour, khorasan (kamut) wheat flour and many others.** These are used at lower levels because they lack gluten. Often, their contribution is 10 to 30% of the total flour weight to avoid any imperfections in the dough.

YEAST

There are several forms of yeast. In bread baking, the most common is fresh compressed yeast, a microscopic fungus (*Saccharomyces cerevisiae*) that is responsible for the fermentation process. Mixed with water and flour, the yeast feeds on the various sugars contained in the flour and causes a fermentation process that releases carbon dioxide (CO_2).

The different types of yeast

• **Fresh compressed yeast.** It comes in the form of a creamy white block, with a crumbly texture and a pleasant odour.

• **Dried yeast (also called freeze-dried).** If fresh yeast is not available, dried yeast is generally used in half the amount.

• **Active dried yeast.** It is sold in large granules, and like fresh yeast, it requires rehydration before use.

Yeast quantities

The amount of yeast to use in a recipe can vary depending on several factors.

• **Climate.** More yeast is used in winter than in summer. In hot and humid countries, the amount of yeast will be reduced.

• **The ingredients.** Adding fat to a dough tends to make it heavier, which makes it necessary to increase the amount of yeast.

• **The bread-making process.** A bread made quickly requires more yeast than one made over a greater length of time.

Storage

Fresh compressed yeast should be stored in the refrigerator between 4 and 6°C. Below 0°C, the cells deteriorate and their fermenting power decreases. Above 50°C, the cells are destroyed, making the yeast unusable.

It should not be left in direct contact with sugar or salt, otherwise it will be less effective.

WATER

During the bread-making process, water triggers all the chemical reactions. During the kneading process, it allows the yeast to multiply and the gluten to hydrate.

The water's quality is important. A high mineral water tightens the glutinous network and accelerates the fermentation. Water also affects the consistency of the dough: using the same amount of flour, the consistency of the dough can vary depending on the proportion of water incorporated.

Depending on the degree of hydration (see p. 30), there are three types of dough.

• **Soft dough.** It is obtained from a flour hydrated at a rate greater than 70%. First rising and fermentation of the dough is longer in order to acquire strength and body (e.g.: Lodève bread).

• **Intermediate (bâtarde) dough.** This dough has a hydration rate of 62%. It is very easy to shape (e.g.: country-style bread).

• **Firm dough.** It is a dough with a hydration rate between 45 and 60% (e.g.: white baguette without pre-fermentation).

SALT

Playing several important roles in the production of bread, salt acts on the extensibility and tenacity of the dough, and promotes uniform and constant fermentation. Salt also acts on the bread's crust and colour. Its presence makes the crust thinner, crisper and more colourful (a bread without salt is always paler).

Finally, salt improves the preservation of bread thanks to its hygroscopic properties: in dry weather, salt delays the drying of bread and the hardening of the crust, thus promoting its preservation. In humid weather, it helps the crust to soften and thus accelerates the staling process.

Sea salt can be used instead of fine salt.

OTHER INGREDIENTS

• **Fats.** They give the products a finer crumb and a softer crust and allow for a longer shelf life. Butter and oil are the most common fats.

• **Sugar.** It stimulates fermentation, as well as gives taste and colour to the product. It also contributes to preserving the product.

• **Eggs.** They give the bread a softer dough, a softer and more colourful crumb and more volume.

• **Milk or cream.** They make the dough heavier and slow down the fermentation process, making the rise more even and uniform. As a result, it is sometimes necessary to increase the amount of yeast used.

HYDRATION OF THE DOUGH

Hydration refers to the amount of water in the recipe. It is expressed as a percentage and is generally between 50 and 80% (see types of dough on p. 29); however, a dough's hydration can be much higher depending on the flour used.

The rate of hydration varies according to several factors:

• **The baking strength of the flour and its gluten content.** The amount of gluten plays an important role in the dough's hydration, since gluten has a high capacity for absorbing moisture. In fact, it absorbs three times its weight in water.

• **Flour humidity.** It should not exceed 16%.

• **Flour type.** Whole wheat flours absorb more water than white flours due to the fibre they contain.

• **The bakery's hygrometric state.** It varies according to its humidity. Soft doughs should be processed in a dry atmosphere, while firm doughs should be made in a humid climate.

BASIC TEMPERATURE

Each baker makes sure that their breads have the same properties every day of the week. For optimal fermentation, the dough must reach a final temperature (at the end of kneading) of between 23 and 25°C and, in cases of cold bulk fermentation, of between 20 and 22°C. To obtain this temperature, the only parameter that can be influenced is the temperature of the water added to the dough.

In order to reach the desired dough temperature at the end of the kneading process, the baker incorporates the concept of 'basic temperature' into the production of each recipe. Knowing it will help the baker to calculate the temperature of the 'pouring' water used in the recipe.

The basic temperature is determined by a professional baker according to the type of kneading machine used and the duration and intensity of the kneading. If the bread is kneaded manually, the basic temperature will be higher since the manual action heats the dough less than a kneading machine. In addition, low-gluten doughs such as rye also require a high basic temperature.

Calculating the pouring water temperature

There is a simple formula for calculating the temperature of the pouring water: you just need to know the basic temperature (usually indicated in the bread recipe), the ambient temperature and the temperature of the flour used.

For example, for a recipe with a basic temperature of 75, the room temperature (21°C) and the flour temperature (22°C) are first added together and then subtracted from the basic temperature.

This gives:

21 + 22 = 43

75 – 43 = 32

The temperature of the pouring water will therefore be 32°C so that, at the end of the kneading process, the temperature of the dough will be between 23 and 25°C.

Pre-fermentation *methods*

There are several types of (and names for) pre-ferments (also called starters or sponges), with particular characteristics that are useful as a leavening agent in bread-making: fermented dough, yeast-based leaven, poolish, and liquid and stiff leavens need to be refreshed every day. They are prepared in advance with fresh compressed yeast or natural 'wild' yeasts and added to the dough ingredients.

These pre-ferments have the advantage of accelerating the fermentation process and reducing the kneading and final proofing time. A bread made with a pre-ferment has many advantages: its flavour is more pronounced, it develops a more honeycomb-like open crumb, and its nutritional value and digestibility are superior to those of other breads. Finally, it has an extended shelf life.

Poolish

Poolish is made of flour, water and yeast. It is a highly hydrated, wet pre-ferment that contains as much water as flour. Fermentation using poolish has several advantages, both in terms of bread-making and taste. It increases elasticity and strength when working with the dough. It also increases fermentation tolerance during the final proofing period.

Breads made using poolish have a strong flavour, a cream-coloured crumb, a very open crumb and a crispy crust. They also have a longer shelf life.

Usage. There are two types of poolish, French and Viennese. They are distinguished by the amount of 'bassinage' water incorporated. The French poolish is made up of 50% water in relation to the total kneaded dough, which is called a 'half poolish'. For the Viennese poolish, it is elaborated with 80% water compared to the total kneaded dough. Note: for some speciality breads, the flour weight can be replaced with grains. The calculation of the amount of fresh compressed yeast can vary depending on the fermentation time.

MAKES 200 G POOLISH

DIFFICULTY ✿ ✿ ✿

___

Preparation: 3 mins (the day before)
• Chilling: 12 hrs

___

100 g water • 100 g T65 flour • 1 g fresh compressed yeast

- The day before, prepare all the ingredients **(1)**. In a bowl, whisk together the water, flour and crumbled yeast **(2)**.

- Using a rubber spatula, scrape down the sides of the bowl. Cover with cling film and refrigerate for 12 hours **(3)**.

- The next day, the poolish should have bubbles **(4)**. Take a small amount of water from the final recipe to loosen the poolish from the side of the bowl **(5)** before adding it to the final kneading of the dough **(6)**.

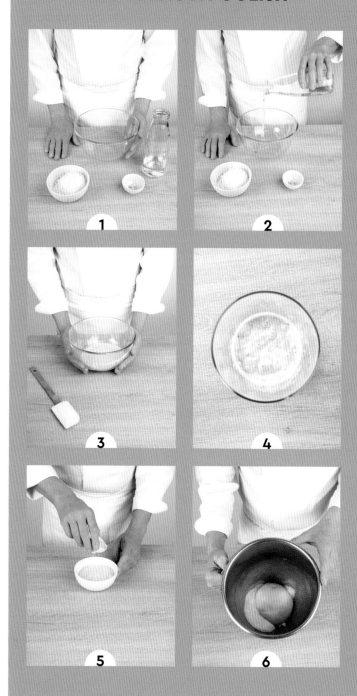

Fermented dough

Fermented dough is one of the easiest starters to prepare. It reinforces the glutinous network and makes the crust crisp and colourful. The salt it contains helps to regulate acidity and yeast multiplication, giving the bread a slightly acidic aroma and a particularly fruity taste.

Usage. Fermented dough is used in bread recipes and contains the same basic ingredients: yeast, water, flour and salt. Viennese fermented dough, which is used in viennoiserie recipes, contains milk and fat.

Quantity. The amount of fermented dough used in the final kneading is generally between 10 and 50% of the weight of the flour.

MAKES 520 G FERMENTED DOUGH

DIFFICULTY ♙

Preparation: 10 mins (the day before)
• **Chilling:** 12 hrs

3 g fresh compressed yeast • 192 g cold water • 320 g 'French tradition' flour • 5 g salt

- The day before, add the yeast to the water in the bowl of a stand mixer. Add the flour and salt. Knead for 10 minutes on a low speed.
- Remove the dough from the mixer, form it into a ball and put it into a bowl. Cover the bowl and refrigerate overnight.

MAKES 457 G VIENNESE FERMENTED DOUGH

DIFFICULTY ♙

Preparation: 8 mins (the day before)
• **Chilling:** 12 hrs

80 g water • 50 g milk • 125 g T45 flour • 125 g T55 flour • 5 g salt • 17 g fresh compressed yeast • 30 g sugar • 25 g cold dry butter (see p.313)

- The day before, put the water, milk, flours, salt, yeast, sugar and butter into the bowl of a stand mixer. Mix on a low speed for 4 minutes until the dough is smooth, then increase the speed for 4 minutes to make it elastic.
- Remove the dough from the mixer and form it into a bowl. Cover with cling film and refrigerate at least overnight.

Yeast-based leaven

A yeast-based leaven is a quick preparation based on fresh compressed yeast, flour and water, resulting in a starter of firm consistency. The amount of yeast varies according to the fermentation time and is often the only yeast used in the final recipe.

This starter gives the product tenacity, body, strength and softness. It also allows for better preservation. Its shelf life is short because of the amount of fresh compressed yeast, which can lead to overfermentation if the starter waits too long before being incorporated into the dough.

Usage. This method is used with specific flours, which are sometimes lower in gluten, especially to make viennoiseries and certain speciality breads, e.g. products rich in sugar and fat, which tend to soften the dough.

Quantity. The amount of starter used in the final kneading is usually between 5 and 40% of the flour weight.

MAKES 350 G YEAST-BASED LEAVEN

DIFFICULTY ♙

Preparation: 3 mins • **Fermentation:** 1 hr

120 g water • 200 g T65 flour • 30 g fresh compressed yeast

- In the bowl of a stand mixer, whisk together the water, flour and crumbled yeast.
- Cover with cling film and leave to ferment at room temperature for 1 hour.

Natural leaven

A natural leaven can be made without fresh compressed yeast by using natural 'wild' yeasts for fermenting a leaven base. To do this, the water obtained from macerated raisins or apples is added to a liquid leaven base (called chef). It takes several days of waiting before fermentative activity appears. Raisins and apples are the most commonly used, as their skins are a source of bacteria and additional leavening.

TO OBTAIN MACERATION WATER

DIFFICULTY ♡

Preparation: 5 mins (4–5 days in advance)

100 g raisins or organic apples, cut into pieces with the skin and seeds • Water

- Put the fruit into a bowl and cover with water. Cover with cling film and leave in a warm place for at least 4 to 5 days.

- Drain the macerated fruit and collect the water. The latter can be used to make a liquid leaven in place of apple juice, for example.

Liquid leaven

A liquid leaven is derived from the enzymatic degradation of sugars in a dough prepared over several days at relatively high temperatures. This is called lactic fermentation. The bacteria present do not produce gas in the dough.

The choice of flour is important when making a liquid leaven. It is advisable to use a stoneground or whole wheat flour, as they include part of the outer shells of the grain, which contain the bacteria essential for starting the leaven. These flours are much more nutritious for a leaven than others.

Maintenance. When making bread often, this leaven needs to be refreshed every day – in other words, they need to be fed flour and water by repeating the day 4 step (see opposite). Indeed, the natural sugars in the flour will help the wild yeasts to develop, while the water, through its humidity, will contribute to their growth. For occasional use, a liquid leaven can be stored in the refrigerator and refreshed for 2 days before use.

Storage. A liquid leaven is more likely to oxidize and, as a result, is more difficult to maintain. The leaven can be stored in the refrigerator for 3 days before use. You can store it in the freezer and resume after 3 days. It will remain active.

Quantity. Once ready to use, the liquid leaven, added to the final kneading, represents between 20 and 50% of the weight of the flour.

PREPARING A LIQUID LEAVEN

DIFFICULTY ♢ ♢ ♢

Preparation: 4 days

DAY 1: BASIC LEAVEN (STARTER)
100 g T80 fine stoneground flour • 35 g honey
• 35 g organic apple juice (or raisin or apple maceration water from natural leavening) • 50 g water at 50°C

DAY 2: LEAVEN CHEF (1ST RECIPE ADDITION)
220 g basic leaven • 220 g water at 40°C
• 220 g T80 fine stoneground flour

DAY 3: LEAVEN CHEF (2ND RECIPE ADDITION)
660 g leaven chef (1st recipe addition)
• 660 g water at 40°C • 660 g T80 fine stoneground flour

DAY 4: FINAL LEAVEN (OR 'LIQUID LEAVEN')
300 g leaven chef (2nd recipe addition)
• 1 kg water at 40°C • 1 kg T65 flour

- **Day 1.** Prepare the ingredients. In a large bowl, whisk together the flour, honey, apple juice and water. Cover and leave at 35°C for 24 hours **(1)**.

- **Day 2.** Add the water and flour to the basic leaven and whisk together. Cover and leave at 30 °C for 18 hours **(2)**.

- **Day 3.** Add the water and flour to the leaven chef from day 2, then whisk together **(3)**. Cover and leave at 28°C for 18 hours **(4)**.

- **Day 4.** Add the water and flour to the leaven chef from day 3, then whisk together. Cover and leave at 28°C for 3 hours **(5)**. The liquid leaven is ready to use **(6)**.

Stiff leaven

A stiff leaven can be made from a liquid leaven base following its 4-day preparation. It is an anaerobic medium, because the dough contains less water, which favours the development of acetic acid. A stiff leaven contains about 50% less water than a liquid leaven. During its transformation, and because of the lower temperatures, the leaven gives off acetic acid and carbon dioxide.

A stiff leaven gives the bread a more pronounced taste, revealing the natural flavour of the flour used. Its presence improves the crumb's colouring and provides a good thickness to the crust, which has a nice finish in the mouth and produces more chewiness.

Usage. It is mainly used in so-called 'character' breads such as country-style bread and is combined with semi-whole wheat flours, rye and stoneground.

Maintenance. To maintain a stiff leaven, it is best to refresh it every day. To do this, take 500 g of stiff leaven from the day before, then mix it with 1 kg of T80 fine stoneground flour and 500 g of water. It is possible to maintain smaller quantities for home use.

Storage. Stiff leaven can be stored in the refrigerator for 3 to 4 days without refreshing, or even in the freezer. In fact, don't hesitate to keep a piece of stiff leaven in the freezer. It can be used in case of a problem in maintaining the leaven.

Quantity. The amount of stiff leaven used in the final kneading is usually between 10 and 40% of the flour weight.

MAKES 1 KG STIFF LEAVEN

DIFFICULTY ✿ ✿ ✿

Preparation: 3 mins • **Fermentation:** 3 hrs

250 g liquid leaven (see p. 35) • 250 g water at 40°C
• 500 g T80 fine stoneground flour

- Put the liquid leaven, water and flour into the bowl of a stand mixer **(1) (2).** Mix for 3 minutes on low speed. Place in a bowl and cover with cling film **(3).** Leave for 3 hours at room temperature before use. If the leaven is not used after this resting time, store it in the refrigerator **(4)** where it will continue to release acetic acid.

Note: it is possible to refresh a stiff leaven with soft wheat flour instead of stoneground flour. For a rye-based stiff leaven, replace the T80 fine stoneground flour with T170 dark rye flour.

PREPARING A STIFF LEAVEN

CONSISTENCY OF LIQUID AND STIFF LEAVEN

1 Comparison between a liquid leaven (left) and a stiff leaven (right).

2 Texture of a stiff leaven.

Fermentation

Louis Pasteur once said: 'Fermentation is life without air.' Fermentation is a degradation. In order to optimise it, a support (sugars and starches) and micro-organisms (ferments) are needed to obtain the product of fermentation (ethyl alcohol, carbon dioxide/CO_2 and heat).

The different types of fermentation

The quality of a dough depends on the type of fermentation. The baker makes his choice according to his work method, the time he has available and the flavours he wants to bring to the bread.

• **Lactic fermentation (liquid leaven):** the transformation of simple sugars into lactic acid and heat gives a light milky taste to the preparations (e.g. baguette using liquid leaven).

• **Alcoholic fermentation (fresh yeast):** simple sugars are transformed into alcohol and carbon dioxide (e.g. croissant).

• **Acetic fermentation (stiff leaven):** the transformation of ethyl alcohol into acetic acid gives a slightly acidic taste to the preparations (e.g. stoneground bread).

Fermentation times during bread making

During the first fermentation, or 'rising', the physical qualities of the dough (related to the texture) develop and continue to strengthen.

During the second fermentation, or 'second and final proofing', a gaseous development occurs, giving the bread a balanced and open crumb. The room temperature (20 to 23°C) facilitates the final proofing and thus the fermentation. If the first fermentation period is long, the second (final) proofing period will be quite short.

The timing of the baking is very important. Indeed, the gas development of the dough must be at its maximum (with an increase in volume corresponding to two or three times the initial volume) without having exceeded the threshold, otherwise the dough would collapse while it is baking. In addition, fermentation will continue for a few minutes after being in contact with the heat of the oven, until the yeast cells are destroyed (when the temperature reaches 50°C).

Factors related to fermentation

• **Dough hydration.** Insufficient hydration slows down fermentation.

• **Temperature of the dough.** Fermentation accelerates as soon as the temperature of the dough increases. In general, the temperature should be between 23 and 25°C at the end of the kneading process. For a classic fermentation it should be 24°C, and for cold bulk fermentation, between 20 and 22°C.

• **The dough's acidity.** A natural phenomenon, the acidity of a bread dough occurs as soon as the first rising period. If the dough has too much acidity, it will not ferment well. This acidity is linked to the quality of the pre-ferment used. For example, if the leaven has fermented too much, the dough will be too acidic.

• **External factors.** The room temperature in the bakery will affect the fermentation of the dough: it is accelerated when hot and slowed down when cold. The ideal temperature for the bakery is between 20 and 25°C.

The basic steps of making *bread*

KNEADING

The process of kneading involves mixing a bread's ingredients in the correct order – namely flour, water, yeast and salt – in order to obtain a homogeneous and smooth dough. Do not forget to incorporate the yeast evenly so that the glutinous network can develop.

Manual kneading and mechanical kneading

Manual kneading includes the following steps.

• **Mixing:** the flour, water, yeast and salt are mixed together in a homogeneous way.

• **Cutting:** the dough is divided into pieces with a dough scraper to build up the glutinous network.

• **Stretching and folding:** the dough is stretched horizontally, then folded over on itself in a rapid movement to incorporate a maximum of air. This action is performed several times.

Mechanical kneading includes the following steps.

• **Mixing:** identical to manual mixing, at low speed to avoid dough ejections.

• **Kneading:** reproducing the steps of manual kneading (cutting and stretching).

• **Folding:** essential at the end of kneading, it enables the incorporation of air, relaxes the glutinous network and provides the dough with additional strength.

Kneading methods

There are two main methods of kneading. The method used will depend on the desired characteristics, the objective being to get the best out of the dough. For example, for a 'French tradition' baguette with a very open crumb, a slow kneading is preferable. On the other hand, for a country-style bread with a denser crumb and a more structured glutinous network, opt for an improved kneading.

• **Kneading at low speed.** It takes about 10 minutes on low speed and is used for flours that are not particularly strong, in order to obtain a less oxidised dough and a more tasty and colourful crumb. In addition, the resulting dough will be softer and require a longer fermentation to compensate for the lack of strength. The crumb will have a nice irregular open texture, the bread will take less volume when baked and the crust will be thinner.

• **Improved kneading.** It takes about 4 minutes at low speed and 5 minutes at medium speed. This is the most commonly used technique. It gives more structure to the glutinous network and gives the bread a nice volume, a slightly open and denser crumb, and a thicker crust. This technique is recommended for country-style or whole wheat breads.

AUTOLYSE

Autolyse promotes the hydration of the flour, which helps to soften the glutinous network. Thanks to it, we can increase the hydration rate of the dough (in the 'bassinage' step) since the flour will better absorb water. This promotes the development of a more open crumb.

To start the autolyse process, the flour and water are mixed and kneaded for 4 minutes at low speed, then the resulting dough is left to rest for 30 minutes to 48 hours before adding the salt and yeast or leaven.

Since the kneading time is reduced (with the flour and water having been previously mixed), less oxidation occurs, the dough is more extensible, more manageable and smoother. Being less sticky, it will be easier to work. Finally, autolyse promotes a finer and more pronounced slash.

KNEADING THE DOUGH BY HAND

- Place the flour on the work surface and make a well **(1)**. Crumble in the yeast and dilute it with the water **(2)**. Add the salt **(3)**.

- Gradually mix in the flour with your fingers, using a circular motion to incorporate it into the centre **(4)**.

- Make a homogeneous mixture with flour, water, yeast and salt (the mixing stage), then knead the dough: form a ball, flatten it and fold it on itself, then form a ball again, flatten it again and so on **(5)**.

- Once the dough is homogeneous, cut it with a dough scraper to develop the glutinous network **(6)**. Repeat this action until it becomes difficult to cut.

- By hand, push and stretch the dough at the same time, then fold it on itself in a quick movement to incorporate a maximum of air (stretching and folding). Repeat this action several times until the dough is smoother and less sticky **(7)** **(8)**.

- Once the dough is kneaded, form it into a ball **(9)**.

'BASSINAGE'

In a dough that is not sufficiently hydrated, a small quantity of liquid, generally water, is added at the end of the kneading. Originating in French bread-making, this 'bassinage' step softens the dough and relaxes the glutinous network. It is not customary to moisten all doughs, especially not doughs that lack strength such as those made with a low-gluten flour.

FIRST RISING

This is the fermentation period that occurs between the end of kneading and the division of the dough into pieces. The role of the first rise is to give strength to the dough, defined by the physical modification of the gluten. During this process, the gluten becomes more tenacious, more elastic and less extensible. The first rise is also used to develop the aromas due to the fermentation.

If the dough is soft, the first rising period will be long. Conversely, if the dough is firm, the first rising will be shorter.

FOLDING (RABATTRE)

This operation consists of stretching the dough before folding it on itself. To make a fold (rabat), stretch and fold each side towards the centre to release the gas from the dough, before turning it over so that the smooth side is on top and the folds are underneath.

Air is thus incorporated while expelling carbon dioxide (CO_2) and alcohol, resulting in a smooth dough and a restart of the fermentation.

The purpose of folding is to lengthen the gluten fibrils and to allow the glutinous network to continue to be structured. This increases the elasticity and the dough shape is more homogeneous, promoting uniform fermentation and better strength distribution.

DIVIDING THE DOUGH

At the end of the first rising and fermentation, the dough is usually divided into pieces of equal weight.

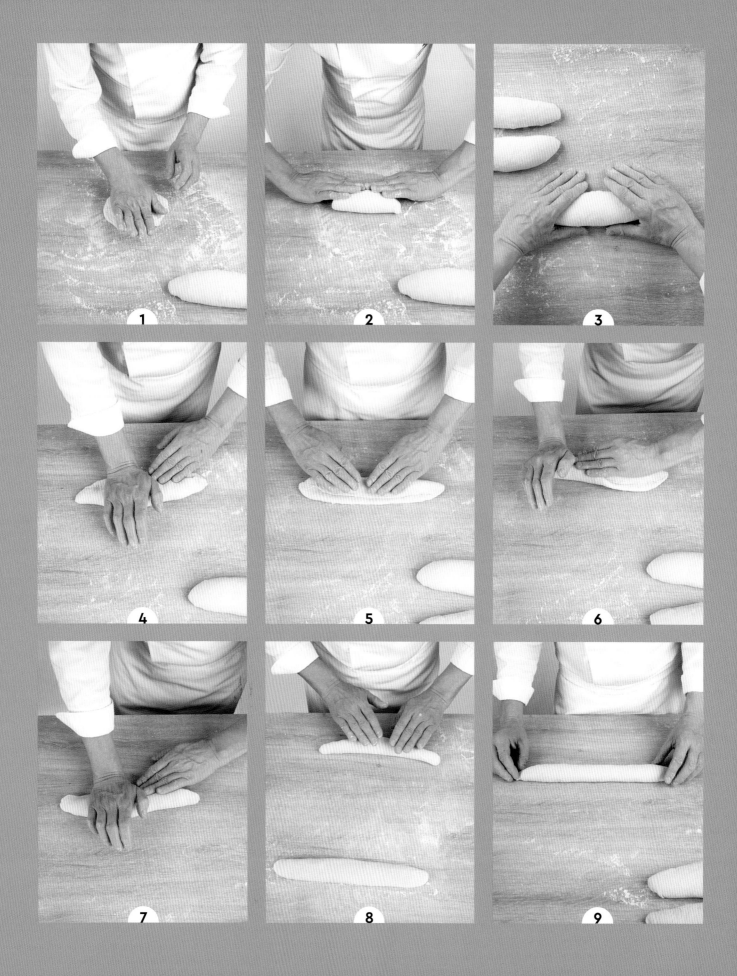

PRE-SHAPING AND FINAL SHAPING OF DOUGH INTO A LONG SHAPE

- Place the piece of dough on the work surface with the smooth side down and flatten with the palm of your hand to release the gas (see p.41) **(1)**.
- Fold the top third of the dough towards the centre and press the edge with your fingers. Turn the dough 180 degrees, fold the opposite third towards the centre and press the edge with your fingers **(2)**.
- Fold the dough in half lengthways, seal with the base of your palm and roll the oval on itself very slightly **(3)**. The dough is now pre-shaped into an elongated form.
- After resting, take the dough, place it smooth side down and flatten it with the palm of your hand to release the gas. Fold the top edge towards the centre and seal with the base of your palm **(4)**.
- Turn the dough 180 degrees and fold the top edge towards the centre. Seal with the base of your palm.
- Fold the dough in half lengthways **(5)**. Do the final seal of the two edges with the base of your palm **(6)** **(7)**.
- To shape the dough into a baguette, roll it backwards and forward to lengthen it **(8)** **(9)**.

PRE-SHAPING

Pre-shaping is an optional step to facilitate the final shaping. It regulates the shape of the dough and prepares it for the final shaping. It should not be too compact.

The dough pieces are pre-shaped into a long form for baguettes and long loaves, and into a ball for semi-long (bâtard) loaves, short loaves and rolls.

For soft doughs or those lacking strength, but also for making 'boule' or round breads and wreaths, the technique known as 'boulage' (forming a ball) is used. It consists of flattening the dough into a disc, folding the outer edges towards the centre,

and then turning the dough over so that the seam is at the base and the smooth part is at the top.
The ball obtained is then turned with the hands while drawing the dough down to the base.

Please note that some round breads are shaped into a ball without this pre-shaping (e.g. buckwheat loaf).

RESTING (BENCH REST)

This is a resting period between the pre-shaping and final shaping stages. The resting stage facilitates stretching and shaping, and prevents the dough tearing. This step lasts between 10 and 45 minutes depending on the strength of the dough pieces and the intensity of the previous stages. The dough is still fermenting as it rests.

FINAL SHAPING

Also called 'tourne', the final shaping gives the dough its definitive form. This step sometimes requires the use of specific equipment (rollers, scissors, moulds, trays, bannetons).

Depending on the product, the shaping can be more or less long, more or less compact, with the dough pieces more or less floured. It is divided into three phases: releasing the gas (degassing), folding and stretching.

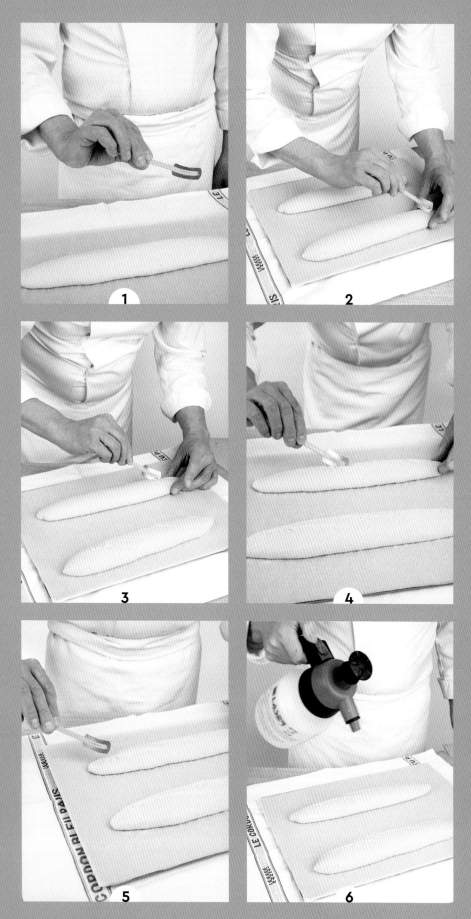

SLASHING THE DOUGH PIECES

- Hold the baker's blade between your thumb and forefinger, keeping the handle loose **(1)**.

- With your other hand, gently hold the dough, then tilt the blade slightly **(2)** **(3)**. Keep the handle loose and score the surface of the dough evenly and in a clean motion so as not to tear it **(4)**.

- Lift the blade at the end of each incision to avoid tearing the dough **(5)**.

- Once the slashing is finished, spray the dough pieces before putting them into the oven **(6)**.

SECOND (FINAL) PROOFING

The last period of fermentation occurs between the final shaping and the baking: the dough 'gets ready' to go into the oven. Final proofing lasts from 20 minutes to 4 hours at room temperature and up to 72 hours in the refrigerator.

SLASHING (OR SCORING)

Slashing, also called scoring, consists of incising a dough piece before putting it into the oven. It is the baker's signature, but that isn't the only reason for doing it. Thanks to slashing, the gas created during fermentation as well as the humidity present in the dough can escape evenly, allowing the dough to keep its shape. Without slashing, the gas escapes in an irregular manner and may cause deformation in the product.

During the baking process, the incisions made on the bread will give it its definitive shape and appearance. For the bread to be totally successful, the crust must have clear and regular 'grignes' (signatures) or scores.

The incisions on the dough are made mainly with a special baker's blade or a razor blade. It must always be clean. For a perfect incision, the blade must be directed with flexibility and skill. The incisions should be regular and of equal length. For a baguette, the incisions should cover the entire length of the dough and overlap by at least a third. They should be made as straight as possible on the surface of the dough to allow for greater harmony at the 'jets' (the openings where the incised dough swells during baking).

The depth of the scores made by the blade is determined by the strength of the dough and its degree of fermentation. If the dough pieces are not very developed, the incisions will be deep and, conversely, if the dough lacks strength or is well risen, the incisions will be shallow.

COOKING AND 'RESSUAGE' (STEAM ESCAPE)

These are the final steps in the bread-making process. For a good bake, the oven should be preheated for at least 30 minutes to obtain sufficient heat. Then flour if necessary and slash the dough before putting it into the oven.

The dough should be put into the oven once it has risen enough. If it doesn't rise enough, it will lack flexibility (bending in the oven). However, if it rises too much, the glutinous network will be at breaking point (collapsing during cooking).

For baking breads, the conventional oven setting is mostly used because the heat source is static, coming from the bottom and the top of the oven. The fan-assisted setting is more appropriate for baking viennoiseries well.

Steam escape is the stage that follows baking, when the bread is placed on a wire rack to allow excess moisture to escape and prevent the bread crust softening.

Loading methods

• **Loading with a peel.** You can use a baker's peel to place the dough pieces one by one on a preheated baking tray. Lift the baker's cloth to turn the dough over on to the peel, then turn the dough over on to the hot tray.

• **Loading on a baking tray.** Using a baking tray reduces handling. For home baking, it is best to preheat the baking tray before carefully placing the dough by hand or with a peel.

Steam

As soon as the bread is put into the oven, steam must be injected into the oven. It is an essential element for baking breads.

First, the steam allows the crust to remain soft enough for the dough to rise in the oven. Without it, the crust forms too early and the crumb cannot develop properly. In addition, the water vapour limits the evaporation of the water contained in the dough. Finally, it allows the crust to caramelise, shine and develop properly.

Tip: if you have a home oven that does not have a steam option, spray the dough with water when you put it into the oven, then add three large ice cubes to a preheated grill pan.

The stages of baking

In bakery, baking refers to the transformation of a dough that has undergone fermentation into a stable product (bread). During the baking process, the dough undergoes several phases of chemical and physical transformations.

• **The development phase.** The dough increases in volume. The ferments present in the dough break down the sugars into carbon dioxide (CO_2). From 50°C onwards, the ferments are destroyed and the production of CO_2 is consequently interrupted.

• **The colouring phase.** As the enzymes break down, they lead to the caramelisation of the crust. The coagulation of the starch gives structure to the crumb.

• **The drying phase.** Some of the water in the bread evaporates, resulting in a tough crust and a non-sticky crumb. As a result, the bread loses weight.

Checking if the bread is baked

Baking time varies depending on the weight, size and shape of the bread. The baker can evaluate the baking by lightly pressing the bread on the sides: the crust should be resistant and crispy. If you tap the base of the bread with your fingertips, it should make a hollow sound.

THE POINTS TO FOLLOW FOR A GOOD BREAD BAKE

• It is important to leave the oven empty between two bakes so that the bottom (the lower, heated part of the oven) can build up its heat again.

• Undercooked bread is indigestible and tasteless. That being said, and while it is essential to bake bread well, you don't want to overcook it either to avoid it drying out.

• Large loaves are best baked using decreasing temperatures, while small pieces are best baked in high heat.

LOADING THE BREAD INTO THE OVEN AND BAKING

- Preheat the oven and baking tray, placing it in the centre. Protect your hands with a dry cloth or gloves, then remove the hot baking tray **(1)** from the oven and place it on to a wire rack.

- If the bread has been proved on a baker's cloth or towel, gently lift the cloth to turn the dough on to a peel, turn or place the dough on to the hot baking tray covered with baking parchment **(2)**.

- If the bread has been proved on a baking tray covered with baking parchment, grasp the edge of the sheet and carefully slide it with the dough pieces on to the hot tray **(3)**.

- When ready to bake, spray the dough pieces with water, then add 3 large ice cubes to the preheated grill pan at the base of the oven to produce steam **(4)**.

- When removed from the oven, place the bread on a wire rack to allow excess moisture to escape and prevent the crust softening.

The evolution of bread after baking

- **Unloading.** When removing bread from the oven, it is imperative to place it carefully on a wire rack and not in direct contact with other bread, because the crust will be hot and still fragile.

- **'Ressuage' (steam escape).** The period during which the bread cools down starts as soon as the bread is removed from the oven. Steam escapes, resulting in a 2% weight loss. During this phenomenon, the crust flakes slightly due to the temperature contrast between the oven and the room. The duration of the cooling process varies according to the size and shape of the bread: the larger the bread, the longer the 'ressuage' (steam escape) and cooling period.

- **Staling.** Whatever the environment in which the bread is stored, it inevitably undergoes the natural phenomenon of staling. The crust softens or, on the contrary, hardens. At the gustative level, the bread loses its flavour. Staling varies according to several factors: large loaves stale much more slowly than baguettes, as do those fermented using poolish or leaven.

Imperfections
in the dough

During the bread-making process, the dough may sometimes have imperfections that may or may not be corrected. The baker must have a good knowledge of flours, know about possible dough imperfections and know how to remedy them.

IMPERFECTIONS RELATED TO FLOUR

Flours have certain characteristics that must be known before starting to work with them. Moreover, a flour can also have anomalies that, if present, will affect the quality of the dough and therefore the bread.

• **Flour too fresh:** the dough slackens, the bread lacks volume, the slashes are torn, the crust is red.

• **Flour too old:** the dough is too firm and dry, the bread lacks volume.

CHANGE IN STRENGTH

During the bread-making process, certain factors (desired or not) can change the strength of the dough.

• **Factors contributing to increased dough strength:**

- water is too warm
- too much yeast
- tight shaping
- rising periods are too long
- dough is too firm.

• **Factors contributing to reduced dough strength:**

- water is too cold
- not enough yeast
- rising periods are too short
- dough is too soft.

A DOUGH THAT SLACKENS

It holds up particularly well when kneaded, but softens during resting. During the first rising, it oozes (releases water). Once out of the oven, the bread reddens and lacks volume.

This factor is primarily related to:

- a wheat poor in gluten and of bad quality
- an overly hydrated dough.

To remedy this:

- increase the duration of the first rising to add strength to the dough
- make a fold (rabat).

A DOUGH THAT IS TOO FIRM

It is hard to the touch and brittle. It may crust and the fermentation will be insufficient.

This factor is primarily related to:

- an error in weighing
- the flour is too dry
- poor hydration of the dough.

To remedy this:

- decrease the first rising time
- reduce the amount of dusting flour
- do not form into a ball.

TOO SHORT A DOUGH

It lacks body, suppleness and elasticity, and tears during kneading. During the fermentation process, the dough crusts and breaks – it can also be said to be earthy. After baking the bread will be pale.

This factor is primarily related to:
- using flour that is too old
- the dough being too firm or too hot
- the first rising being too long.

To remedy this:
- make a softer dough
- reduce the resting time
- bake at a lower temperature.

MAIN BREAD DEFECTS

• **Bread not colourful enough and flat bread** (lack of strength and excess rising).

• **Bread too rounded or curved** (it has not developed properly during baking).

• **Dough too hard** (lack of steam, oven not hot enough).

• **Dull bread** (kneading problem, excess force, problem during fermentation, lack of salt or steam).

• **Bread that lacks slashed lines, bread that does not bear the baker's signature** (too much force, inappropriate shaping, too long a final proofing time, too much steam).

The equipment

KNEADING MACHINE

The kneading machine is an integral part of the baker's equipment. Its role is to ensure a regular and homogeneous mixture. To make bread dough at home, a stand mixer can be used. If necessary, increase the speed to mimic a professional kneading machine (speed 1 on a professional kneading machine may correspond to speed 3 on a stand mixer, for example).

COLD STORAGE APPLIANCES

• **The refrigerator.** It allows keeping the preparations at a low but positive temperature, between 0 and 8°C, thus slowing down the fermentation for a short period (a few days).

• **The freezer.** Freezing allows you to quickly block a dough and to quickly cool a product for future use. It should be noted that freezing causes the formation of ice crystals and changes the cellular structure of the product.

• **Deep freezer.** This freezer allows the stabilisation of food in its original state by a very rapid lowering of the temperature (from 0 to – 40°C in a few minutes). This process preserves the product's texture and hold during thawing.

PROVING OVEN

Professionals use specially designed fermentation chambers to control the temperature, humidity and proving time of the products.

THE OVEN

To replicate the bottom of a baker's oven, you can preheat a baking tray in the oven before placing the dough on it. It is also possible to use a cast-iron casserole.

UTENSILS

• **Kitchen scales.** For accurate weighing of ingredients, an electronic scale is ideal. It is also used for dividing preparations and dough.

• **Flour brush.** Very useful for removing flour from a surface or a dough.

• **Dough scraper.** A very useful tool for cutting the dough during manual kneading, scraping the work surface or emptying a container.

• **Baker's blade.** Also called a lame, a baker's blade is essential for slashing the dough before loading it into the oven. It is composed of a rod handle and a razor blade that does not tear the dough.

• **Baker's cloth.** Called a 'baker's couche' by the professionals, often of natural linen, it is used dry or damp to cover and protect the dough, and to hold the dough pieces in place during the fermentation.

• **Peel.** A flat wooden board to help transfer a dough piece to the oven.

• **Rolling pin.** Used in many recipes to roll out a dough.

• **Cooking thermometer.** To check the temperature of preparations and cooking.

CREATING THE CONDITIONS OF A PROVING OVEN

It is possible to reproduce an environment that provides the heat and humidity necessary to rise dough at home.

• Bring a saucepan of water to the boil, then place it in a turned-off oven.

• Using a cooking thermometer, check the oven temperature every 30 minutes to make sure it is between 22 and 25°C for breads and between 25 and 28°C for viennoiseries. If the temperature drops, add boiling water to allow for proper fermentation without drying out.

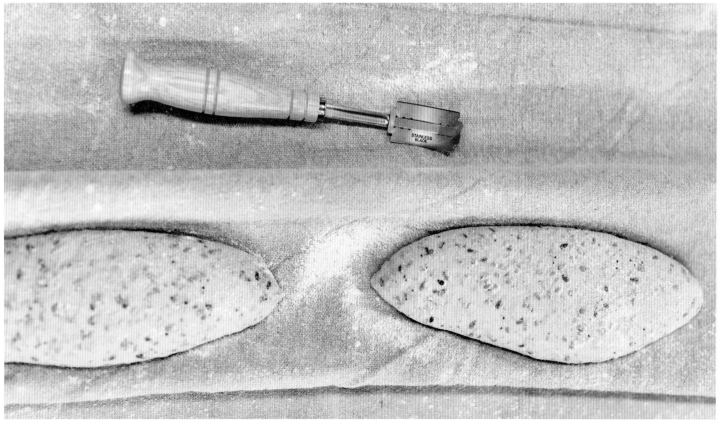

TRADITIONAL BREADS

'French tradition' baguette using stiff leaven

'French tradition' baguette (cold bulk fermentation) without pre-fermentation

'French tradition' baguette using stiff leaven

Baguette using poolish

Baguette using fermented dough

'French tradition' baguette (cold bulk fermentation) using liquid leaven

White baguette without pre-fermentation

White baguette

without pre-fermentation

DIFFICULTY ♡

Preparation: 10 mins • Fermentation: 20 mins • Proofing: 1hr 20 mins • Baking: 20–25 mins • Basic temperature: 75

MAKES 3 BAGUETTES

500 g T55 flour • 10 g fresh compressed yeast • 310 g water • 9 g salt

KNEADING

- Place the flour on the work surface. Make a well in the centre, crumble the yeast into it and dilute with water. Add the salt. Gradually mix in the flour with your fingers, using a circular motion to incorporate the flour **(1)**.

- Knead for about 10 minutes, cutting with a dough scraper to develop the glutinous network **(2) (3) (4)**. After kneading, the temperature of the dough should be 23–25°C.

FIRST RISING AND FERMENTATION

- Cover the dough and leave to ferment for 20 minutes at room temperature.

DIVIDING AND SHAPING

- Divide the dough into three pieces of about 270 g each. Pre-shape each dough piece into an elongated form **(5)** (see pp. 42–43). Leave to rest for 20 minutes.

- Finish shaping the dough **(6)** and place on a floured cloth.

SECOND (FINAL) PROOFING

- Leave to proof, covered with a damp cloth, for 1 hour at room temperature.

BAKING

- Using the conventional setting, preheat the oven to 240°C with a 30 x 38 cm baking tray in the centre.

- Remove the hot tray and place it on a wire rack. Using a peel, gently place the dough pieces on top, then, make three incisions on the surface with a baker's blade.

- Place directly in the oven, add steam (see p. 50) and bake for 20–25 minutes.

- Remove the baguettes from the oven and place on a wire rack to allow the steam to escape and cool.

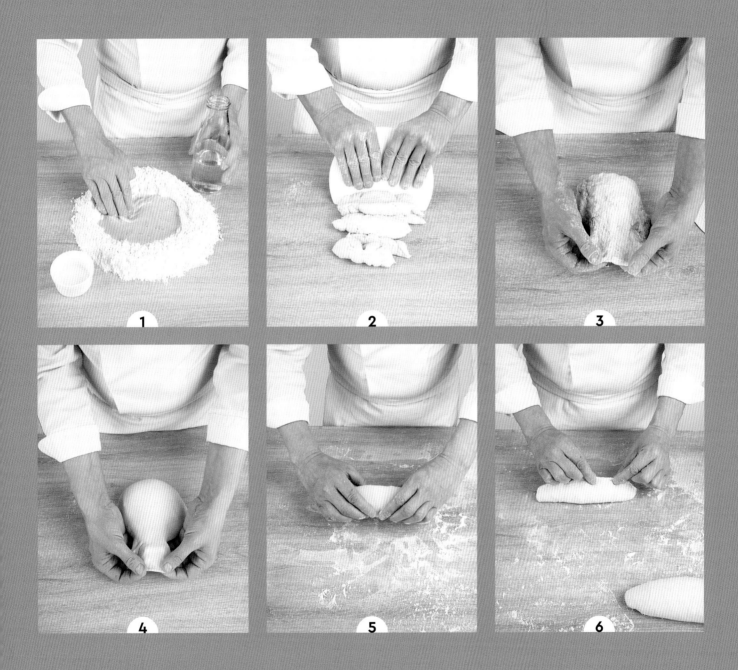

Baguette
using fermented dough

DIFFICULTY ♙

THE DAY BEFORE **Preparation:** 10 mins • **Fermentation:** 30 mins • **Chilling:** 12 hrs
ON THE DAY **Preparation:** 10 mins • **Fermentation:** 1 hr • **Proofing:** 1 hr 20 mins • **Baking:** 20–25 mins
• **Basic temperature:** 54

MAKES 3 BAGUETTES

100 g fermented dough

....

400 g T55 flour • 8 g salt • 4 g fresh compressed yeast • 260 g water

FERMENTED DOUGH (THE DAY BEFORE)

• Prepare the fermented dough and refrigerate overnight (see p. 33).

KNEADING (ON THE DAY)

• Put the flour, salt, yeast and water **(1)** into the bowl of a stand mixer. Mix for 4 minutes on low speed. Add the 100 g of fermented dough, cut into small pieces **(2)**, then knead for 6 minutes on medium speed. After kneading, the temperature of the dough should be 23–25°C.

FIRST RISING AND FERMENTATION

• Take the dough out of the mixer, cover and leave it to ferment at room temperature for 1 hour **(3)**.

DIVIDING AND SHAPING

• Divide the dough into three pieces of about 250 g each **(4)**. Pre-shape each piece into an elongated form (see pp. 42–43). Leave to rest for 20 minutes.

• Finish shaping the dough and place on a cloth.

SECOND (FINAL) PROOFING

• Leave to proof, covered with a damp cloth, for 1 hour at room temperature.

BAKING

• Using the conventional setting, preheat the oven to 240°C with a 30 x 38 cm baking tray in the centre.

• Remove the hot tray and place it on a wire rack. Using a peel, gently place the dough pieces on top, then make three incisions on the surface with a baker's blade. Place directly in the oven, add steam (see p. 50) and bake for 20–25 minutes.

• Remove the baguettes from the oven and place on a wire rack to allow the steam to escape and cool.

Baguette
using poolish

DIFFICULTY ♟ ♟ ♟

THE DAY BEFORE Preparation: 5 mins • **Chilling:** 12 hrs
ON THE DAY Preparation: 10 mins • **Autolyse:** 30 mins • **Fermentation:** 1 hr • **Proofing:** 1 hr 5 mins–1 hr 20 mins
• **Baking:** 20–25 mins • **Basic temperature:** 54

MAKES 2 BAGUETTES

POOLISH
30 g T65 flour • 30 g water • 0.3 g fresh compressed yeast

AUTOLYSE
270 g T65 flour • 175 g water

FINAL KNEADING
5 g salt • 1 g fresh compressed yeast • 10 g water

POOLISH (THE DAY BEFORE)

• Prepare the poolish and refrigerate overnight (see p. 32).

AUTOLYSE (ON THE DAY)

• Put the flour and water into the bowl of a stand mixer. Mix on low speed to form a dough **(1)**. Cover and leave in the mixer bowl for 30 minutes.

FINAL KNEADING

• Add the salt and yeast to the autolyse. Use the water to remove 60.3 g of poolish from the side of the bowl and put it into the mixer bowl **(2)**. Mix for 5 minutes on low speed, then knead for 2 minutes on medium speed. After kneading, the temperature of the dough should be 23–25°C **(3)**.

FIRST RISING AND FERMENTATION

• Cover the dough and leave it to ferment for 20 minutes.

• Take the dough out of the bowl and make a fold (rabat) on the work surface. Leave to ferment, covered with a damp cloth, for 40 minutes at room temperature.

DIVIDING AND SHAPING

• Divide the dough into two pieces of about 260 g each. Pre-shape each piece into an elongated form (see pp. 42–43). Leave to rest for 20 minutes.

• Finish shaping the dough and place on a cloth.

SECOND (FINAL) PROOFING

• Leave them to proof, covered with a cloth, at room temperature for 45 minutes–1 hour.

BAKING

• Using the conventional setting, preheat the oven to 240°C with a 30 x 38 cm baking tray in the centre.

• Remove the hot tray and place it on a wire rack. Using a peel, gently place the dough pieces on top, then make three incisions on the surface with a baker's blade. Place directly into the oven, add steam **(4)** (see p. 50) and bake for 20–25 minutes.

• Remove the baguettes from the oven and place on a wire rack to allow the steam to escape and cool.

'French tradition' baguette
using stiff leaven

DIFFICULTY ♢♢♢

This bread requires 4 days to establish a stiff leaven.

THE DAY BEFORE Preparation: 10 mins • **Fermentation:** 2 hrs • **Chilling:** 12–48 hrs
ON THE DAY Preparation: 8–10 mins • **Autolyse:** 1 hr • **Fermentation:** 1 hr 15 mins • **Proofing:** 1 hr 20 mins
• **Baking:** 20–25 mins • **Basic temperature:** 68

MAKES 2 BAGUETTES

50 g stiff leaven

AUTOLYSE
250 g 'French tradition' flour • 162 g water

KNEADING
5 g salt • 1 g fresh compressed yeast • 25 g water for 'bassinage'

STIFF LEAVEN (4 DAYS IN ADVANCE)

• Prepare a stiff leaven using a liquid leaven (see p. 36).

STIFF LEAVEN (THE DAY BEFORE)

• Refresh the stiff leaven (see p. 36) and refrigerate overnight.

AUTOLYSE (ON THE DAY)

• Put the flour and water into the bowl of a stand mixer. Mix on low speed to form a dough. Cover and leave in the mixer bowl for 1 hour.

KNEADING

• Add the salt, yeast and 50 g of stiff leaven, cut into small pieces, to the autolyse. Knead for 8–10 minutes on low speed. Add the water for 'bassinage' in the last 2 minutes. After kneading, the temperature of the dough should be 23–25°C.

FIRST RISING AND FERMENTATION

• Take the dough out of the bowl and put it into a covered container **(1)**. Leave to ferment at room temperature for 1 hour 15 minutes.

DIVIDING AND SHAPING

• Divide the dough into two pieces of about 240 g each. Pre-shape each piece into an elongated form **(2)** (see pp. 42–43). Leave to rest for 20 minutes.

• Finish shaping the dough and place on a cloth **(3)**.

SECOND (FINAL) PROOFING

• Leave to proof, covered with a cloth, for 1 hour at room temperature.

BAKING

• Using the conventional setting, preheat the oven to 240°C with a 30 x 38 cm baking tray in the centre.

• Remove the hot tray and place it on a wire rack. Using a peel, gently place the dough pieces on top, then make three incisions on the surface with a baker's blade. Place directly in the oven, add steam (see p. 50) and bake for 20–25 minutes.

• Remove the baguettes from the oven, place on a wire rack to allow the steam to escape and cool. **(4)**.

'French tradition' baguette

(cold bulk fermentation) without pre-fermentation

DIFFICULTY ⬠

THE DAY BEFORE Preparation: 13 mins • **Autolyse:** 1 hr • **Fermentation:** 30 mins • **Chilling:** 12 hrs

ON THE DAY Proofing: 1 hr 5 mins–1 hr 20 mins • **Baking:** 20–25 mins

• **Basic temperature:** 54

MAKES 2 BAGUETTES

AUTOLYSE

300 g 'French tradition' flour • 195 g water

FINAL KNEADING

5 g salt • 2 g fresh compressed yeast • 15–30 g water for 'bassinage'

FINISH

Flour • Fine semolina

AUTOLYSE (THE DAY BEFORE)

• Put the flour and water into the bowl of a stand mixer. Mix for 3 minutes on low speed until the flour absorbs the water. Cover and leave in the mixer bowl for 1 hour.

FINAL KNEADING

• Add the salt and yeast to the autolyse. Knead for 10 minutes on low speed. Add the water for 'bassinage' in the last 2 minutes. After kneading, the temperature of the dough should be 22°C.

FIRST RISING AND FERMENTATION

• Cover the dough and leave to ferment for 30 minutes at room temperature.

• Take the dough out of the bowl, make a fold (rabat) **(1)**, then put it into a covered container and refrigerate overnight **(2)**.

DIVIDING AND SHAPING (ON THE DAY)

• Divide the dough into two pieces of about 260 g each **(3)**. Pre-shape each piece into an elongated form (see pp. 42–43). Leave to rest for 20 minutes.

• Finish shaping the dough into baguette shapes. Place, with the seam on top, on a cloth floured with a mixture of flour and semolina **(4)**.

SECOND (FINAL) PROOFING

• Leave to proof for 45 minutes–1 hour at room temperature.

BAKING

• Using the conventional setting, preheat the oven to 240°C with a 30 x 38 cm baking tray in the centre.

• Remove the hot tray and place it on a wire rack. Using a peel, gently place the dough pieces on top, then make three incisions on the surface with a baker's blade. Place directly in the oven, add steam (see p. 50) and bake for 20–25 minutes.

• Remove the baguettes from the oven and place on a wire rack to allow the steam to escape and cool.

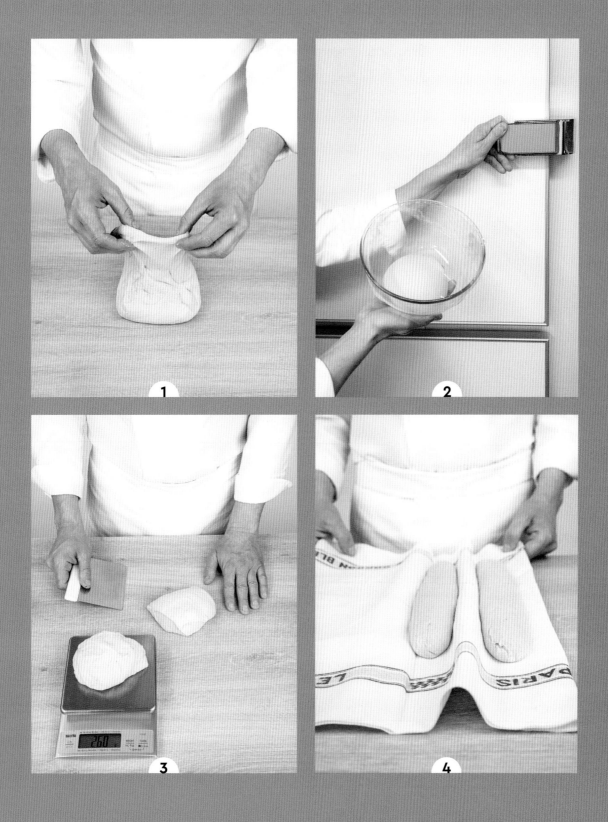

'French tradition' baguette

(cold bulk fermentation) using liquid leaven

DIFFICULTY ♙ ♙

This bread requires 4 days to establish a liquid leaven.

1 OR 2 DAYS IN ADVANCE Preparation: 20 mins • **Autolyse:** 30 mins
• **Fermentation:** 30 mins • **Chilling:** 12–24 hrs
ON THE DAY Preparation: 10 mins • **Proofing:** 1 hr 20 mins–1 hr 50 mins • **Baking:** 20–25 mins
• **Basic temperature:** 54

MAKES 2 BAGUETTES

38 g liquid leaven

AUTOLYSE
250 g 'French tradition' flour • 163 g water

FINAL KNEADING
4 g salt • 2 g fresh compressed yeast • 12 g water for 'bassinage'

FINISH
Flour • Fine semolina

LIQUID LEAVEN (4 DAYS IN ADVANCE)

• Prepare a liquid leaven (see p. 35).

AUTOLYSE (1 OR 2 DAYS IN ADVANCE)

• Put the flour and water into the bowl of a stand mixer. Mix on low speed until the flour absorbs the water **(1)**. Cover and leave in the mixer bowl for 30 minutes.

FINAL KNEADING

• Add the salt, yeast and liquid leaven to the autolyse. Knead for 8–10 minutes on low speed. Add the water for 'bassinage' in the last 2 minutes **(2)**. After kneading, the temperature of the dough should be 22°C.

FIRST RISING AND FERMENTATION

• Cover the dough and leave to ferment for 30 minutes at room temperature. Take the dough out of the bowl, make a fold (rabat) **(3)**, then put it into a covered container and refrigerate for 12–24 hours.

DIVIDING AND SHAPING (ON THE DAY)

• Divide the dough into two pieces of about 230 g each. Pre-shape each piece into an elongated form (see pp. 42–43). Leave to rest for 20 minutes.

• Finish shaping into baguettes. Place, with the seam on top, on a cloth floured with a mixture of flour and semolina **(4)**.

SECOND (FINAL) PROOFING

• Leave to proof at room temperature for 45 minutes.

BAKING

• Using the conventional setting, preheat the oven to 240°C with a 30 x 38 cm baking tray in the centre.

• Remove the hot tray and place it on a wire rack. Using a peel, gently turn the dough pieces right side up on the baking tray, then make three incisions on the surface with a baker's blade. Place directly in the oven, add steam (see p. 50) and bake for 20–25 minutes.

• Remove the baguettes from the oven and place on a wire rack to allow the steam to escape and cool.

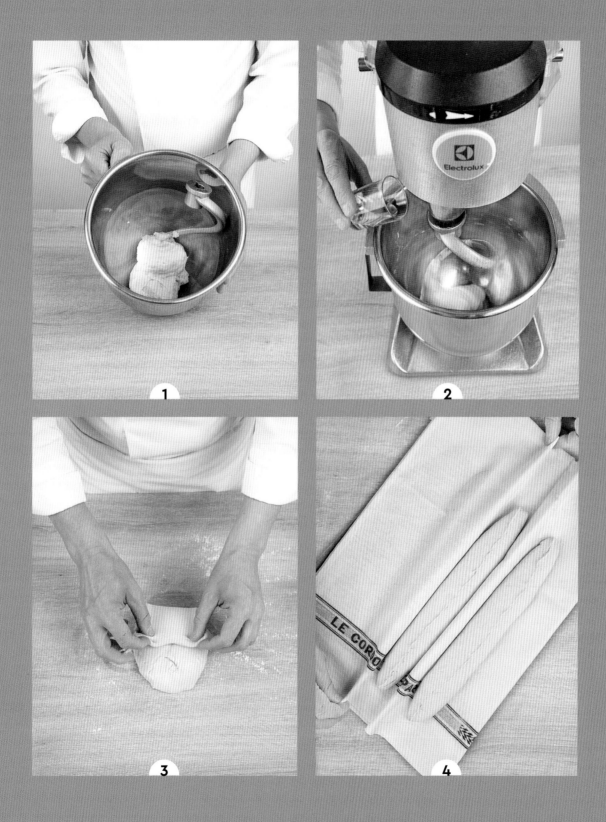

Milk bread baguette

DIFFICULTY ⌂

THE DAY BEFORE **Preparation:** 10 mins • **Chilling:** 12 hrs
ON THE DAY **Preparation:** 12–14 mins • **Fermentation:** 20 mins • **Proofing:** 2 hrs 10 mins
• **Baking:** 20–25 mins • **Basic temperature:** 60

MAKES 3 BAGUETTES

45 g Viennese fermented dough

KNEADING

300 g T45 fine wheat flour • 8 g fresh compressed yeast • 6 g salt • 18 g sugar • 40 g egg (½ large egg) • 150 g milk

FINISH

1 egg + 1 egg yolk, beaten together • 30 g room-temperature unsalted butter

VIENNESE FERMENTED DOUGH (THE DAY BEFORE)

• Prepare the Viennese fermented dough and refrigerate overnight (see p. 33).

KNEADING (ON THE DAY)

• Put the flour, yeast, salt, sugar, egg, milk and the 45 g of Viennese fermented dough, cut into small pieces, into the bowl of a stand mixer. Mix for 4 minutes on low speed, then knead for 8 –10 minutes on high speed. After kneading, the temperature of the dough should be 25°C.

FIRST RISING AND FERMENTATION

• Cover the dough with a damp cloth and leave to ferment for 20 minutes at room temperature.

DIVIDING AND SHAPING

• Divide the dough into three pieces of about 190 g each. Pre-shape each piece into an elongated form (see pp. 42–43). Leave to rest for 10 minutes.

• Finish shaping into very tight baguette shapes with seven folds. Place them on a 30 x 38 cm baking tray covered with baking parchment. Make 'saucisson' incisions on the surface (see p. 44) and brush them with egg wash.

SECOND (FINAL) PROOFING

• Leave to proof for 2 hours in a proving oven at 25°C (see p. 54).

BAKING

• Preheat a fan-forced oven to 210°C. Brush a second time with egg wash, place them in the centre of the oven and bake for 20–25 minutes.

• Remove the baguettes from the oven, place them on a wire rack and brush with the butter.

VARIATION

Milk bread baguette with white chocolate

590 g Milk bread baguette dough • 150 g white chocolate chips • Grated zest of ½ lime

• After kneading the milk bread baguette dough, add the white chocolate chips and lime zest. Mix for 1 minute on low speed, then continue as for the milk bread baguettes. Bake for 20 minutes at 180°C.

TRADITIONAL BREADS

T110 Stoneground bread

using stiff leaven

DIFFICULTY ♙ ♙ ♙

This bread requires 4 days to establish a liquid leaven.

THE DAY BEFORE Preparation: 4 mins • Fermentation: 2 hrs • **Chilling:** 12 hrs
ON THE DAY Preparation: 10 mins • Fermentation: 1 hr 15 mins • **Proofing:** 2 hrs 20 mins
• Baking: 40 mins • **Basic temperature:** 75

MAKES 1 LOAF

STONEGROUND STIFF LEAVEN
250 g T110 stoneground whole wheat flour • 125 g liquid leaven • 125 g water at 40°C

KNEADING
400 g T110 stoneground whole wheat flour • 100 g 'French tradition' flour • 13 g Guérande sea salt • 1 g fresh compressed yeast • 350 g water • 300 g stoneground stiff leaven from the day before • Water for 'bassinage' (up to 50 g)

·················
Flour for the finish

LIQUID LEAVEN (4 DAYS IN ADVANCE)

• Prepare a liquid leaven (see p. 35).

STONEGROUND STIFF LEAVEN (THE DAY BEFORE)

• Put the flour, liquid leaven and water into the bowl of a stand mixer. Mix for 4 minutes on low speed. Leave to ferment at room temperature for 2 hours, then place in a large covered container and refrigerate for at least 12 hours.

KNEADING (ON THE DAY)

• Put the two flours, the salt, yeast, water and stoneground stiff leaven, cut into small pieces, into the bowl of a stand mixer. Knead for 10 minutes on low speed. Add the water for 'bassinage' in the last 2 minutes. After kneading, the temperature of the dough should be 25–27°C.

• Put the dough into a floured container and make a light fold (rabat) without giving too much force.

FIRST RISING AND FERMENTATION

• Leave to ferment, covered with a cloth, for 1 hour 15 minutes at room temperature.

SHAPING

• Pre-shape the dough into a ball and leave it to rest for 20 minutes. Lengthen the dough and place it, with the seam on top, on a floured cloth.

SECOND (FINAL) PROOFING

• Leave to proof at room temperature for 2 hours.

BAKING

• Using the conventional setting, preheat the oven to 250°C with a 30 x 38 cm baking tray in the centre.

• Remove the hot tray and place it on a wire rack. Using a peel, gently turn the dough right side up on the baking tray. Flour, then make an incision along the entire length with a baker's blade. Place directly in the oven, then lower the temperature to 220°C. Add steam (see p. 50) and bake for 40 minutes.

• Remove the bread from the oven and place on a wire rack to allow the steam to escape and cool.

Country-style bread
(cold bulk fermentation) using liquid leaven
DIFFICULTY ♙ ♙

This bread requires 4 days to establish a liquid leaven.

1 OR 2 DAYS IN ADVANCE **Preparation:** 11 mins • **Fermentation:** 30 mins • **Chilling:** 12–24 hrs
ON THE DAY **Proofing:** 1 hr 5 mins • **Baking:** 25–30 mins • **Basic temperature:** 65

MAKES 2 LOAVES

100 g liquid leaven

KNEADING
425 g 'French tradition' flour • 75 g T170 dark rye flour • 10 g Guérande sea salt • 350 g water
• 1 g fresh compressed yeast • 25 g water for 'bassinage'

LIQUID LEAVEN (4 DAYS IN ADVANCE)

• Prepare a liquid leaven (see p. 35).

KNEADING (1 OR 2 DAYS IN ADVANCE)

• Put the two flours, the salt, liquid leaven, water and yeast into the bowl of a stand mixer. Mix for 7 minutes on low speed, then knead for 4 minutes on medium speed. Add the water for 'bassinage' in the last 2 minutes and smooth the dough. After kneading, the temperature of the dough should be 23°C.

FIRST RISING AND FERMENTATION

• Take the dough out of the mixer and put it into a covered container. Leave to ferment for 30 minutes at room temperature.

• Make a fold (rabat), cover and refrigerate for 12–24 hours.

DIVIDING AND SHAPING (ON THE DAY)

• Divide the dough into two pieces of about 490 g each. Pre-shape each piece into a ball (see p. 43). Leave to rest for 20 minutes.

• Finish shaping into semi-long oval (bâtard). Place the pieces, with the seam on top, on a floured cloth.

SECOND (FINAL) PROOFING

• Leave to proof for 45 minutes at room temperature.

BAKING

• Using the conventional setting, preheat the oven to 250°C with a 30 x 38 cm baking tray in the centre.

• Remove the hot tray and place it on a wire rack. Using a peel, gently turn the pieces right side up on the baking tray, then make two incisions on the surface with a baker's blade. Place directly in the oven and lower the temperature to 230°C. Add steam (see p. 50) and bake for 25–30 minutes.

• Remove from the oven and place on a wire rack to allow the steam to escape and cool.

Nutritional bread
with mixed grains
DIFFICULTY ⌂

This bread requires 4 days to establish a liquid leaven.

THE DAY BEFORE Preparation: 5 mins • **Chilling:** 12 hrs

ON THE DAY Preparation: 11 mins • **Fermentation:** 1 hr 30 mins • **Proofing:** 1 hr 20 mins–1 hr 50 mins • **Baking:** 40 mins
• **Basic temperature:** 54

MAKES 1 LOAF

80 g liquid leaven

MIXED GRAIN POOLISH

80 g mixed grains (brown flax (linseed), golden flax (linseed), millet, poppy seeds, sunflower seeds) • 32 g roasted sesame seeds • 32 g T170 dark rye flour • 200 g water • 0.5 g fresh compressed yeast

KNEADING

400 g T65 flour • 8 g salt • 2 g fresh compressed yeast • 170 g water

Sunflower oil for the loaf tin • Fine wheat flour for the finish

---

LIQUID LEAVEN (4 DAYS IN ADVANCE)

• Prepare a liquid leaven (see p. 35).

MIXED GRAIN POOLISH (THE DAY BEFORE)

• In a bowl, whisk together the mixed grains, roasted sesame seeds, flour, water, yeast and liquid leaven. Cover and refrigerate overnight.

KNEADING (ON THE DAY)

• Put the flour, salt, yeast, water and mixed grain poolish into the bowl of a stand mixer. Mix for 7 minutes on low speed, then knead for 4 minutes on medium speed. After kneading, the temperature of the dough should be 23°C.

FIRST RISING AND FERMENTATION

• Leave to ferment, covered with a cloth, for 30 minutes at room temperature.

• Make a fold (rabat), cover and leave to ferment again for 1 hour at room temperature.

DIVIDING AND SHAPING

• Divide the dough into four pieces of about 250 g each or leave it in a single piece of 1 kg. Pre-shape the dough into a ball. Leave to rest for 20 minutes.

• Re-round each small ball, giving the dough the necessary strength, or shape the 1 kg ball into an elongated shape (see pp. 42–43). Place the four balls together or the elongated dough in a 28 x 11 x 9 cm loaf tin previously oiled.

SECOND (FINAL) PROOFING

• Leave the dough to proof for 1 hour–1 hour 30 minutes at room temperature.

BAKING

• Preheat the oven to 240°C with the shelf in the centre.

• Dust the top of the dough with flour using a sieve, then place in the oven. Lower the temperature to 220°C, add steam (see p. 50) and bake for about 40 minutes.

• Remove from the oven, unmould the loaf and place on a wire rack to allow the steam to escape and cool.

Whole wheat bread

using stiff leaven

DIFFICULTY ♙ ♙

This bread requires 4 days to establish a stiff leaven.

THE DAY BEFORE **Preparation:** 8 mins • **Fermentation:** 1 hr • **Chilling:** 12–18 hrs
ON THE DAY **Preparation:** 10 mins • **Proofing:** 2 hrs 20 mins • **Baking:** 40–45 mins
• **Basic temperature:** 58

MAKES 1 LOAF

150 g stiff leaven

KNEADING

500 g T150 whole wheat flour • 280 g water • 10 g salt • 4 g fresh compressed yeast

Plain flour for the finish

STIFF LEAVEN (4 DAYS IN ADVANCE)

• Prepare a stiff leaven (see p. 36).

KNEADING (THE DAY BEFORE)

• Put the flour, water, salt, yeast and stiff leaven, cut into small pieces, into the bowl of a stand mixer. Knead for 8 minutes on low speed. After kneading, the temperature of the dough should be 22°C.

FIRST RISING AND FERMENTATION

• Cover the dough and leave to ferment for 1 hour at room temperature. Fold (rabat) and refrigerate for 12–18 hours.

DIVIDING AND SHAPING (ON THE DAY)

• Pre-shape the dough into a ball. Leave to rest for 20 minutes.

• Finish shaping into a ball. Place the dough, with the seam on top, on a well-floured cloth in a large bowl. Cover the bowl with cling film.

SECOND (FINAL) PROOFING

• Leave to proof for 2 hours at room temperature.

BAKING

• Using the conventional setting, preheat the oven to 250°C with a 24 cm-diameter cast-iron casserole and its lid.

• Cut out a 24 cm disc of baking parchment. Gently turn the dough out on to the parchment, then spread the flour over the surface by hand. Make four incisions to form a square, then a cross in the centre.

• Put three ice cubes in the bottom of the hot casserole, then lower the dough with the baking parchment on top. Cover the casserole and place it in the oven. Bake for 40–45 minutes. Remove the lid after 30 minutes and continue baking for 10–15 minutes.

• Remove the casserole from the oven, take out the loaf and place on a wire rack to allow the steam to escape and cool.

Buckwheat loaf

DIFFICULTY ♙ ♙ ♙

This bread requires 4 days to establish a stiff leaven.

THE DAY BEFORE Preparation: 13–14 mins • **Chilling:** 12 hrs
ON THE DAY Preparation: 10 mins • **Fermentation:** 2 hrs 15 mins • **Proofing:** 15 mins • **Baking:** 40 mins

MAKES 1 LOAF

REFRESHED STIFF LEAVEN

125 g stiff leaven

·················

250 g T110 stoneground whole wheat flour • 125 g water at 40°C

STONEGROUND LEAVEN

218 g fermented dough from the day before

·················

62.5 g buckwheat flour • 62.5 g water at 80°C

KNEADING

187.5 g water at 70°C • 150 g 'French tradition' flour • 37.5 g buckwheat flour • 7.5 g salt

---

STIFF LEAVEN (4 DAYS IN ADVANCE)

• Prepare a stiff leaven (see p. 36).

REFRESHED STIFF LEAVEN (THE DAY BEFORE)

• Put the flour, stiff leaven and water into the bowl of a stand mixer fitted with the paddle attachment. Mix on low speed for 3–4 minutes. Remove the dough from the bowl, then place it in a covered bowl and refrigerate overnight.

FERMENTED DOUGH FOR THE STONEGROUND LEAVEN (THE DAY BEFORE)

• Prepare the fermented dough and refrigerate overnight (see p. 33).

STONEGROUND LEAVEN (ON THE DAY)

• Put the flour, 218 g of refreshed stiff leaven, 218 g of fermented dough, cut into small pieces, and water into the bowl of a stand mixer. Knead on low speed until the dough becomes homogeneous. Cover the dough in the bowl with cling film and leave to ferment for 1 hour.

KNEADING

• Add the water to the stoneground leaven mixture, followed by the two flours and the salt. Mix on low speed for 3–4 minutes, then knead on medium speed for 2 minutes. After kneading, the temperature of the dough should be 30–35°C.

FIRST RISING AND FERMENTATION

• Cover the dough in the mixer bowl with cling film and leave to ferment for 1 hour and 15 minutes.

SHAPING AND SECOND (FINAL) PROOFING

• Flour the work surface well, then put the dough on to it. Quickly fold the edges over the centre. Shape the dough into a ball, place it with the seam on top in a well-floured 22 cm-diameter banneton and pinch the seam with your fingers. Cover with a damp cloth. Leave to proof for 15 minutes at room temperature.

BAKING

• Using the conventional setting, preheat the oven to 260°C with a 30 x 38 cm baking tray in the centre.

• Remove the hot baking tray, place it on a wire rack and cover with baking parchment. Gently turn the banneton over on to the baking tray and make four incisions to form a square, then put in the oven. Add steam (see p. 50) and bake, releasing the steam after 10 minutes, then turn off the oven and continue baking for 30 minutes. Remove from the oven and place on a wire rack to allow the steam to escape and cool.

Spelt bread

using liquid leaven

DIFFICULTY ♧ ♧

This bread requires 4 days to establish a liquid leaven.

Preparation: 8 mins • **Fermentation:** 1 hr 30 mins • **Proofing:** 2 hrs 20 mins • **Baking:** 40–45 mins • **Basic temperature:** 65

MAKES 1 LOAF

150 g liquid leaven

KNEADING

500 g spelt flour • 280 g water • 10 g salt • 4 g fresh compressed yeast

LIQUID LEAVEN (4 DAYS IN ADVANCE)

• Prepare a liquid leaven (see p. 35).

KNEADING

• Put the flour, water, salt, yeast and liquid leaven into the bowl of a stand mixer. Knead for 8 minutes on low speed. After kneading, the temperature of the dough should be 23–25°C.

FIRST RISING AND FERMENTATION

• Cover the dough and leave to ferment for 1 hour 30 minutes at room temperature.

SHAPING

• Pre-shape the dough into a ball. Leave to rest for 20 minutes.

• Finish shaping into a ball. Place the dough, with the seam on top, on a floured cloth.

SECOND (FINAL) PROOFING

• Leave to proof for 2 hours at room temperature.

BAKING

• Using the conventional setting, preheat the oven to 250°C with a 24 cm-diameter cast-iron casserole and its lid.

• Cut out a 24 cm disc of baking parchment. Gently turn the dough over on to the parchment, then spread the flour over the surface by hand. Make four incisions to form a square.

• Put three ice cubes in the bottom of the hot casserole, then lower the dough with the baking parchment on top. Cover the casserole and put it into the oven. Bake for 40–45 minutes. Remove the lid after 30 minutes and continue baking for 10–15 minutes.

• Remove the casserole from the oven, take out the loaf and place on a wire rack to allow the steam to escape and cool.

Festive rolls

DIFFICULTY ♙

Preparation: 15 mins • **Fermentation:** 30 mins • **Proofing:** 1 hr • **Baking:** 15 mins
• **Basic temperature:** 54

500 g T45 fine wheat flour • 325 g milk • 9 g salt • 20 g sugar • 15 g fresh compressed yeast • 125 g cold unsalted butter

FINISH
Poppy seeds • Sunflower oil for sticking • Flour

REFINED BREADS

Stencilled and personalised, these rolls are served in honour of special events and celebrations. A multitude of stencils are available to purchase on the Internet. The themes vary endlessly, and you can also make your own stencils from a drawing or an image. Print the stencil on a semi-rigid material for durability.

KNEADING

- Put the flour, milk, salt, sugar and yeast into the bowl of a stand mixer. Mix for 5 minutes on low speed until the flour absorbs the liquid well and the dough is soft and sticky. Add the butter all at once and continue to knead for 10 minutes on high speed until the dough is soft and smooth.

FIRST RISING AND FERMENTATION

- Shape into a ball and put it into a large bowl. Leave to ferment, covered with a damp cloth or cling film, for 30 minutes at room temperature.

DIVIDING AND SHAPING

- Take 350 g of dough and, using a rolling pin, roll it out to a thickness of 2 mm. Place on a baking tray covered with baking parchment, moisten and cover well with poppy seeds **(1)**. Put the baking tray into the freezer until the dough hardens. Remove any excess poppy seeds and cut out eight discs 7 cm in diameter **(2)**. Set aside in the freezer.

- With the remaining dough, weigh out eight pieces of dough of about 80 g each and form fairly tight balls. Put them on to a 30 x 38 cm baking tray covered with baking parchment.

SECOND (FINAL) PROOFING

- Leave to proof for 1 hour in a proving oven at 25°C (see p. 54).

- Turn the poppy-covered discs over and brush the outline with oil **(3)**. Using the brush, lightly moisten the centre of each dough ball with water and place a poppy seed disc on top **(4)**. Place different stencils on the discs and using a sieve, sprinkle them with flour, then carefully remove the stencils **(5) (6)**.

BAKING

- Preheat a fan-forced oven to 145°C. Bake in the centre of the oven for 15 minutes.

- Remove the buns from the oven and place on a wire rack to allow the steam to escape and cool.

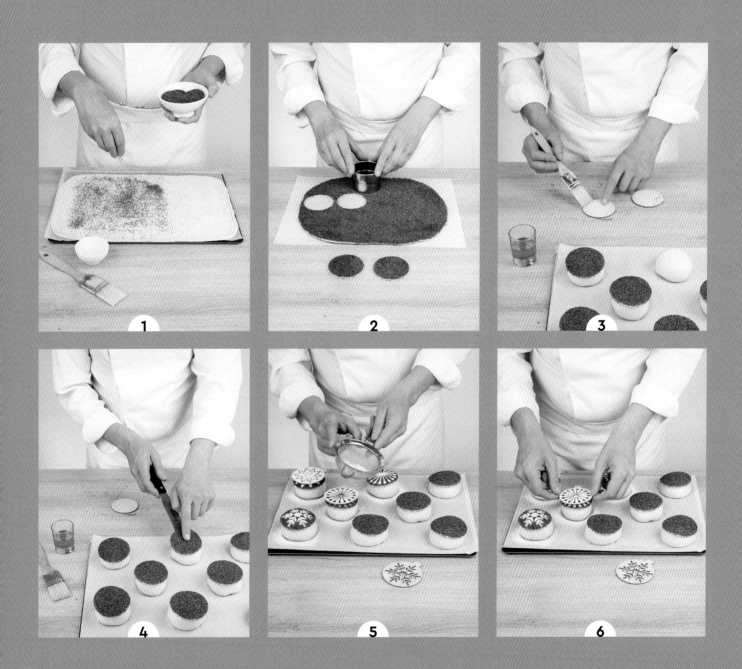

Party bread

DIFFICULTY ⌂

Preparation: 10–11 mins • **Fermentation:** 30 mins • **Proofing:** 1hr • **Baking:** 20–25 mins
• **Basic temperature:** 58

MAKES 1 PARTY BREAD

500 g T150 whole wheat flour • 300 g T130 medium rye flour • 200 g T55 flour • 600 g water
• 20 g salt • 20 g fresh compressed yeast • 25 g butter

DECORATION (OPTIONAL)
Poppy seeds • White sesame seeds • Flour or spices

EDIBLE PASTE
250 g T130 medium rye flour + 215 g water mixed with a silicone spatula
....
Flour for the finish

TECHNICAL BUT PLAYFUL CREATIONS

Various shapes, colours and heights provide the greatest pleasure when working a bread dough in an artistic way. Little known to the general public, party bread is made by professionals in prestigious baking competitions. It is a notable highlight at buffets and requires both technical skill and dexterity.

KNEADING

- Put the flours, water, salt, yeast and butter into the bowl of a stand mixer. Mix for 4 minutes on low speed, then knead for 6–7 minutes on medium speed. After kneading, the temperature of the dough should be 25°C. Leave to ferment, covered with cling film, for 30 minutes at room temperature.

BASE

- Take 800 g of dough and, using a rolling pin, roll it out to a thickness of 1 cm **(1) (2)**, then cut out a shape of your choice. Cut clean edges with a cutter. Dust with flour using a sieve and make incisions along the edge **(3)**. (You can use a stencil to cut out and decorate the shape.)

- Put on to a 30 x 38 cm baking tray covered with baking parchment and leave it to proof for about 1 hour in a proving oven at 25°C (see p.54).

MAIN SUBJECT

- Roll out 500 g of dough to an 8 mm thickness with a rolling pin. Moisten and sprinkle with poppy seeds **(4)**. Place on a 30 x 38 cm baking tray covered with baking parchment and place in the freezer so that the dough hardens for easy cutting.

- Remove from freezer and brush off any excess poppy seeds before cutting out the main subject **(5)**. Using a stencil, cut out the shape **(6)**. Put it on to a 30 x 38 cm baking tray covered with baking parchment. Leave it to proof for about 1 hour in a proving oven at 25°C (see p.54).

- Add colour effects (optional) with flour or spices **(7)**, then, make small incisions around it using a small knife **(8)**.

SMALL SUBJECTS

- Using the rolling pin, roll out the remaining dough to a thickness of 6 mm and cut out three small shapes. You can moisten one and cover it with poppy seeds, cover another with white sesame seeds and sift flour or spices over the last one using a fine-mesh sieve. Put them on to a 30 x 38 cm baking tray covered with baking parchment and leave them to proof for about 1 hour in a proving oven at 25°C (see p.54).

- Gather up all the dough scraps and roll them out to a 5 mm thickness. Using a fork, dock and then cut two triangles the height of the main subject and at least three triangles the size of the smaller subjects. Using stencils of different designs, sift all the elements with flour.

BAKING

- Using a conventional setting, preheat the oven to 230°C. Place the trays in the oven, add steam (see p.50) and bake for 20–25 minutes. Let the pieces cool on wire racks.

ASSEMBLING

- After cooling, position the main subject on the base and, using a small knife, mark the location of the triangles that will support it. Carve into the location 5 mm deep.

- Using a small spoon or piping bag, fill the hollow part with the edible paste and press in the triangles **(9)**. Add paste to the support side and attach the main subject. Proceed in the same way with the small subjects.

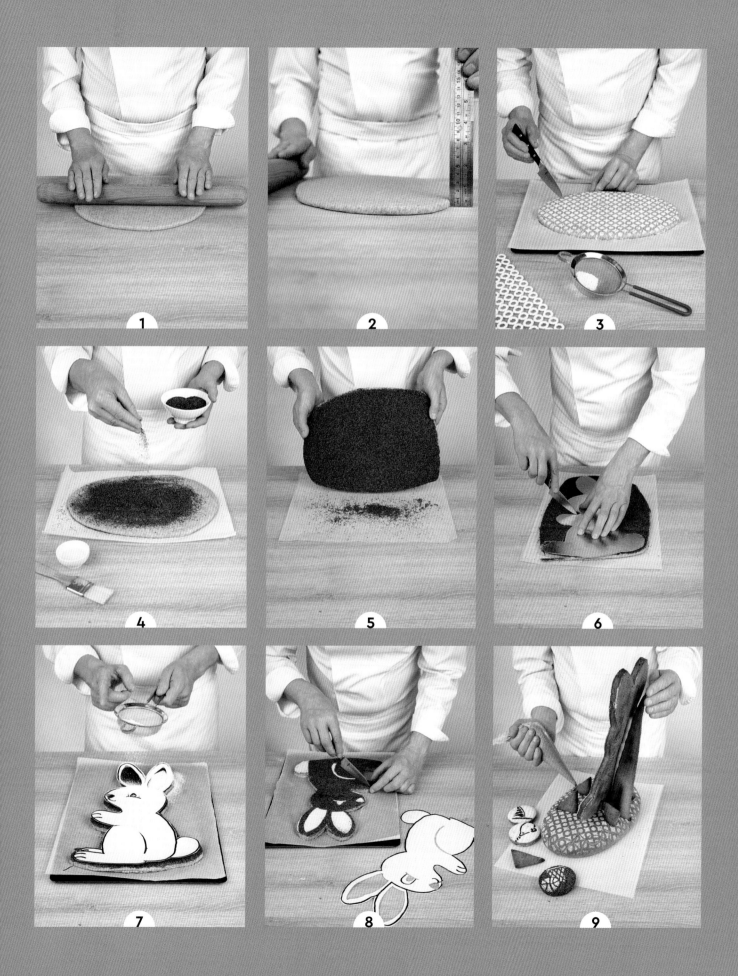

AROMATIC BREADS

Cider bread
with apples

DIFFICULTY ♙ ♙

THE DAY BEFORE Preparation: 10 mins • **Fermentation:** 30 mins • **Chilling:** 12 hrs
ON THE DAY Preparation: 12 mins • **Fermentation:** 1 hr 30 mins • **Proofing:** 1 hr 20 mins • **Baking:** 30 mins
• **Basic temperature:** 58

MAKES 2 LOAVES

MACERATION
138 g dry cider • 150 g apples, cut into small cubes • 100 g sultanas

150 g fermented dough

KNEADING
25 g dry cider • 325 g water • 500 g 'French tradition' flour • 12.5 g salt • 7.5 g fresh compressed yeast • Sunflower oil

MACERATION AND FERMENTED DOUGH (THE DAY BEFORE)

• In a bowl, combine the cider, apples and sultanas. Cover with cling film and refrigerate overnight.

• Prepare the fermented dough and refrigerate overnight (see p. 33).

KNEADING (ON THE DAY)

• Decant the macerated fruit and reserve 50 g of the macerating liquid.

• Put the maceration liquid, cider, water, flour, salt, yeast and the 150 g of fermented dough, cut into small pieces, into the bowl of a stand mixer. Mix for 7 minutes on low speed, then knead for 4 minutes on medium speed. Add the macerated fruit and mix for about 1 minute on low speed until incorporated. After kneading, the temperature of the dough should be 23°C.

FIRST RISING AND FERMENTATION

• Cover the dough with a cloth and leave to ferment for 30 minutes at room temperature. Make a fold (rabat), cover and leave to ferment for 1 hour at room temperature.

DIVIDING AND SHAPING

• Divide the dough into two pieces of about 535 g each. Pre-shape each piece of dough into a ball. Leave to rest for 20 minutes. Finish shaping into a semi-long oval (bâtard).

• Place the dough pieces on a well-floured work surface. Using a rolling pin, roll out one-third of each dough piece, from a long side, so that the dough spreads out far enough to be folded over the entire surface of the bread. Lightly brush 5 mm around the edge of the rolled-out part with oil, then the central part with water. Fold the rolled-out part over the dough, then place with the seam on top on a lightly floured cloth.

SECOND (FINAL) PROOFING

• Cover with a damp cloth and leave it to proof for 1 hour at room temperature.

BAKING

• Using the conventional setting, preheat the oven to 240°C with a 30 x 38 cm baking tray in the centre. Transfer the hot baking tray to a wire rack and cover with baking parchment.

• Using a peel, gently turn the dough pieces right side up on to the baking tray. With a baker's blade, make an incision lengthways, then small incisions diagonally on both sides.

• Place directly into the oven, then lower the temperature to 220°C, add steam (see p. 50) and bake for 30 minutes.

• Remove from the oven and place on a wire rack to allow the steam to escape and cool.

Provençal laminated bread

DIFFICULTY ♙ ♙

THE DAY BEFORE Preparation: 10 mins • **Chilling:** 24 hrs
ON THE DAY Freezing: 20 mins • **Proofing:** 2 hrs • **Baking:** 2 hrs
• **Basic temperature:** 54

MAKES 1 LOAF

360 g T65 flour • 7 g salt • 9 g fresh compressed yeast • 17 g unsalted butter • 180 g water

TURNS
140 g dry butter (see p.313)

FILLING
85 g black olives, cut into quarters • 85 g green olives, cut into quarters • 140 g sundried tomatoes, cut into quarters • Chopped fresh basil

....

Sunflower oil for the mould

KNEADING (THE DAY BEFORE)

• Put the flour, salt, yeast, butter and water into the bowl of a stand mixer. Mix for 4 minutes on low speed, then knead for 6 minutes on medium speed. Form the dough into a ball, cover with cling film and refrigerate for 24 hours.

TURNS (ON THE DAY)

• Prepare a 14 cm-square of dry butter (see p. 206). Using a rolling pin, roll the dough into a disc wide enough that the corners of the butter come to the edge of the disc. Place the butter on top and fold the dough towards the centre to enclose.

• Make one double and one single turn (see p. 208), then cover with cling film and freeze for 20 minutes.

SHAPING

• Using a rolling pin, roll out the dough into a 40 x 30 cm rectangle with a thickness of 3 mm. Using a brush, moisten the entire surface with water and sprinkle with the filling.

• Roll the dough and cut in half lengthways. Twist and place in an oiled 28 x 9 x 10 cm mould with a lid.

SECOND (FINAL) PROOFING

• Leave to proof for at least 2 hours in a 25°C proving oven (see p. 54) until the dough reaches the lid.

BAKING

• Using the conventional setting, preheat the oven to 220°C. Put the mould into the centre of the oven, then lower the temperature to 160°C and bake for 2 hours.

• Remove from the oven, unmould the bread and place on a wire rack to allow the steam to escape and cool.

Pulse and grain bread

DIFFICULTY ♙ ♙ ♙

This bread requires 4 days to establish a liquid leaven.

THE DAY BEFORE **Preparation:** 20 mins • **Cooking:** 20 mins • **Chilling:** 12 hrs
ON THE DAY **Preparation:** 8 mins • **Fermentation:** 1 hr–1 hr 15 mins • **Proofing:** 1 hr 25 mins • **Baking:** 40 mins
• **Basic temperature:** 90

MAKES 1 LOAF

80 g liquid leaven

MIXED GRAIN POOLISH

45 g red lentils • 45 g black lentils • 25 g roasted sesame seeds • 20 g pumpkin seeds • 1 g fresh compressed yeast
200 g lentil cooking liquid supplemented with water

KNEADING

400 g 'French tradition' flour • 9 g salt • 2 g fresh compressed yeast • 150 g water + 15 g water for 'bassinage' (optional)

'GIRAFFE' (DUTCH CRUNCH) COATING

90 g T130 medium rye flour • 100 g lager beer (5.5% vol.)
• 2 g fresh compressed yeast • ¼ tsp black curry powder
....
Sunflower oil for the loaf tin

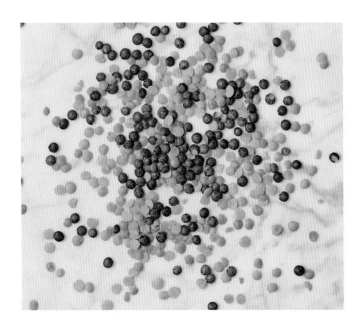

AN ORIGINAL HEALTHY BREAD

The addition of pulses, a source of vegetable protein and fibre, increases the nutritional value of this bread. Cook the lentils thoroughly and reserve their cooking liquid to add to the poolish. Be sure to mix all the ingredients of this poolish well.

LIQUID LEAVEN (4 DAYS IN ADVANCE)

• Prepare a liquid leaven (see p. 35).

MIXED GRAIN POOLISH (THE DAY BEFORE)

• In a saucepan, add the two types of lentils and cover with water. Bring to the boil and cook over a low heat for about 20 minutes (1). At the end of cooking, drain the lentils and set aside the cooking liquid (2). Leave it to cool.

• In a bowl, mix the lentils with the sesame and pumpkin seeds, yeast and lentil cooking liquid with added water (3). Cover with cling film and refrigerate overnight.

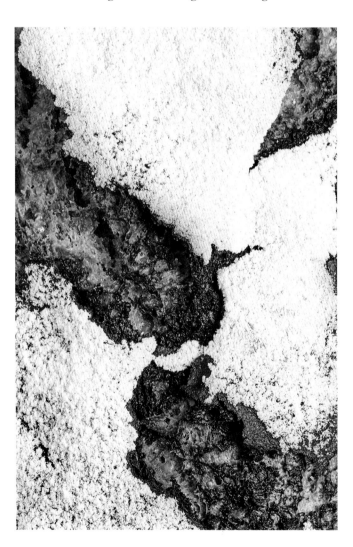

KNEADING (ON THE DAY)

• Put the poolish, flour, salt, yeast, 80 g of the liquid leaven (4) and the 150 g of water into the bowl of a stand mixer. Mix for 3 minutes on low speed, then knead for 5 minutes on medium speed. When the dough comes away from the sides of the bowl, incorporate the 15 g of water for 'bassinage'. The dough should come away from the bowl again. After kneading, the temperature of the dough should be 23–25°C.

FIRST RISING AND FERMENTATION

• Cover the dough in the bowl with a damp cloth and leave it to ferment for 30 minutes.

• Take the dough out of the bowl and make a fold (rabat) on the work surface. Cover with a damp cloth and leave it to ferment for 30–45 minutes at room temperature.

SHAPING AND MAKING A 'GIRAFFE' (DUTCH CRUNCH) COATING

• Pre-shape into an elongated dough (see pp. 42–43) and allow to rest for 10–15 minutes.

• During the resting time, prepare the 'giraffe' (Dutch Crunch) coating. In a bowl, whisk together flour, beer, yeast and curry powder (5). Set aside.

• Make the final elongated shape, then place the loaf in a 28 x 9 x 10 cm loaf tin previously oiled (6). Brush with the 'giraffe' (Dutch Crunch) coating using a silicone spatula (7). Dust the top of the loaf with flour and leave for 10 minutes before dusting with flour again (8) (9).

SECOND (FINAL) PROOFING

• Leave it to proof for about 1 hour at room temperature without covering.

BAKING

• Using a conventional setting, preheat the oven to 240°C.

• Put the tin into the centre of the oven, then lower the temperature to 210°C. Bake for 40 minutes.

• Remove from the oven, unmould the bread and place on a wire rack to allow the steam to escape and cool.

Special bread for foie gras

DIFFICULTY ♙

THE DAY BEFORE Preparation: 15 mins • **Fermentation:** 30 mins • **Chilling:** 12 hrs
ON THE DAY Preparation: 11 mins • **Fermentation:** 1 hr 30 mins • **Proofing:** 1 hr 20 mins
• **Baking:** 20–25 mins • **Basic temperature:** 58

MAKES 3 LOAVES

MIXED GRAIN POOLISH

100 g mixed grains (brown flax (linseed), golden flax (linseed), millet, poppy seeds) • 40 g roasted sesame seeds
• 40 g T170 dark rye flour • 267 g water • 1 g fresh compressed yeast

....

113 g fermented dough

KNEADING

534 g 'French tradition' flour • 10 g salt • 13 g fresh compressed yeast • 220 g water

....

100 g dried apricots, cut into small pieces • 100 g dried figs, cut into small pieces • 67 g sultanas
• 67 g roasted hazelnuts

....

Room-temperature unsalted butter, for the loaf tins

MIXED GRAIN POOLISH (THE DAY BEFORE)

• In a bowl, whisk together the mixed grains, roasted sesame seeds, flour, water and yeast. Cover with cling film and refrigerate overnight.

FERMENTED DOUGH (THE DAY BEFORE)

• Prepare the fermented dough and refrigerate overnight (see p. 33).

KNEADING (ON THE DAY)

• Put the flour, salt, yeast, fermented dough, cut into small pieces, and water into the bowl of a stand mixer. Add the poolish. Mix for 7 minutes on low speed, then knead for 4 minutes on medium speed. Add the dried fruit at low speed. After kneading, the temperature of the dough should be 23°C.

FIRST RISING AND FERMENTATION

• Leave to ferment for 30 minutes at room temperature. Make a fold (rabat) and leave to ferment for 1 hour at room temperature.

DIVIDING AND SHAPING

• Divide the dough into three pieces of about 550 g each. Pre-shape each piece of dough into a ball. Leave to rest for 20 minutes.

• Make a final elongated shape (see pp. 42–43). Put the dough pieces into three buttered 19 x 9 x 7 cm loaf tins.

SECOND (FINAL) PROOFING

• Leave to proof for 1 hour at room temperature.

BAKING

• Using the conventional setting, preheat the oven to 240°C.

• Make seven diagonal incisions on the surface of the dough pieces, then place the tins directly in the centre of the oven. Add steam (see p. 50) and bake for 20–25 minutes.

• Remove from the oven, unmould the loaves and place on a wire rack to allow the steam to escape and cool.

Harlequin bread

DIFFICULTY ♔ ♔

Preparation: 10–12 mins • Fermentation: 1 hr 20 mins • Proofing: 2 hrs • Baking: 1 hr 2 mins
• Basic temperature: 58

MAKES 1 LOAF

TURMERIC BREAD
150 g T45 fine wheat flour • 3.6 g fresh compressed yeast • 15 g sugar • 3 g salt • 25 g egg (½ egg)
• 15 g room-temperature unsalted butter • 100 g milk • 1.5 g turmeric

CUTTLEFISH INK DOUGH
150 g T45 fine wheat flour • 3.6 g fresh compressed yeast • 15 g sugar • 3 g salt • 25 g egg (½ egg)
• 15 g room-temperature unsalted butter • 100 g milk • 10 g cuttlefish ink

BEETROOT DOUGH
150 g T45 fine wheat flour • 3.6 g fresh compressed yeast • 15 g sugar • 3 g salt • 15 g room-temperature unsalted butter
• 37 g milk • 80 g beetroot juice

Oil for the loaf tin

SYRUP
100 g water • 130 g sugar

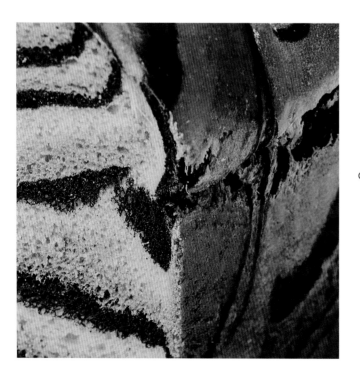

A BREAD WITH A MULTICOLOURED CRUMB

The originality of this bread lies in the stripes of its crumb. Other natural colourings can be substituted for those in the recipe: curry instead of turmeric, tomato juice instead of beetroot juice, spinach juice, red cabbage juice and many others.

TIP: To prevent the coloured dough pieces staining the work surface, roll them out on a silicone mat.

KNEADING

- Put the flour, yeast, sugar, salt, egg, butter, milk and turmeric into the bowl of a stand mixer. Mix for 3–4 minutes on low speed, then 7–8 minutes on medium speed.

- Repeat for cuttlefish ink and beetroot doughs **(1) (2) (3)**. After kneading, the temperature of the doughs should be 23°C.

FIRST RISING AND FERMENTATION

- Remove one dough after the other from the bowl and place each in a bowl covered with cling film. Leave to ferment for 20 minutes at room temperature.

- Make a fold (rabat), cover with cling film and refrigerate for 1 hour.

SHAPING

- On a silicone mat, using a rolling pin, roll out each dough into a 28 x 9 cm rectangle **(4)**.

- Using a brush, lightly brush the top of the turmeric dough with water, then place the cuttlefish ink dough on top. Brush it and place the beetroot dough on top **(5)**.

- Roll the dough tightly into an elongated shape **(6)**, then cut it in half lengthways **(7)**. Make a twist with the two pieces **(8)**, then place in a well-oiled 28 x 9 x 10 cm loaf tin **(9)**.

SECOND (FINAL) PROOFING

- Leave to proof for 2 hours in a proving oven at 25°C (see p. 54).

BAKING

- Preheat the fan-forced oven to 145°C. Put the tin in the centre of the oven and bake for 1 hour.

- Prepare a syrup in a small saucepan by bringing the water and sugar to the boil. Remove from the heat and leave to cool. When the bread is baked, brush it with syrup and return it to the oven for 2 minutes.

- Remove from the oven, unmould the bread and place on a wire rack to allow the steam to escape and cool.

Note: for a plain version of the bread, prepare the dough with the following ingredients: 450 g T45 fine wheat flour, 11 g fresh compressed yeast, 45 g sugar, 9 g salt, 50 g egg (1 egg), 45 g room-temperature unsalted butter, and 300 g milk.
After first rising, shape the dough into a long, tight shape and place it in the tin. Then follow the above proofing and baking steps.

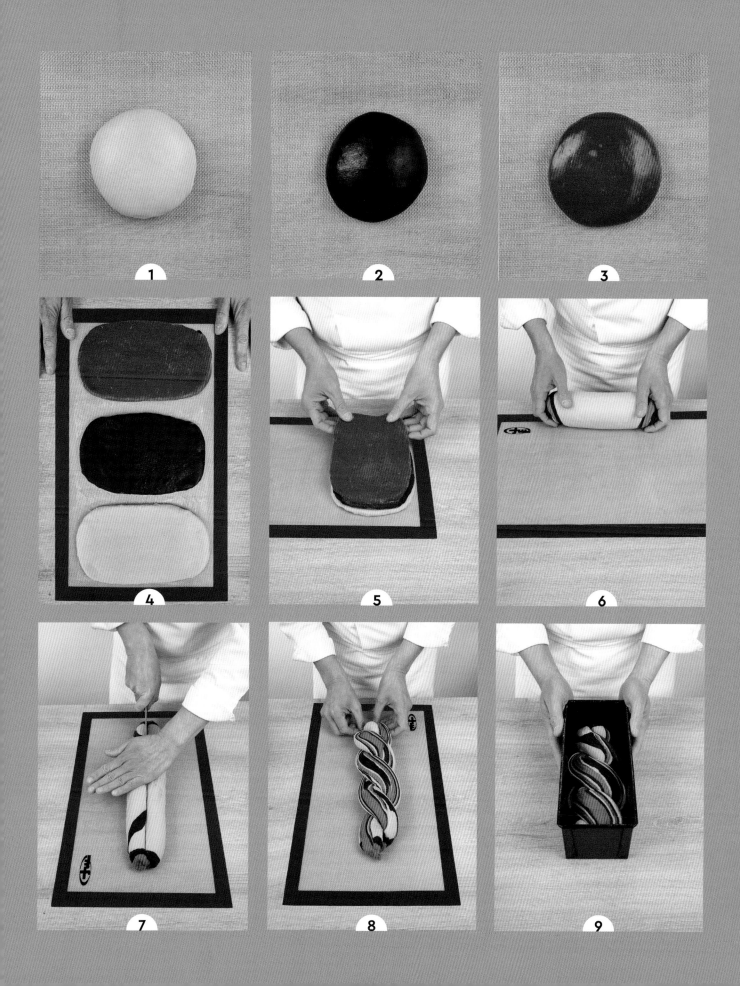

Short rye loaves
with raisins

DIFFICULTY ♙ ♙

THE DAY BEFORE Preparation: 10 mins • **Fermentation:** 30 mins • **Chilling:** 12 hrs
ON THE DAY Preparation: 10 mins • **Fermentation:** 15 mins • **Proofing:** 45 mins
• **Baking:** 20 mins • **Basic temperature:** 77

MAKES 6 SHORT LOAVES

200 g fermented dough

KNEADING

200 g water • 250 g T130 medium rye flour • 5 g Guérande sea salt • 0.8 g fresh compressed yeast • 80 g sultanas

FERMENTED DOUGH (THE DAY BEFORE)

• Prepare the fermented dough and refrigerate overnight (see p. 33).

KNEADING (ON THE DAY)

• Pour the water into the bowl of a stand mixer, then add the fermented dough, cut into small pieces, the flour, salt and yeast. Mix for 4 minutes on low speed, then knead for 4 minutes on medium speed. Add sultanas and knead on low speed until well incorporated. After kneading, the temperature of the dough should be 25 to 27°C.

FIRST RISING AND FERMENTATION

• Cover with a damp cloth and leave to ferment on the work surface for 15 minutes at room temperature.

DIVIDING AND SHAPING

• Flour the work surface, then roll out the dough into a 18 x 12 cm rectangle with a thickness of 1.5 cm. Cut six pieces 3 cm wide and weighing about 120 g each. Transfer to a baking tray covered with baking parchment and dusted with flour.

SECOND (FINAL) PROOFING

• Cover with a damp cloth and leave it to proof for 45 minutes at room temperature.

BAKING

• Using the conventional setting, preheat the oven to 260°C with a 30 x 38 cm baking tray in the centre.

• Remove the hot baking tray and place it on a wire rack, then slide the baking parchment with the dough on to the hot tray. Bake for a maximum of 20 minutes to avoid burning the sultanas. Remove from the oven and place on a wire rack to allow the steam to escape and cool.

VARIATION

Rye bread with pink pralines

• Prepare the dough but replace the sultanas with 160 g of pink pralines. Leave to rise for 45 minutes at room temperature, then put into two buttered 18 x 5.5 x 5.5 cm loaf tins. Cover with a damp cloth and leave to rise for 45 minutes at room temperature.

• Preheat the oven to 220°C. Flour the loaves, then place in the centre of the oven on two baking trays. Lower the temperature to 180°C and bake for 30 minutes. Remove from the oven and leave the breads to cool on a wire rack covered with baking parchment.

AROMATIC BREADS

Beaujolais bread
with Rosette de Lyon sausage

DIFFICULTY ♙

THE DAY BEFORE Preparation: 10 mins • **Fermentation:** 30 mins • **Chilling:** 12 hrs
ON THE DAY Preparation: 12 mins • **Fermentation:** 1 hr 30 mins • **Proofing:** 1 hr 20 mins • **Baking:** 20–25 mins
• **Basic temperature:** 58

MAKES 2 LOAVES

100 g fermented dough

KNEADING

500 g 'French tradition' flour • 7 g salt • 10 g fresh compressed yeast • 180 g Beaujolais wine • 120 g water
200 g thinly sliced Rosette de Lyon (salami-style) sausage

....

Flour for the finish

FERMENTED DOUGH (THE DAY BEFORE)

• Prepare the fermented dough and refrigerate overnight (see p. 33).

KNEADING (ON THE DAY)

• Put the flour, salt, yeast, fermented dough, cut into small pieces, Beaujolais wine and water into the bowl of a stand mixer. Mix for 7 minutes on low speed, then knead for 4 minutes on medium speed. Add the sausage and mix for 1 minute on low speed until it shreds and blends into the dough. After kneading, the temperature of the dough should be 23°C.

FIRST RISING AND FERMENTATION

• Leave to ferment for 30 minutes at room temperature covered with a cloth. Make one fold (rabat) and leave to ferment for 1 hour at room temperature.

DIVIDING AND SHAPING

• Divide the dough into two pieces of about 550 g each. Pre-shape each dough into a ball. Leave to rest for 20 minutes.

• Make a final elongated shape (see pp. 42–43). With the edge of your hand, make three marks across the width of the doughs, then roll in the flour. Place with the seam underneath on a lightly floured cloth.

SECOND (FINAL) PROOFING

• Leave to proof for 1 hour at room temperature.

BAKING

• Using the conventional setting, preheat the oven to 240°C with a 30 x 38 cm baking tray in the centre.

• Remove the hot tray and place it on a wire rack. Using the peel, carefully place the dough on to it. Place in the oven, add steam (see p. 50) and bake for 20–25 minutes.

• Remove from the oven and place on a wire rack to allow the steam to escape and cool.

Gluten-free bread

with grains

DIFFICULTY ♙

This bread requires 4 days before the final preparation to establish
a strong-enough leaven that has good acidity.

PREPARING THE LEAVEN 4 days

THE DAY BEFORE (DAY 4) **Baking:** 10 minutes

ON THE DAY (DAY 5) **Preparation:** 7 mins • **Fermentation:** 45 mins • **Proofing:** 45 mins–1 hr • **Baking:** 50 mins
• **Basic temperature:** 60

MAKES 3 LOAVES

CHESTNUT FLOUR LEAVEN
80 g chestnut flour • 160 g water

ROASTED GRAINS
25 g poppy seeds • 25 g white sesame seeds • 25 g golden flax (linseed) • 60 g water

KNEADING
10 g fresh compressed yeast • 500 g water • 300 g rice flour • 200 g chestnut flour • 12 g salt • 15 g xanthan gum
• 240 g chestnut flour leaven

DECORATION
15 g poppy seeds • 15 g white sesame seeds • 15 g golden flax (linseed)

A TASTY LEAVENED BREAD

Leaven plays a major role in gluten-free bread. Also,
the fermentation time is important since the taste
qualities of the bread depend on it. Xanthan gum
absorbs water and makes the dough more viscous,
compensating in part for the lack of structure due to
the absence of gluten.

CHESTNUT FLOUR LEAVEN (DAYS 1-4)

- **Day 1.** In a bowl, using a silicone spatula mix 20 g of flour with 40 g of water at 28°C. Cover with cling film and leave at room temperature overnight.

- **Day 2.** Add 20 g of flour and 40 g of water at 28°C to the Day 1 preparation. Mix, cover and leave at room temperature overnight **(1)**.

- **Day 3.** Add 20 g of flour and 40 g of water at 28°C to the Day 2 preparation. Mix, cover and leave at room temperature overnight.

- **Day 4.** Add 20 g of flour and 40 g of water at 28°C to the Day 3 preparation. Mix, cover and leave at room temperature overnight.

ROASTED MIXED GRAINS (DAY 4)

- Using a conventional setting, preheat the oven to 180°C. Place the poppy seeds, white sesame seeds and golden flax (linseed) on a 30 x 38 cm baking tray and roast for 10 minutes. Turn the tray around after 5 minutes for an even roast. Put the seeds into the water as soon as they come out of the oven **(2)**. Refrigerate overnight.

KNEADING (DAY 5)

- Put the yeast, water, both flours, salt, xanthan gum, 240 g of chestnut flour leaven and the roasted mixed grains with water into the bowl of a stand mixer fitted with the paddle attachment **(3)**. Mix for 5 minutes on low speed, then knead for 2 minutes on high speed.

FIRST RISING AND FERMENTATION

- Cover the bowl with cling film and leave to ferment for 45 minutes at room temperature.

SHAPING

- Line three 18 x 8 x 7 cm baking tins with baking parchment **(4)**. Fill each tin with one-third of the dough. Even out the height of the dough in the tins with the back of a wet spoon **(5)**.

SECOND (FINAL) PROOFING

- Leave to proof for 45 minutes–1 hour at room temperature.

BAKING

- Using the conventional setting, preheat the oven to 210°C.

- In a small container, mix together the grains for the decoration. Using a brush, gently brush the tops of the loaves with water and sprinkle with the mixed grains **(6)**. Put the tins into the centre of the oven, add steam (see p. 50) and bake for 20 minutes at 210°C, then at 180°C for 30 minutes.

- Remove from the oven, unmould the loaves and place on a wire rack to allow the steam to escape and cool.

Spinach-goat's cheese bars

with dried apricots, pumpkin seeds and rosemary

DIFFICULTY ♢

Preparation: 10 mins • **Fermentation:** 45 mins • **Proofing:** 50 mins • **Baking:** 15 mins

MAKES 10 BARS

250 g T45 flour • 150 g baby spinach leaves, washed and stalks removed
• 5 g salt • 10 g sugar • 10 g fresh compressed yeast
• 50 g water • 30 g unsalted butter

FILLING
130 g fresh goat's cheese • 60 g dried apricots, chopped into small pieces
• 1 g chopped rosemary

FINISH
1 egg + 1 egg yolk beaten together • Roasted pumpkin seeds • Olive oil

KNEADING

- Put the flour, spinach, salt, sugar and yeast into the bowl of a stand mixer. Mix for 4 minutes at low speed until you obtain a smooth dough, adding the water little by little. Knead at high speed to obtain an elastic dough. Add the butter and knead again at high speed until the dough is elastic again.

FIRST RISING AND FERMENTATION

- Cover with a damp cloth and leave to ferment for 45 minutes at room temperature.

DIVIDING AND SHAPING

- Divide the dough into two pieces and pre-shape each piece into an oval. Cover with a damp cloth and leave to rest for 20 minutes.

- Using a rolling pin, roll the dough into 32 x 20 cm rectangles. Moisten the edges, spread one of the rectangles with goat's cheese, then sprinkle with dried apricots and rosemary. Cover with the second rectangle. Place on a 30 x 38 cm baking tray covered with baking parchment. Cover with cling film and place in the freezer to harden; to make it easier to cut the bars.

- Cut into 18 x 3 cm bars and arrange on a 30 x 38 cm baking tray.

SECOND (FINAL) PROOFING

- Leave to proof for 30 minutes in a proving oven at 25°C (see p.54).

BAKING

- Preheat the oven to 155°C. Brush the bars with egg wash and sprinkle with pumpkin seeds. Place in the oven, then lower the temperature to 140°C and bake for 15 minutes.

- Remove from the oven, transfer to a wire rack and brush with olive oil.

Special buffet milk bread rolls

DIFFICULTY ♙

Preparation: 12 mins • **Chilling:** 1 hr • **Freezing:** 1–1 hr 30 mins • **Proofing:** 1 hr 30 mins–2 hrs
• **Baking:** 10–15 mins • **Basic temperature (spinach rolls):** 56

MILK BREAD DOUGH

1 kg T45 fine wheat flour • 650 g milk • 18 g salt
• 40 g sugar • 30 g fresh compressed yeast
• 250 g cold unsalted butter

EGG WASH FOR ALL ROLLS

2 eggs + 2 egg yolks, beaten together

MAKES 12 ROLLS, MORNAY SAUCE, ESPELETTE PEPPER

480 g milk bread dough • 360 g Mornay sauce

MORNAY SAUCE

24 g unsalted butter • 32 g T55 flour
• 242 g cold milk • 14 g egg yolk (1 small yolk)
• 48 g cheese, grated • Salt, pepper, Espelette pepper

....
Olive oil
Espelette pepper

MAKES 10 SEAWEED ROLLS

400 g milk bread dough • 50 g seaweed butter

MAKES 12 CUTTLEFISH INK ROLLS

475 g milk bread dough • 25 g cuttlefish ink

....
White sesame seeds

MAKES 10 TURMERIC AND CARAMELISED HAZELNUT AND WALNUT ROLLS

550 g milk bread dough • 6 g turmeric

CARAMELISED HAZELNUTS AND WALNUTS

40 g sugar • 10 g water • 40 g walnuts • 40 g hazelnuts
• 10 g unsalted butter

....
10 hazelnuts
Room-temperature unsalted butter, for the moulds

MAKES 10–12 SPINACH ROLLS

250 g T45 flour • 150 g baby spinach leaves, washed and
stalks removed • 5 g salt • 10 g sugar • 10 g fresh
compressed yeast • 30 g unsalted butter • 25 g water (to
be adjusted based on the spinach's humidity)

....
Black sesame seeds

TIP

Once kneaded, the milk bread dough can be refrigerated in a large container for 24 hours.
This way, it will gain strength and the aromas will have time to develop properly.

MILK BREAD DOUGH

- Put the flour, milk, salt, sugar, yeast and butter into the bowl of a stand mixer. Mix for 4 minutes on low speed, then knead for 8 minutes on medium speed.

- Take the dough out of the bowl and place it on the work surface, then cover with a damp cloth.

BREAD ROLLS, MORNAY SAUCE, ESPELETTE PEPPER

- Prepare the Mornay sauce. In a saucepan, melt the butter, then stir in the flour and cook for a few minutes over low heat, stirring. Pour in the cold milk and bring to the boil, stirring with a whisk. Remove from heat and add egg yolk, grated cheese, salt, pepper and Espelette pepper, then mix. Fill 4 cm-diameter silicone insert moulds with 30 g of Mornay sauce **(1)** and place in the freezer until hardened (for about 1 hour).

- Divide 480 g of milk bread dough into 12 pieces of about 40 g each. Pre-shape each into a ball, then place on two 30 x 38 cm baking trays lined with baking parchment. Cover with cling film and refrigerate for 1 hour.

- Using a rolling pin, roll out dough balls into 8 cm-diameter discs. Add the frozen Mornay sauce to the centre and seal with the dough like a purse to form a seam **(2)**. Place the dough rolls on two baking trays. Brush with egg wash and leave to stand for 1 hour 30 minutes in a proving oven at 25°C (see p.54).

- Using a conventional setting, preheat the oven to 200°C. Place 3 cm high spacers at each corner of the baking trays and cover with a sheet of baking parchment and another baking tray **(3)**. Bake for 8 minutes. Remove the baking tray and baking parchment from the top and bake for another 3–4 minutes.

- When the rolls come out of the oven, brush them with olive oil and sprinkle with Espelette pepper. Place on a wire rack to allow the steam to escape and cool.

SEAWEED ROLLS

- Weigh out 10 x 5 g portions of seaweed butter. Roll each piece into a 4 cm-long sausage, cover with cling film and place in the freezer until hardened (for about 20 minutes).

- Divide 400 g of milk bread dough into 10 pieces of about 40 g each. Shape into a ball **(4)**, then place on a 30 x 38 cm baking tray covered with baking parchment. Brush with egg wash and leave to stand for 45 minutes–1 hour in a proving oven at 25°C (see p.54).

- Slide the sheet of baking parchment on to the work surface. Dip a small rolling pin (1.5 cm in diameter) into water and press it into the middle of each small ball **(5)** before gently removing it. Brush with egg wash a second time, then add a seaweed butter sausage to the hollow **(6)** before sliding the baking parchment on to the baking tray.

- Using a conventional setting, preheat the oven to 160°C. Bake in the centre of the oven for 10 minutes. Remove from the oven and place on a wire rack to allow the steam to escape and cool.

CUTTLEFISH INK ROLLS

- Put 475 g of milk bread dough into the bowl of a stand mixer fitted with the paddle attachment, then add the cuttlefish ink. Mix on low speed until the dough is evenly coloured. Take the dough out of the bowl, make a fold (rabat), cover it with a cloth and leave it to ferment for 30–40 minutes at room temperature.

- Divide the dough into 12 pieces of about 40 g each and shape into balls **(1).** Place on a 30 x 38 cm baking tray covered with baking parchment. Brush with egg wash and sprinkle with sesame seeds **(2).** Leave to proof for 1 hour in a proving oven at 25–28°C (see p. 54).

- Using a conventional setting, preheat the oven to 145°C and bake in the centre for 12 minutes. Remove from the oven and place the rolls on a wire rack to allow the steam to escape and cool.

TURMERIC AND CARAMELISED HAZELNUT AND WALNUT ROLLS

- Prepare the caramelised hazelnuts and walnuts. In a small saucepan, add the sugar and water and cook until amber in colour. Add the hazelnuts and walnuts. Stir constantly with a plastic spatula until the nuts are well coated with caramel. Add the butter and mix, then place on a sheet of baking parchment. Separate the hazelnuts and walnuts and leave to cool. Using a large knife, coarsely chop the nuts.

- Put 550 g of milk bread dough into the bowl of a stand mixer fitted with a dough hook, then add the turmeric and caramelised hazelnuts and walnuts **(3).** Mix on low speed until the dough is smooth. Take the dough out of the bowl, make a fold (rabat), cover with a cloth and leave to ferment for 30 minutes at room temperature.

- Divide the dough into ten pieces of about 60 g each. Shape into balls, then place into 6 cm-diameter 4.5 cm-high moulds that have been buttered and lined with baking parchment extending 1 cm above the moulds. Brush with egg wash, place on a 30 x 38 cm baking tray covered with baking parchment and leave to proof for 1 hour 30 minutes in a proving oven at 25°C (see p. 54).

- Using a conventional setting, preheat the oven to 145°C. With scissors, cut the top of each dough into a cross **(4),** then press a hazelnut into each. Bake in the centre of the oven for 12–15 minutes. Remove from the oven and place on a wire rack to allow the steam to escape and cool.

SPINACH ROLLS

- Put the flour, spinach, salt, sugar, yeast, butter and water into the bowl of a stand mixer **(5).** Mix for 4 minutes on low speed, then knead for 8 minutes on medium speed. Take the dough out of the bowl, make a fold (rabat), cover with a damp cloth and leave to ferment 30–40 minutes at room temperature.

- Divide the dough into 10–12 pieces of about 40 g each. Shape each into a ball and place on a 30 x 38 cm baking tray covered with baking parchment. Brush with egg wash and sprinkle with sesame seeds **(6).** Leave to proof for 1 hour in a proving oven at 25–28°C (see p. 54).

- Preheat oven to 145°C and bake for 12 minutes. Remove from the oven and place on a wire rack to allow the steam to escape and cool.

REGIONAL BREADS

Rye loaf

AUVERGNE

DIFFICULTY ♔ ♔ ♔

This bread requires 4 days to establish a liquid leaven and a stiff rye leaven.

THE DAY BEFORE Preparation: 3–4 mins • **Fermentation:** 2 hrs • **Chilling:** 12 hrs
ON THE DAY Preparation: 6–7 mins • **Fermentation:** 2 hrs 15 mins • **Proofing:** 15 mins • **Baking:** 40 mins

MAKES 1 LOAF

STIFF RYE LEAVEN REFRESHMENT
150 g stiff rye leaven

....

500 g T170 dark rye flour • 300 g water at 40°C

RYE LEAVEN FROM AUVERGNE
220 g liquid leaven

....

50 g water at about 80 °C • 65 g T170 dark rye flour

KNEADING
190 g water at about 70°C • 190 g T130 medium rye flour • 7 g Guérande sea salt

....

Flour for the banneton

LIQUID LEAVEN AND STIFF RYE LEAVEN (4 DAYS IN ADVANCE)

- Prepare the leavens (see pp. 35 and 36).

RYE LEAVEN REFRESHMENT (THE DAY BEFORE)

- Put the flour, 150 g of stiff rye leaven and the water into the bowl of a stand mixer fitted with the paddle attachment **(1)**. Mix for 3–4 minutes on low speed. Form a ball with the dough and wrap in cling film. Leave to rise for 2 hours at room temperature. Refrigerate overnight.

RYE LEAVEN FROM AUVERGNE (ON THE DAY)

- Put the water, 220 g of the liquid leaven, 220 g of the stiff rye leaven, cut into small pieces, and the rye flour into the bowl of a stand mixer **(2)**. Mix for 4 minutes on low speed. Cover the dough in the bowl with cling film and leave to ferment for 1 hour.

KNEADING

- Add the hot water, rye flour and salt to the bowl **(3)**. Knead for 2–3 minutes on medium speed. After kneading, the temperature of the dough should be 30–35°C **(4)**.

FIRST RISING AND FERMENTATION

- Cover and leave the dough to ferment in the mixer bowl for 1 hour 15 minutes.

SHAPING

- Put the dough into a floured 24 cm-diameter banneton **(5)**.

SECOND (FINAL) PROOFING

- Leave to proof for 15 minutes at room temperature **(6)**.

BAKING

- Using the conventional setting, preheat the oven to 260°C with a 30 x 38 cm baking tray in the centre.

- Remove the hot tray and place it on a wire rack. Turn the banneton over on to a sheet of baking parchment **(7)**, then carefully slide the dough on to the hot baking tray. Return the tray to the oven and add steam (see p. 50). Let the steam out after 10 minutes. Turn off the oven and continue baking for 30 minutes or until the core temperature of the bread reaches at least 98°C **(8) (9)**.

- Remove from the oven and place on a wire rack to allow the steam to escape and cool.

Traditional Normandy bread

DIFFICULTY ♙

THE DAY BEFORE Preparation: 10 mins • Fermentation: 30 mins • **Chilling:** 12 hrs
ON THE DAY Preparation: 11 mins • Fermentation: 5 mins • **Proofing:** 2 hrs • **Baking:** 40 mins
• **Basic temperature:** 60

MAKES 2 LOAVES

350 g fermented dough

KNEADING

140 g water • 5 g fresh compressed yeast • 350 g T65 flour • 7 g salt • 10 g room-temperature unsalted butter

FERMENTED DOUGH (THE DAY BEFORE)

• Prepare the fermented dough and refrigerate overnight (see p. 33).

KNEADING (ON THE DAY)

• Put the water, yeast, flour, fermented dough, cut into small pieces, salt and butter into the bowl of a stand mixer. Knead for 10 minutes on low speed, then 1 minute on medium speed. The resulting dough will be quite stiff and dry.

DIVISION

• Divide the dough into two pieces of about 430 g each and pre-shape each piece into a tight ball.

FIRST RISING AND FERMENTATION

• Cover the balls with a cloth and leave to ferment for 5 minutes at room temperature.

SHAPING

• Shape into 20 cm-long pieces and place on a baking tray covered with baking parchment. With a baker's blade, make an incision lengthways in the middle, then three incisions at regular intervals on each side.

SECOND (FINAL) PROOFING

• Leave to proof for 2 hours in a proving oven at 25°C (see p. 54).

BAKING

• Using the conventional setting, preheat the oven to 210°C with a 30 x 38 cm baking tray in the centre.

• Transfer the hot baking tray to a wire rack and slide the baking parchment over the hot tray. Place in the oven, add steam (see p. 50) and bake for 40 minutes, reducing the temperature to 200°C after 30 minutes if the bread is turning too dark.

• Remove from the oven and place on a wire rack to allow the steam to escape and cool.

Lodève bread

OCCITANIE

DIFFICULTY ♙ ♙

This bread requires 4 days to establish a liquid leaven.

THE DAY BEFORE Preparation: 8 mins • **Fermentation:** 1 h 30 mins • **Chilling:** 12 hrs
ON THE DAY Fermentation: 1 hr • **Proofing:** 45 mins–1 hr • **Baking:** 20–25 mins

• Basic temperature: 56

MAKES 4 LOAVES
250 g liquid leaven

KNEADING
3 g fresh compressed yeast • 270 g water • 500 g 'French tradition' flour
• 15 g salt • 40 g water for 'bassinage'

Flour for the finish

LIQUID LEAVEN (4 DAYS IN ADVANCE)

• Prepare the liquid leaven (see p. 35).

KNEADING (THE DAY BEFORE)

• Put the yeast, water, flour, 250 g of liquid leaven and salt into the bowl of a stand mixer. Mix for 3 minutes on low speed, then knead for 5 minutes on medium speed. Gradually add the water for 'bassinage' in the final 2 minutes.

• Place in a container, cover with a damp cloth and leave to ferment for 1 hour 30 minutes at room temperature. Make a fold (rabat) and refrigerate overnight.

PRE-SHAPING (ON THE DAY)

• Fold the dough twice, from the base to the centre and from the top to the centre, to shape it into an elongated dough piece to obtain a 25 x 20 cm rectangle. Place on a cloth with the seam underneath.

FIRST RISING AND FERMENTATION

• Leave to ferment for 1 hour at room temperature. Flour the top of the dough.

DIVIDING AND FINAL SHAPING

• Using a large knife, cut four triangles of about 260 g, turn them over and place on a baking tray covered with a cloth so that they do not touch each other.

SECOND (FINAL) PROOFING

• Cover with a cloth and proof for 45 minutes–1 hour at room temperature.

BAKING

• Using the conventional setting, preheat the oven to 230°C with a 30 x 38 cm baking tray in the centre.

• Remove the hot tray and place it on a wire rack. Using a peel, gently turn each triangle over on to the baking tray, then lightly slash the top of the dough pieces with a baker's blade. Place in the oven, add steam (see p. 50) and bake for 20–25 minutes.

• Remove from the oven and place on a wire rack to allow the steam to escape and cool.

Sübrot bread

ALSACE

DIFFICULTY ♙ ♙

This bread requires 4 days to establish a stiff leaven.

Preparation: 10 mins • **Fermentation:** 45 mins • **Proofing:** 1 hr 45 mins • **Baking:** 20–30 mins • **Basic temperature:** 56

MAKES 2 LOAVES

100 g stiff leaven

KNEADING
325 g 'French tradition' flour • 6 g salt • 2 g fresh compressed yeast • 205 g water
....
Sunflower oil

A 'PENNY LOAF'

Sübrot bread, formerly called 'one penny bread', originates from Alsace, in particular from Strasbourg. Dating from 1870 (and probably before), it was very successful between the two wars thanks to its low price. It is much appreciated at breakfast for its crispy crust and its light crumb, it is also delicious with regional deli meats.

STIFF LEAVEN (4 DAYS IN ADVANCE)

- Prepare the stiff leaven (see p. 36).

KNEADING

- Put the flour, leaven, salt, yeast and water into the bowl of a stand mixer and mix for 5 minutes on low speed, then knead for 5 minutes on high speed. The dough obtained will be of firm consistency. After kneading, the temperature of the dough should be 23–25°C.

FIRST RISING AND FERMENTATION

- Transfer to a container, cover with a damp cloth and leave to ferment for 45 minutes at room temperature.

DIVIDING AND SHAPING

- Divide the dough into two pieces of about 310 g each **(1)**. Slightly shape into a ball and leave to rest for 15 minutes at room temperature **(2)**.

- Using a rolling pin, roll the dough into two rectangles of 15 x 13 cm **(3)**. Brush a thin layer of oil on one of the rectangles and place the second one on top **(4) (5)**.

- Cut two strips lengthways and divide each strip into two rectangles of 7.5 x 6.5 cm **(6) (7)**. Place two rectangles side by side on a cloth so that they touch each other, standing with a corner pointing up, to form a diamond shape **(8)**.

SECOND (FINAL) PROOFING

- Cover with a damp cloth and leave to proof for 1 hour 30 minutes at room temperature.

BAKING

- Using the conventional setting, preheat the oven to 250°C with a 30 x 38 cm baking tray in the centre. Remove the hot tray and place it on a wire rack. By hand, carefully place the dough pieces on a sheet of baking parchment and slide them on to the hot baking tray **(9)**. Place in the oven, add steam (see p. 50) and bake for 20–30 minutes.

- Remove from the oven and place on a wire rack to allow the steam to escape and cool.

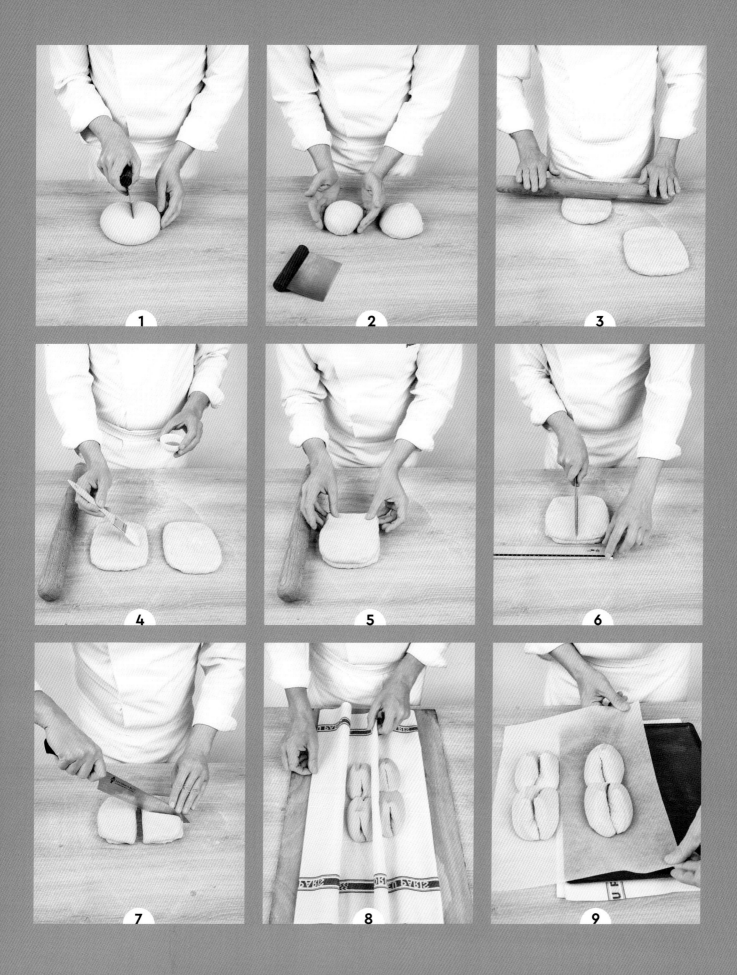

Fougasse with olives

PROVENCE

DIFFICULTY ♙

Preparation: 13 mins • **Fermentation:** 2 hrs • **Proofing:** 40 mins–55 mins • **Baking:** 20–25 mins • **Basic temperature:** 54

MAKES 2 FOUGASSES

5 g fresh compressed yeast • 330 g water • 540 g T65 flour • 11 g salt • 40 g olive oil for 'bassinage'

....

150 g Kalamata olives, chopped into large pieces

....

Olive oil for the finish

KNEADING

- Put the yeast, water, flour and salt into the bowl of a stand mixer. Mix for 5 minutes on low speed, then knead for 8 minutes on medium speed. Pour in the olive oil for 'bassinage' at low speed, then mix until smooth. Add the olives and mix on low speed until incorporated.

- Oil the sides of a container with olive oil, then add the dough.

FIRST RISING AND FERMENTATION

- Cover with a damp cloth and leave to rest for 1 hour at room temperature. Make a fold (rabat), cover and leave to ferment for 1 hour at room temperature.

DIVIDING AND SHAPING

- Divide the dough into two pieces of about 530 g each. Pre-shape each dough piece into an oval without making the dough too tight. Cover with a cloth and leave to rest for 10 minutes at room temperature.

- Using your hands or a rolling pin, flatten into 25 x 18 cm rectangles **(1)**. Place them on two 30 x 38 cm baking trays covered with baking parchment.

- Using a dough cutter, make seven slits to create the specific shape of the fougasse **(2)**. Gently open the slots **(3)** by hand.

SECOND (FINAL) PROOFING

- Cover with a cloth and leave to proof for 30–45 minutes at room temperature.

BAKING

- Using a conventional setting, preheat the oven to 230°C. Place the two trays in the oven, add steam (see p. 50) and bake for 20–25 minutes.

- After removing them from the oven, place the fougasses on a wire rack and brush with olive oil.

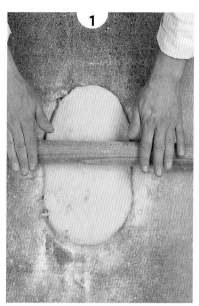

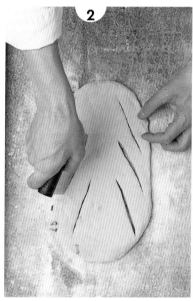

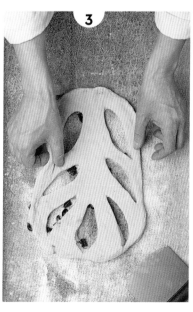

Beaucaire bread

OCCITANIE

DIFFICULTY ♔ ♔

This bread requires 4 days to establish a stiff leaven.

Preparation: 15 mins • **Fermentation:** 20 mins • **Proofing:** 3 hrs 15 mins • **Baking:** 20–25 mins
• **Basic temperature:** 58

MAKES 3 LOAVES

100 g stiff leaven

KNEADING
250 g 'French tradition' flour • 0.5 g fresh compressed yeast
• 5 g salt • 165 g water

PASTE
125 g water • 25 g T55 flour

A VERY TASTY
OLD FASHIONED BREAD

This pretty small loaf, characterised by its beautiful slit, is considered one of the best in France. It is traditionally made with a high quality flour from the soft wheat of the Limagne plain in Auvergne, known for its rich soils. It contains a high percentage of leaven and is characterised by an open crumb and a thin crust.

STIFF LEAVEN (4 DAYS IN ADVANCE)

- Prepare the stiff leaven (see p. 36).

KNEADING

- Put the flour, yeast, salt, water and 100 g of stiff leaven, cut into small pieces, into the bowl of a stand mixer **(1)**. Mix for 15 minutes on low speed. After kneading, the temperature of the dough should be 25°C **(2)**.

FIRST RISING AND FERMENTATION

- Cover with a damp cloth and leave to ferment for 20 minutes at room temperature.

PASTE

- In a small bowl, mix the water and flour to form a 'paste' **(3)**.

DIVIDING AND SHAPING

- Flatten the dough by hand, then shape into a rectangle of about 30 x 18 cm **(4)**. Leave to rest for 20 minutes at room temperature.

- Do a single turn (see p. 206) **(5)**. Leave to rest for 30 minutes.

- Using a rolling pin, roll the dough into a 22 x 17 cm rectangle with a thickness of 2.5 cm. Brush the top with the paste **(6)**. Leave to rest for 10 minutes.

- Cut the dough into two pieces (11 x 17 cm each) **(7)** and place one on top of the other. Leave to rest for at least 15 minutes.

- Using a dough cutter or a large knife, cut three pieces of dough (5.5 x 11 cm each) weighing about 170 g **(8)**. Place them with the cut side on a floured cloth-lined baking tray **(9)**, and make folds in the cloth high enough to prevent the dough pieces opening.

SECOND (FINAL) PROOFING

- Cover with a cloth and leave to proof for 2 hours at room temperature.

BAKING

- Using the conventional setting, preheat the oven to 260°C with a 30 x 38 cm baking tray in the centre.

- Remove the hot tray and place it on a wire rack. Using a peel, carefully place the dough pieces on it. Place in the oven, add steam (see p. 50) and bake for 20–25 minutes.

- Remove from the oven and place on a wire rack to allow the steam to escape and cool.

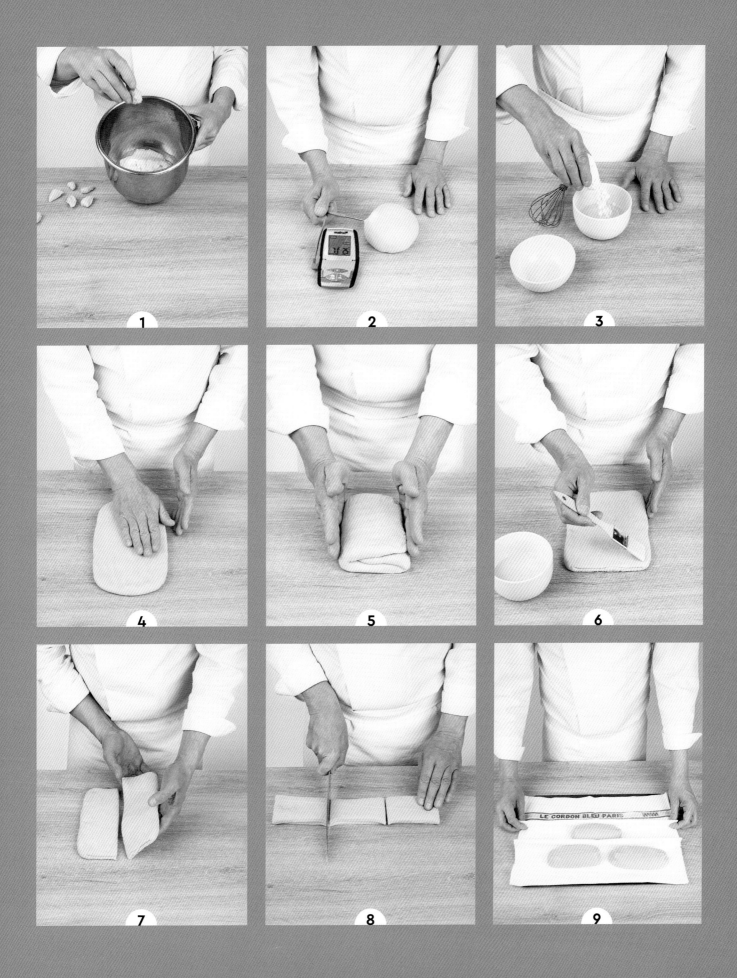

Hand of Nice

PROVENCE

DIFFICULTY ♙ ♙

---

2 DAYS IN ADVANCE Preparation: 10 mins • **Fermentation:** 30 mins • **Chilling:** 12 hrs

THE DAY BEFORE Preparation: 8 mins • **Fermentation:** 30 mins • **Chilling:** 12 hrs

ON THE DAY Proofing: 1 hr 30 mins • **Baking:** 20 mins

• **Basic temperature:** 54

MAKES 2 LOAVES

50 g fermented dough

KNEADING
330 g 'French tradition' flour • 185 g water • 6 g salt
• 3 g fresh compressed yeast • 26 g olive oil

A REGIONAL BREAD THAT BECAME FAMOUS

Shaped like a hand with four fingers, this bread was immortalised in 1952, thanks to a photo of Pablo Picasso signed by Robert Doisneau.

TIP: to roll out the dough thinly over 1 m long, proceed in several steps so as not to tear it, and flour the work surface to prevent it sticking. Finally, brush off excess flour before shaping the fingers.

FERMENTED DOUGH (2 DAYS IN ADVANCE)

• Prepare the fermented dough and refrigerate overnight (see p. 33).

KNEADING (THE DAY BEFORE)

• Put the flour, water, salt, yeast, 50 g of fermented dough, cut into small pieces, and olive oil into the bowl of a stand mixer. Mix for 3 minutes on low speed, then knead for 5 minutes on medium speed. After kneading, the temperature of the dough should be 23°C.

FIRST RISING AND FERMENTATION

• Put the dough into a container, cover with a cloth and leave to ferment for 30 minutes at room temperature. Refrigerate overnight.

DIVIDING AND SHAPING (ON THE DAY)

• Take the container out of the refrigerator 30 minutes before use. Divide the dough into two pieces of about 300 g each. Pre-shape each dough into a long oval (1) and leave to rest for 30 minutes.

• Using a rolling pin, roll out the dough pieces very thinly into strips of about 1 m x 15 cm (2).

• Slit the ends of each strip in two for about 45 cm (3). Take the inner edge of each strip and roll it diagonally outwards to form a cone (4).

• Once the four fingers are rolled up, bring the bottom two fingers over the top two fingers, spreading them outwards to form a hand (5). Place the two hands on two 30 x 38 cm baking trays covered with baking parchment (6).

SECOND (FINAL) PROOFING

• Cover with a damp cloth and leave to proof for 1 hour at room temperature.

BAKING

• Using a conventional setting, preheat the oven to 250°C. Place the trays in the centre of the oven, add steam (see p. 50) and bake for 20 minutes.

• Remove from the oven and place on a wire rack to allow the steam to escape and cool.

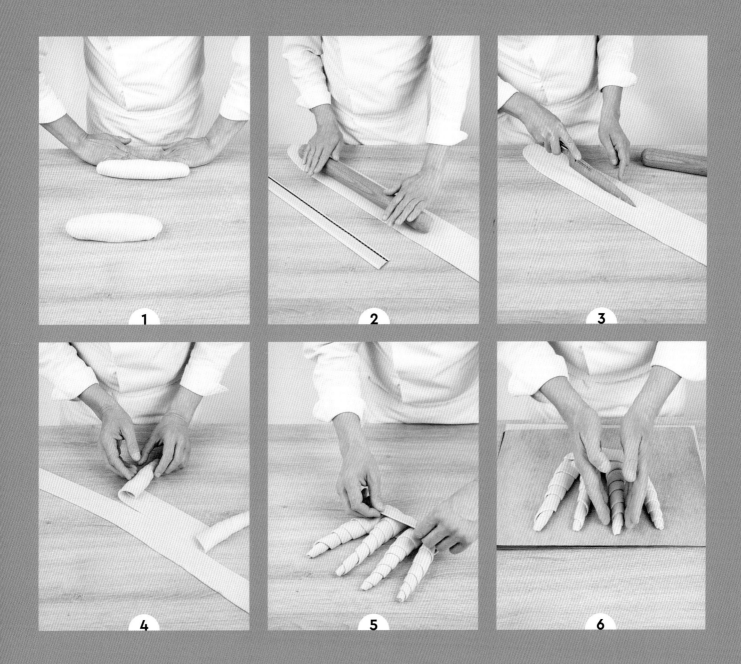

INTERNATIONAL BREADS

Focaccia

ITALY

DIFFICULTY ♙

THE DAY BEFORE Preparation: 10 mins • **Fermentation:** 30 mins • **Chilling:** 12 hrs
ON THE DAY Preparation: 8 mins • **Fermentation:** 1 hr 30 mins • **Proofing:** 45 mins • **Baking:** 20–25 mins
• **Basic temperature:** 54

MAKES 1 FOCACCIA

100 g fermented dough

KNEADING

425 g T55 flour • 350 g water • 75 g potato flakes • 10 g salt • 7.5 g fresh compressed yeast
• 5 g herbes de Provence • 100 g olive oil for 'bassinage'

FINISH

Olive oil • Fleur de sel (fine sea salt) • Rosemary sprigs

FERMENTED DOUGH (THE DAY BEFORE)

• Prepare the fermented dough and refrigerate overnight (see p. 33).

KNEADING (ON THE DAY)

• Put the flour, water, fermented dough, cut into small pieces, potato flakes, salt, yeast and herbes de Provence into the bowl of a stand mixer. Mix for 4 minutes on low speed, then knead for 4 minutes on medium speed. Pour in the olive oil for 'bassinage' on low speed, then finish on medium speed until the dough pulls away from the sides of the bowl. After kneading, the temperature of the dough should be 25°C.

FIRST RISING AND FERMENTATION

• Take the dough out of the bowl and place into a container oiled with olive oil. Cover and leave to ferment for 20 minutes. Make a fold (rabat) and leave to ferment for another 40 minutes. Make another fold and leave to ferment for 30 minutes.

SHAPING

• Line the base of a 38 x 28 cm rimmed baking tray with baking parchment. By hand, flatten the dough into the shape of the baking tray.

SECOND (FINAL) PROOFING

• Leave to proof for 45 minutes at room temperature.

BAKING

• Using a conventional setting, preheat the oven to 240°C. Make indentations on the surface of the dough by pressing your fingers into it, then fill with olive oil. Place in the centre of the oven, add steam (see p. 50) and bake for 20–25 minutes.

• Remove from the oven, transfer the focaccia to a wire rack and allow the steam to escape and cool. Brush with olive oil, sprinkle with fleur de sel and add a few sprigs of rosemary.

Ciabatta

ITALY

DIFFICULTY ♡

THE DAY BEFORE Preparation: 10 mins • **Fermentation:** 30 mins • **Chilling:** 12 hrs
ON THE DAY Preparation: 10 mins • **Fermentation:** 2 hrs • **Proofing:** 45 mins • **Baking:** 20–25 mins
• **Basic temperature:** 54

MAKES 3 CIABATTAS

100 g fermented dough

KNEADING
500 g T45 fine wheat flour • 12.5 g salt • 8 g fresh compressed yeast • 375 g water
• 40 g olive oil • 75 g water for 'bassinage'

FINISH
Olive oil • Flour • Fine semolina

FERMENTED DOUGH (THE DAY BEFORE)

• Prepare the fermented dough and refrigerate overnight (see p. 33).

KNEADING (ON THE DAY)

• Put the flour, salt, yeast, fermented dough, cut into small pieces, and 375 g of water into the bowl of a stand mixer. Mix for 4 minutes on low speed, then knead for 4 minutes on medium speed.

• Add the olive oil in a slow stream and finish on medium speed. Add the 75 g of water for 'bassinage' until the dough comes away from the sides of the bowl. After kneading, the temperature of the dough should be 25°C.

FIRST RISING AND FERMENTATION

• Put the dough into a container oiled with olive oil. Cover and leave to ferment for 20 minutes. Make a fold (rabat) and leave to ferment for another 40 minutes. Make another fold and leave to ferment for 1 hour.

DIVIDING AND SHAPING

• Dust a work surface with flour, then flatten the dough on it by hand. Using a large knife, cut out three pieces of dough weighing about 370 g. Dust a cloth with a mixture of flour and fine semolina, then turn the dough pieces over on to the cloth.

SECOND (FINAL) PROOFING

• Cover with a damp cloth and leave to proof for 45 minutes at room temperature.

BAKING

• Using the conventional setting, preheat the oven to 240°C with a 30 x 38 cm baking tray in the centre.

• Remove the hot tray and place on a wire rack. Using a peel, gently turn the dough pieces right side up on to the baking tray. Place in the oven, add steam (see p. 50) and bake for 20–25 minutes.

• Remove from the oven and place on a wire rack to allow the steam to escape and cool.

Ekmek

TURKEY

DIFFICULTY ♙

Preparation: 11 mins • **Fermentation:** 45 mins • **Proofing:** 1 hr 15 mins–1 hr 30 mins • **Baking:** 30–40 mins
• **Basic temperature:** 65

MAKES 1 EKMEK

3 g fresh compressed yeast • 5 g sugar • 125 g water • 175 g T65 flour • 4 g baking powder
• 35 g fromage blanc • 3 g salt • 75 g T130 medium rye flour

FINISH
Flour • Olive oil • White sesame seeds

KNEADING

• Put the yeast, sugar, water, flour, baking powder, fromage blanc, salt and flour into the bowl of a stand mixer. Mix for 4 minutes on low speed, then knead for 7 minutes on medium speed until the dough is smooth and elastic.

FIRST RISING AND FERMENTATION

• Transfer the dough to the work surface and form into a ball. Lightly flour the top, then cover with a dry cloth and leave to ferment for 45 minutes at room temperature.

FINAL SHAPING

• Pre-shape the dough into an elongated form (see pp. 42–43). Using a rolling pin, roll the dough to a 1.5 cm-thick oval. Brush with olive oil, then sprinkle the top with white sesame seeds. Place on a 30 x 38 cm baking tray covered with baking parchment and make five slits with a dough cutter.

SECOND (FINAL) PROOFING

• Leave to proof for 1 hour 15 minutes–1 hour 30 minutes in a proving oven at 25°C (see p. 54).

BAKING

• Using the conventional setting, preheat the oven to 220°C, then place the baking tray in the centre of the oven for 30–40 minutes.

• Remove from the oven and place on a wire rack to allow the steam to escape and cool.

Pitta

MIDDLE EAST AND SOUTH-EAST EUROPE

DIFFICULTY ⬡

This bread requires 4 days to establish a liquid leaven.

Preparation: 8–10 mins • **Fermentation:** 2 hrs 30 mins–3 hrs • **Proofing:** 45 mins–1 hr • **Baking:** 3–4 mins

MAKES 8 PITTAS

75 g liquid leaven

KNEADING

500 g T55 flour • 10 g salt • 4 g fresh compressed yeast • 10 g olive oil • 300 g water

LIQUID LEAVEN (4 DAYS IN ADVANCE)

• Prepare the liquid leaven (see p. 35).

KNEADING

• Put the flour, salt, yeast, liquid leaven, olive oil and water into the bowl of a stand mixer. Mix for 2–3 minutes on low speed, then knead for 6–7 minutes on medium speed.

FIRST RISING AND FERMENTATION

• Shape the dough into a ball, cover with a damp cloth and leave to ferment for 2 hours 30 minutes–3 hours at room temperature.

DIVIDING AND SHAPING

• Divide the dough into 8 pieces of about 110 g each. Pre-shape each piece into a tight ball.

SECOND (FINAL) PROOFING

• Cover with a damp cloth and leave to proof for 45 minutes–1 hour at room temperature.

BAKING

• Using the conventional setting, preheat the oven to 270°C with two 30 x 38 cm baking trays.

• Using a rolling pin, roll each ball into a disc about 14 cm in diameter.

• Remove the hot trays one by one and place on to wire racks. Using a peel, slide the discs on to the baking trays and bake for 3–4 minutes.

• After removing from the oven, leave the pittas to cool between two cloths.

Batbout

MOROCCO

DIFFICULTY ♙

Preparation: 11 mins • **Fermentation:** 45 mins • **Proofing:** 1 hr 10 mins–1 hr 40 mins • **Cooking:** 5 mins
• **Basic temperature:** 65

MAKES 12 BATBOUTS

320 g water • 7 g fresh compressed yeast • 30 g sugar • 400 g T55 flour
• 50 g T150 whole wheat flour • 50 g durum wheat semolina
• 10 g salt • 50 g olive oil for 'bassinage'

KNEADING

• Put the water, yeast, sugar, the two flours, durum wheat semolina and salt into the bowl of a stand mixer. Mix for 4 minutes on low speed, then knead for 7 minutes on medium speed until the dough is smooth and elastic. Add the olive oil for 'bassinage' in the last 2 minutes. The dough should be fairly soft, but not sticky.

FIRST RISING AND FERMENTATION

• Cover with a cloth and leave to ferment for 45 minutes at room temperature.

DIVIDING AND SHAPING

• Divide the dough into 12 pieces of about 70 g each. Pre-shape each piece into a smooth ball. Cover with a cloth and leave to rest on a lightly floured surface for about 10 minutes.

• Using a rolling pin, roll the balls into 11 cm-diameter discs. Place on a dry cloth and cover.

SECOND (FINAL) PROOFING

• Leave to proof for about 1 hour–1 hour 30 minutes.

COOKING

• Heat a cast-iron frying pan or griddle over a medium heat. Cook the batbout in batches, turning them several times until golden brown on both sides. The colouring will be a little uneven as the breads swell during cooking.

• Once the batbouts are cooked, leave to cool on a wire rack.

Steamed bao buns

VIETNAM

These steamed Asian buns, which can be filled with pork and pickled vegetables, are perfect for celebrating the Chinese New Year.

DIFFICULTY ♙

Preparation: 20 mins • **Fermentation:** 2 hrs • **Proofing:** 1 hr 32 mins– 1 hr 33 mins • **Cooking:** 8 minutes

MAKES 5 BUNS

175 g T55 flour • 3 g sugar • 3 g fresh compressed yeast • 1 small pinch of sugar • 1 tsp warm water • 100 g milk • 3 g sunflower oil • 3 g rice vinegar • 2 g baking powder • 65 g water

Sunflower oil for brushing

KNEADING

- Mix the flour with the sugar in a mixing bowl. Make a well in the centre. In a separate bowl, dilute the yeast and sugar in the warm water, then pour it into the well with the milk, sunflower oil, rice vinegar, baking powder and water. Mix with a dough scraper to obtain a dough.

- Transfer the dough to a lightly floured work surface and knead for 10–15 minutes until smooth and homogeneous. Put the dough into a lightly oiled bowl and cover with a damp cloth.

FIRST RISING AND FERMENTATION

- Leave to ferment for 2 hours at room temperature.

DIVIDING AND SHAPING

- Using a rolling pin, roll the dough to about 3 cm thick. Cut out five pieces of dough weighing 70 g. Roll into balls, cover with a cloth and leave to rest for 2–3 minutes.

- Cut five 15-cm squares of baking parchment. Roll the dough pieces into discs of about 13 cm in diameter. Place each disc on a square of parchment and brush the surface with a little oil.

SECOND (FINAL) PROOFING

- Place the discs on a baking tray, cover with a cloth and leave them to proof for 1 hour 30 minutes at room temperature until double in size.

COOKING

- Heat a large bamboo steamer over medium-high heat. Steam the bao buns on their baking parchment for 8 minutes until puffed.

- Slice the buns in half without cutting all the way through, then fill with the filling of your choice.

Challah

EASTERN EUROPEAN JEWISH CUISINE

DIFFICULTY 🎩

Preparation: 13 mins • **Fermentation:** 1 hr • **Proofing:** 1 hr 45 mins • **Baking:** 20–25 mins

MAKES 2 CHALLAHS

400 g T55 flour • 160 g water • 10 g fresh compressed yeast • 10 g honey • 8 g salt
• 60 g unsalted butter • 100 g eggs (2 eggs) • 5 g sugar

DECORATION
White sesame seeds • Black sesame seeds • Oat flakes

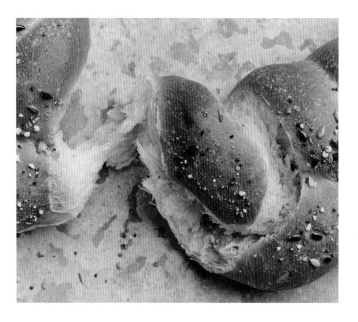

A TRADITIONAL BRAID

Challah, a kind of plaited brioche, is a traditional Jewish bread prepared every week for the Sabbath. On this occasion, two challahs are placed on the table and enjoyed on Friday evening and throughout Saturday. It is also served in honour of most Jewish holidays. For Rosh Hashanah, which celebrates the Jewish New Year, the challah is shaped into a wreath.

KNEADING

- Put the flour, water, yeast, honey, salt, butter, eggs and sugar into the bowl of a stand mixer. Mix for 5 minutes on low speed, then knead for 8 minutes on medium speed. After kneading, the temperature of the dough should be 24°C.

FIRST RISING AND FERMENTATION

- Put the dough into a large container, cover and leave to ferment for 1 hour at room temperature.

DIVIDING AND SHAPING

- Divide the dough into two pieces of about 370 g each, then pre-shape each piece into a 16 cm-long piece (see pp. 42–43). Leave to rest for 15 minutes at room temperature.

- Using a large knife, cut the dough into three pieces lengthways (1). Roll out each new dough piece by hand, working from the centre to the ends, until it is 75 cm long.

- Plait the 3 strands (2). Form into a wreath, then place each wreath on a 30 x 38 cm baking tray covered with baking parchment. Brush with water. Sprinkle with the white and black sesame seeds mixed with the oat flakes (3) (4).

SECOND (FINAL) PROOFING

- Leave to proof for 1 hour 30 minutes in a proving oven at 21–24°C (see p. 54).

BAKING

- Using a conventional setting, preheat the oven to 190°C. Place the 2 baking trays in the oven and lower the temperature to 175°C. Bake for 20–25 minutes.

- Remove from the oven and place the challahs on 2 wire racks, to allow the steam to escape and cool.

Vollkornbrot

GERMANY

DIFFICULTY 🎩

THE DAY BEFORE Preparation: 5 mins • **Fermentation:** 12 hrs

ON THE DAY Baking: 1 hr 30 mins

• **Basic temperature:** 70

MAKES 1 LOAF

1 g fresh compressed yeast • 100 g water • 100 g T110 spelt flour • 10 g rye seeds
• 8 g cracked wheat • 30 g golden flax (linseed) • 60 g sunflower seeds
• 6 g white sesame seeds • 4 g salt • 4 g sugar
• 100 g buttermilk • 50 g brown ale

DECORATION
30 g oat flakes

KNEADING (THE DAY BEFORE)

• Put the yeast, water, flour, rye seeds, cracked wheat, flax (linseed), sunflower and sesame seeds, salt, sugar, buttermilk and brown ale into the bowl of a stand mixer fitted with the paddle attachment. Mix for 5 minutes on medium speed. Cover and leave at room temperature overnight.

SHAPING (ON THE DAY)

• Line an 18 x 8 cm loaf tin with baking parchment. Transfer the dough to the tin, then sprinkle the oat flakes over the entire surface.

BAKING

• Using a conventional setting, preheat the oven to 180°C. Place the tin in the centre of the oven, add steam (see p.50) and bake for 1 hours 30 minutes.

• Remove the bread from the tin and place on a wire rack to allow the steam to escape and cool.

Borodinsky bread

RUSSIA

DIFFICULTY ♙

PREPARATION OF THE LEAVEN 5 days
ON THE DAY (DAY 6) Preparation: 10 mins • **Proofing:** 6 hrs • **Baking:** 1 hr

MAKES 1 LOAF

RYE LEAVEN
270 g T170 dark rye flour • 500 g water

KNEADING
100 g water at 30°C • 250 g T170 dark rye flour • 5 g sea salt
• 20 g black molasses • 15 g malt • 2 g coriander seeds

DECORATION
10 g coriander seeds

RYE LEAVEN (DAYS 1–4)

- **Day 1.** Using a silicone spatula, mix 30 g of the flour with 50 g of the water at 28°C in a mixing bowl. Cover with cling film and leave at room temperature overnight.

- **Day 2.** Add 30 g of the flour and 50 g of the water at 28°C to the Day 1 preparation. Mix, cover and leave at room temperature overnight.

- **Day 3.** Add 30 g of the flour and 50 g of the water at 28°C to the Day 2 preparation. Mix, cover and leave at room temperature overnight.

- **Day 4.** Add 30 g of the flour and 50 g of the water at 28°C to the Day 3 preparation. Mix, cover and leave at room temperature overnight.

LEAVEN REFRESHMENT (DAY 5)

- **Day 5.** Put 50 g of the Day 4 preparation into the bowl of a stand mixer. Add 150 g of flour and 300 g of water at 28°C. Knead for 3 minutes at low speed to obtain a fairly liquid dough. Cover with cling film and leave for 12–18 hours at room temperature.

KNEADING (DAY 6)

- Put the water, flour, salt, molasses, malt, coriander seeds and 270 g of the Day 5 leaven refreshment into the bowl of a stand mixer fitted with the paddle attachment. Knead for 5 minutes on low speed.

- Transfer the dough to a damp work surface, then knead by hand for a few minutes.

SHAPING

- Line a 18 x 8 cm loaf tin with baking parchment, then place the dough into the tin.

SECOND (FINAL) PROOFING

- Cover with a cloth and leave to proof for 6 hours at room temperature. Brush the top gently with water and sprinkle with coriander seeds.

BAKING

- Using a conventional setting, preheat the oven to 180°C. Place the tin in the centre of the oven, add steam (see p. 50) and bake for 1 hour.

- Turn the bread out of the tin and place on a wire rack to allow the steam to escape and cool.

Corn bread (broa)

PORTUGAL

DIFFICULTY ♙

THE DAY BEFORE Preparation: 15 mins • **Chilling:** 12 hrs
ON THE DAY Preparation: 7–9 mins • **Fermentation:** 1 hr 15 mins–1 hr 45 mins
• **Proofing:** 1 hr 15 mins–1 hr 45 mins • **Baking:** 20–30 mins
• **Basic temperature:** 60

MAKES 2 LOAVES

BOILED CORN SEMOLINA/POLENTA
125 g corn semolina/polenta • 125 g boiling water

....

100 g fermented dough

KNEADING
440 g T55 flour • 10 g salt • 3 g fresh compressed yeast
• 75 g mixed sweet corn kernels, fresh or canned • 260 g water

FINISH
Room-temperature unsalted butter, for the loaf tins • Corn semolina/Polenta

---

BOILED CORN SEMOLINA/POLENTA (THE DAY BEFORE)

• In a bowl, whisk together the corn semolina and boiling water. Cover with cling film and refrigerate overnight.

FERMENTED DOUGH

• Prepare the fermented dough and refrigerate overnight (see p. 33).

KNEADING (ON THE DAY)

• Put the boiled corn semolina, flour, salt, yeast, corn kernels, fermented dough, cut into small pieces, and water into the bowl of a stand mixer. Mix for 2–3 minutes on low speed, then knead for 5–6 minutes on medium speed.

FIRST RISING AND FERMENTATION

• Form a ball and leave to rest for 15 minutes, then tighten the dough into a ball once again. Cover with a damp cloth and leave to ferment 1 hour–1 hour 30 minutes at room temperature.

DIVIDING AND SHAPING

• Divide the dough into two pieces of about 560 g, then shape into long pieces of about 15 cm. Cover with a damp cloth and leave to rest for 15 minutes at room temperature.

• Butter two 20 x 8 x 8 cm loaf tins. Tighten and lengthen each dough piece by about 20 cm. Moisten the surface, roll the dough pieces in the corn semolina and place in the tins with the seam underneath.

SECOND (FINAL) PROOFING

• Cover the loaf tins with a damp cloth and leave to proof for 1 hour–1 hour 30 minutes in a proving oven at 25°C (see p. 54).

BAKING

• Using a conventional setting, preheat the oven to 230°C.

• Using a baker's blade, make seven incisions on the surface, then put into the centre of the oven. Add steam (see p. 50) and bake for 20–30 minutes.

• Remove from the oven, unmould, then place the loaves on a wire rack to allow the steam to escape and cool.

SNACKS

Bagel with salmon
and seaweed butter

DIFFICULTY ♙

THE DAY BEFORE Preparation: 10 mins • Fermentation: 30 mins • Chilling: 12 hrs
ON THE DAY Preparation: 9–11 mins • Fermentation: 15 mins • Proofing: 1 hr–1 hr 15 mins • Baking: 13–16 mins

MAKES 10 BAGELS

100 g fermented dough

KNEADING
150 g milk • 150 g water • 500 g T45 fine wheat flour • 10 g salt
• 5 g fresh compressed yeast • 35 g unsalted butter

FINISH
Egg white, beaten • White sesame seeds

FILLING
60 g seaweed butter • 300 g smoked salmon, cut into long slices • 1 lemon • A few dill sprigs

FERMENTED DOUGH (THE DAY BEFORE)
• Prepare the fermented dough and refrigerate overnight (see p. 33).

KNEADING (ON THE DAY)
• Put the milk, water, flour, salt, yeast, butter and fermented dough, cut into small pieces, into the bowl of a stand mixer. Mix for 2–3 minutes on low speed, then knead for 7–8 minutes on medium speed.

FIRST RISING AND FERMENTATION
• Cover with a damp cloth and leave to ferment for 15 minutes at room temperature.

DIVIDING AND SHAPING
• Divide the dough into 10 pieces of about 95 g. Form into sausage shapes about 15 cm long, then cover with a damp cloth and leave to rest for 15 minutes at room temperature.

• Stretch each sausage until it is about 25 cm long. Join the ends to form rings of about 10 cm in diameter, then place on two baking trays covered with baking parchment.

SECOND (FINAL) PROOFING
• Cover with a damp cloth and leave to proof for 45 minutes– 1 hour at room temperature.

BAKING
• Using a conventional setting, preheat the oven to 200°C.

• Bring a large pot of water to a simmer over a low heat, then using a slotted spoon, dip the bagels into the simmering water for about 1 minute or until they rise to the surface. Drain and place back on the trays.

• Brush the bagels with egg white, sprinkle with sesame seeds and bake for 12–15 minutes.

• Remove from the oven and transfer the bagels to a wire rack.

FILLING
• Cut the bagels in half horizontally and spread the seaweed butter on the inside. Fold the salmon slices and place on the bagels. Drizzle with lemon juice and add dill before closing the bagels.

Croque-monsieur with ham,
buckwheat butter and Mornay sauce

DIFFICULTY ♤

Preparation: 10 mins • **Baking:** 5 mins

MAKES 1 CROQUE-MONSIEUR

MORNAY SAUCE
10 g unsalted butter • 10 g flour • 60 g milk • 25 g egg yolk (1 egg yolk) • 10 g Comté cheese, grated

....

20 g buckwheat butter • 3 slices nutritional bread with mixed grains (see p. 80), 1 cm thick • 2 slices cooked ham, 40 g each • Watercress leaves • 30 g Comté cheese, grated

MORNAY SAUCE
• Melt the butter in a saucepan, then add the flour and cook for a few minutes over a low heat while stirring. Pour in the cold milk and bring to the boil, stirring with a whisk. Off the heat, add the egg yolk and cheese.

ASSEMBLING
• Preheat the grill. Spread the buckwheat butter on one side of the three slices of bread. On the bottom slice, thinly spread one-third of the Mornay sauce over the butter. Add one slice of ham and watercress.

• On the middle slice, thinly spread another third of the Mornay sauce over the butter. Add one slice of ham and place on top of the first. Close with the third slice of bread, spread the remaining Mornay sauce over the butter and sprinkle with the Comté cheese.

• Place the croque-monsieur under the grill until golden brown.

Savoury tartlets
with bacon and Béchamel sauce

DIFFICULTY ♡

Preparation: 10 mins • **Proofing:** 1 hr • **Baking:** 22 mins

MAKES 8 TARTLETS

BÉCHAMEL SAUCE
25 g unsalted butter • 32 g flour • 250 g milk • Salt, pepper, nutmeg

....

80 g lardons (small bacon strips) • 320 g croissant dough trimmings (see p. 206)

BÉCHAMEL SAUCE
• Melt the butter in a saucepan, then stir in the flour and cook for a few minutes. Pour in the cold milk and bring to the boil, stirring with a whisk. Season with the salt, pepper and nutmeg.

• Add the lardons to a saucepan and cover with cold water. Bring to the boil, then drain, dry with kitchen paper and refrigerate.

PREPARATION AND BAKING
• Cut croissant dough trimmings into 3.5 mm–1 cm squares. Line eight small 8 x 4 cm rectangular moulds with 40 g of dough.

• Leave to proof for about 1 hour in a proving oven at 28°C (see p. 54).

• Top each mould with 35 g (about 2 tablespoons) of Béchamel sauce, then spread the lardons on top.

• Preheat the fan-forced oven to 165°C. Bake in the centre of the oven for 22 minutes. Enjoy hot.

Neapolitan pizza

DIFFICULTY ○

THE DAY BEFORE Preparation: 10 mins • Fermentation: 30 mins • **Chilling:** 12 hrs
ON THE DAY Preparation: Preparation: 35 mins • Cooking: 20–30 mins • **Fermentation:** 45 mins–1 hr
• **Proofing:** 1 hr • **Baking:** 14 mins

MAKES 1 PIZZA

75 g fermented dough

KNEADING

150 g water • 250 g T55 flour • 5 g salt • 5 g fresh compressed yeast • 4 g herbes de Provence • 20 g olive oil for 'bassinage'

TOPPING

200 g courgettes, thinly sliced • Olive oil • 6 g salt • 0.5 g pepper • Basil • 250 g tomatoes, sliced • 2 g garlic powder
• 300 g mozzarella cheese, grated • 40 g Parmesan cheese, grated

PIZZA SAUCE

20 g olive oil • 60 g onions, chopped • 1 garlic clove, degermed and chopped • Salt, pepper
• 200 g tomatoes, peeled, seeded and chopped • 1 small tin tomato purée • Bay leaves, thyme, oregano • 2 g sugar

Olive oil for the finish

FERMENTED DOUGH (THE DAY BEFORE)

• Prepare the fermented dough and refrigerate overnight (see p.33).

TOPPING (THE DAY BEFORE OR ON THE DAY)

• Marinate the courgettes in a container with the olive oil, salt, pepper and basil for at least a few hours before use, preferably the day before.

PIZZA SAUCE (ON THE DAY)

• Heat a frying pan with olive oil over a medium heat and sweat the onions and garlic for 3 minutes. Season and add the chopped tomatoes, tomato purée, sugar and aromatic herbs. Simmer for 20–30 minutes on a low heat. Reduce the sauce as much as possible to concentrate the flavour, then leave to cool.

KNEADING

• Put the water, flour, salt, yeast, fermented dough, cut into small pieces, and herbes de Provence into the bowl of a stand mixer. Mix for 4 minutes on low speed, then knead for 4 minutes on high speed. Pour in the olive oil for 'bassinage' in a stream until the dough comes away from the sides of the bowl and is smooth. After kneading, the temperature of the dough should be 24–25°C.

FIRST RISING AND FERMENTATION

• Cover with a damp cloth and leave to ferment for 45 minutes–1 hour at room temperature.

SHAPING AND SECOND (FINAL) PROOFING

• Roll out the dough into a 30 x 28 cm rectangle on a lightly floured sheet of baking parchment.

• Leave to proof for 1 hour in a proving oven at 25°C (see p.54).

BAKING

• Using the conventional setting, preheat the oven to 280°C with a 30 x 38 cm baking tray in the lowest position.

• Put the tomato slices into a mixing bowl, then season with salt and pepper and sprinkle with the garlic powder.

• Top the dough with the pizza sauce, then sprinkle with the mozzarella and Parmesan cheeses. Roll up the marinated courgettes and arrange with tomatoes in a harmonious pattern.

• Remove the hot baking tray from the oven and place it on a wire rack, then slide the baking parchment with the pizza dough on to the baking tray. Bake for 14 minutes. Lift the pizza to make sure the base of the dough is golden brown.

• Remove from the oven and brush with olive oil.

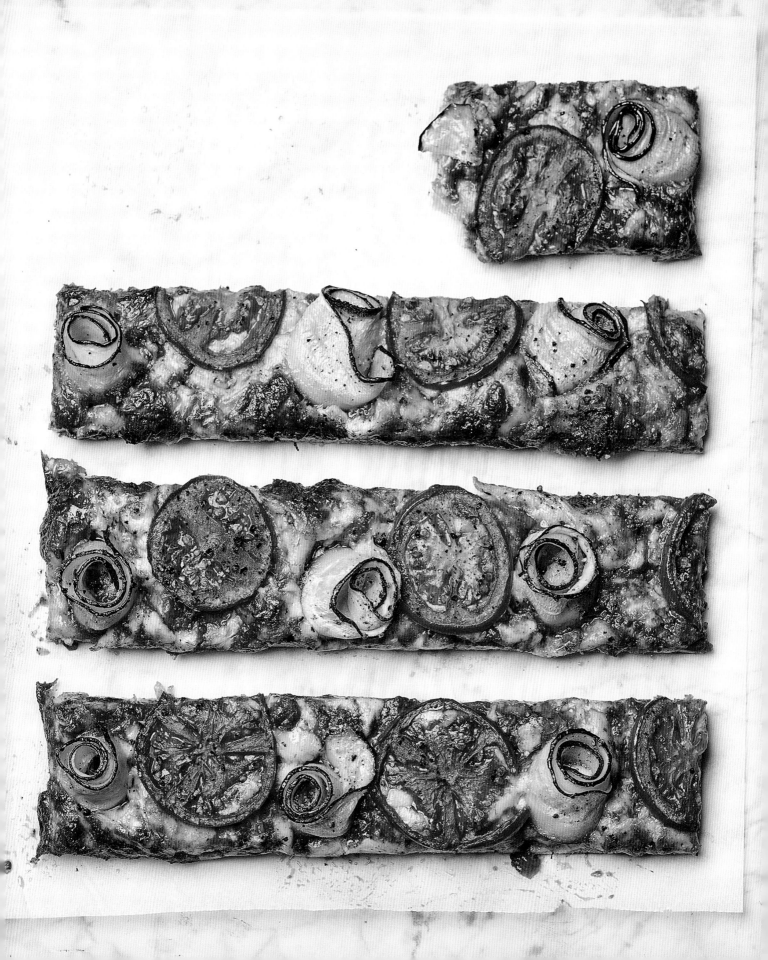

Potato tourte

DIFFICULTY ⌒

THE DAY BEFORE **Preparation:** 5 mins • **Chilling:** 24 hrs
ON THE DAY **Preparation:** 15–20 mins • **Baking:** 40–50 mins

MAKES 1 TOURTE

600 g puff pastry

FILLING

3 potatoes • ½ onion, finely chopped • 1 garlic clove, degermed and chopped
• Parsley, chopped • Salt, pepper

EGG WASH

1 egg + 1 egg yolk, beaten together

....

2 tbsp crème fraîche

PUFF PASTRY (THE DAY BEFORE)

• Prepare the puff pastry with four turns (see p. 212).

ON THE DAY

• Make a fifth single turn with the puff pastry dough, then cut it in half. Using a rolling pin, roll one piece of the dough to 2 mm thick, then cut out a 20 cm-diameter disc for the base.

• Roll the other half to 2.5 mm thick and cut out an 18 cm-diameter disc for the lid.

FILLING AND ASSEMBLY

• Cut the potatoes into thin slices and mix with the onion, garlic, parsley, salt and pepper.

• Put the dough base on a baking tray covered with baking parchment, then moisten 2 cm around the edges. Place the potato mixture on top, leaving the edge free. Seal with the lid.

• Brush with egg wash and make an impression in the centre with a 9 cm-diameter biscuit cutter.

BAKING

• Using the conventional setting, preheat oven to 200°C. Place in the oven, lower the temperature to 180°C and bake for 40–50 minutes. Check the potatoes for doneness with a knife.

• After taking the tourte out of the oven, cut out the impression made in the centre of the lid and remove it. Spread the crème fraîche over the entire surface of the potatoes, then replace the lid's centre.

Pain perdu quiche Lorraine

DIFFICULTY ⬠

Preparation: 10 mins • **Baking:** 20 mins

MAKES 5 PAINS PERDU

30 g lardons (small bacon strips) • 5 x 1 cm thick slices of sandwich bread (see Harlequin bread, note p. 112)
• ½ 'French tradition' baguette from the day before • 25 g Emmental cheese, grated

QUICHE MIXTURE
190 g eggs (4 small eggs) • 150 g milk • 150 g single cream
• Salt, pepper, nutmeg

PAIN PERDU

• Put the lardons into a saucepan and cover with cold water. Bring to the boil, then drain and dry with kitchen paper.

• Cut out 9 cm-diameter discs from slices of bread using a biscuit cutter. Line five 10 cm-diameter quiche moulds with the discs.

• Cut the baguette into 1 cm-thick slices, then cut each slice in half. Place six baguette halves against the sides of each mould. Sprinkle with the Emmental cheese and lardons.

QUICHE MIXTURE

• Using a whisk, beat the eggs in a mixing bowl, then add the milk and cream. Season. Pour the quiche mixture into the prepared moulds.

BAKING

• Preheat the fan-forced oven to 180°C. Bake in the centre of the oven for 20 minutes.

• Remove the moulds from the oven and unmould the quiches.

Vegetarian toast
with red cabbage, carrot, cauliflower and currants

DIFFICULTY ♡

Preparation: 30 mins

MAKES 4 TOASTS

PICKLED CARROTS

50 g organic cider vinegar • 50 g sugar • 50 g water • 350 g yellow carrots, sliced diagonally • 200 g carrots stored in sand, sliced diagonally

SHREDDED RED CABBAGE

30 g white vinegar • 100 g red cabbage, finely shredded • Salt

CHIVE CREAM

1 bunch of chives • 350 g fromage frais, beaten • Juice and zest of 2 limes • Green Tabasco®

....

4 slices cut lengthways of pulse and grain bread (see p. 104) • 200 g cauliflower florets • 50 g olive oil • 100 g currants • Salt, pepper

PICKLED CARROTS

• Bring the vinegar, sugar and water to the boil in a saucepan, then add the carrots. Leave to cool.

SHREDDED RED CABBAGE

• Heat the vinegar and pour it over the red cabbage. Add a pinch of salt. Mix, drain and leave to cool.

CHIVE CREAM

• Cut a few chives into batons for decoration and set aside. Finely chop the rest. Combine the fromage frais, finely chopped chives, lime juice and zest and green Tabasco® in a mixing bowl. Season. Transfer the cream to a piping bag fitted with a no. 12 fluted nozzle.

ASSEMBLING

• Toast the slices of bread and leave to cool.

• Pipe the chive cream on to the toasts. Drain the pickled carrots and place in a bowl. Add the shredded red cabbage and cauliflower florets. Drizzle with olive oil, then arrange nicely on the toasts with the currants. Sprinkle with a few batons of chives.

Smoked duck magret sandwich

with goat's cream cheese, pear and honey

DIFFICULTY ♢

Preparation: 10 mins

MAKES 1 SANDWICH

PEAR WITH HONEY
1 pear • juice of ½ lemon • 10 g acacia honey

....

1 small nutritional baguette with mixed grains
• 60 g goat's cream cheese • 30 g smoked duck magret slices

PEAR WITH HONEY

- Cut the pear in half, core it and slice thinly. Squeeze lemon juice over half of the slices and set aside.

- In a frying pan, heat the honey until it is coloured, then add the plain pear slices and coat them with honey. Leave to cool in a bowl.

ASSEMBLING

- Cut the baguette in half lengthways. Spread the goat's cream cheese on both sides of the baguette. Place the smoked duck magret slices on top, overlapping and with the fat showing on the outside.

- Between each slice of duck magret, place a slice of honeyed pear and a slice of pear with lemon juice. Close the sandwich.

Note: to prepare the nutritional baguette with mixed grains, knead the dough as for the nutritional bread with mixed grains (see p. 80). Divide it into five pieces of 200 g each and shape them into balls. After resting for 20 minutes, shape them into baguettes and proof. Place on two 30 × 38 cm baking trays and bake in a preheated oven at 240°C for 15–18 minutes.

Vegetarian open sandwich

with avocado, horseradish, celery and Granny Smith apple

DIFFICULTY ♢

Preparation: 30 mins

MAKES 20 OPEN SANDWICHES

100 g horseradish cream • 300 g fromage frais, beaten • 4 slices pulse and grain bread (see p. 104)
• 2 lemons • 2 avocados, thinly sliced • 2 Granny Smith apples, thinly sliced
• 4 stalks celery heart, thinly sliced • 200 g walnuts, lightly roasted
• Salt, pepper

PREPARATION

• Whisk together the horseradish cream and fromage frais in a mixing bowl. Fill a piping bag fitted with a no. 10 fluted nozzle and pipe small dots on to the bread slices.

• Squeeze lemon juice over the avocado slices. Cut the apple into discs, then squeeze lemon juice over them.

• Top each slice of bread with the slices from half an avocado and a few apple discs. Add the slices from one stalk of celery and a few roasted walnuts. Season with salt and pepper. Cut each slice of bread into five pieces.

TIP

Choose stalks of celery heart that are crisp and break easily, a sign of their freshness. Lay the stalks flat and then use a peeler to remove the hard strands. Cut off the tender yellow leaves from the centre; you can set aside to decorate the open sandwich, for example.

Cocktail brioche

DIFFICULTY ♙

THE DAY BEFORE **Preparation:** 12–15 mins • **Fermentation:** 30 mins • **Chilling:** 12 hrs
ON THE DAY **Preparation:** 15 mins • **Proofing:** 1 hr • **Baking:** 25 mins

> **MAKES 12 COCKTAIL BRIOCHES OF EACH**

VARIETY
600 g brioche dough

CHEESE BRIOCHES
60 g Comté cheese, grated • Cumin seeds

OLIVE BRIOCHES
50 g black stoned olives, chopped into small pieces

ONION AND PECAN NUT BRIOCHES
40 g red onion (½ onion), finely sliced and caramelised • 10 g pecan nuts

EGG WASH
1 egg + 1 egg yolk beaten together

BRIOCHE DOUGH (THE DAY BEFORE)

• Prepare the brioche dough (see p. 204).

PREPARATION (ON THE DAY)

• Divide the brioche dough into three pieces of about 200 g each, then flatten each one slightly with the palm of your hand.

• Spread three-quarters of the Comté cheese and the cumin seeds on a piece of dough (reserve the remaining Comté cheese and some of the cumin seeds to sprinkle on the brioches once brushed with egg wash).

• Add the olives to the second piece of dough, and the onion and pecan nuts to the third piece of dough.

• Form each piece of dough into a sausage shape and cut each one into 12 pieces of about 20 g. (You can leave them in pieces or shape into balls). Place on two 30 x 38 cm baking trays covered with baking parchment. Brush with egg wash, sprinkle with the remaining Comté cheese and cumin seeds, and leave them to proof for 1 hour at room temperature (25°C).

BAKING

• Preheat the fan-forced oven to 145°C. Bake for 25 minutes.

• After taking the brioches out of the oven, leave to cool on a wire rack.

Spent grain muffins

DIFFICULTY ♡

Preparation: 10 mins • **Baking:** 20 mins

MAKES 9 MUFFINS

85 g T55 flour • 30 g spent grain flour (Maltivor®) • 140 g sugar • 3 g bicarbonate of soda • 2 g salt • 40 g room-temperature unsalted butter • 100 g eggs (2 eggs) • 60 g single cream • Room-temperature unsalted butter, for the muffin tin

PREPARATION

• Preheat the fan-forced oven to 165°C.

• Combine the two flours, sugar, bicarbonate of soda and salt in a mixing bowl. Stir in the butter, then the eggs and cream. Mix with a whisk to obtain a light batter.

• Butter a 5.5 x 4 cm muffin tin and fill each muffin imprint with about 50 g of batter.

• Place in the centre of the oven and bake for 20 minutes.

....

VARIATION

Orange muffins

2 oranges • 35 g sugar • 25 g unsalted butter • 1 vanilla pod, split and scraped • 3 pinches of fleur de sel (fine sea salt) • 1 capful of Cointreau® • Muffin batter (see above) • Icing sugar

• Zest the oranges, then remove the segments. Set aside nine small segments and cut the remainder into two or three pieces. Place them on kitchen paper.

• Put the sugar into a small saucepan and make a dry caramel with an amber colour. Remove from the heat and add the butter, cut into small pieces, vanilla seeds and fleur de sel. Tip the orange peel and pieces into the caramel without stirring. Just before filling the muffin tin, add the Cointreau® to the caramel.

• Divide the batter between the muffin imprints in a buttered muffin tin. Top each muffin with one or two pieces of orange with caramel. Bake in the oven for 20 minutes.

• Remove from oven and leave to cool on a wire rack, then decorate with icing sugar and reserved segments.

VIENNOISERIES

Brioche dough

DIFFICULTY ⌂

THE DAY BEFORE **Preparation:** 12–15 mins • **Fermentation:** 30 mins • **Chilling:** 12 hrs

MAKES 700 G BRIOCHE DOUGH

90 g eggs (2 small eggs) • 45 g egg yolks (2 egg yolks) • 85 g milk • 300 g T45 flour • 6 g salt • 45 g sugar • 9 g fresh compressed yeast • 120 g cold unsalted butter • ½ tsp vanilla extract (2 g)

KNEADING (THE DAY BEFORE)

- Put the eggs, egg yolks, milk, flour, salt, sugar and yeast into the bowl of a stand mixer **(1)**. Mix on low speed until the dough is smooth and comes away from the sides of the bowl **(2)**.

- Add the butter, cut into small pieces, at low speed **(3)** and knead until the dough comes away from the sides again. It is advisable to use low speed to retain the butter's organoleptic qualities. Add the vanilla and finish kneading to completely smooth the dough.

- Take the dough out of the bowl and form it into a ball **(4)**.

FIRST RISING AND FERMENTATION

- Put the dough in a container covered with cling film and leave to ferment for 30 minutes at room temperature.

- Transfer the dough to a work surface. Make a fold (rabat) **(5)**, wrap in cling film and refrigerate overnight **(6)**.

TIP

Brioche dough contains a large quantity of eggs and butter, which gives it a soft and delicate texture. Refrigerate for at least 12 hours to stabilise the butter and develop its taste and aroma. In both sweet or savoury versions, the brioche dough lends itself to many forms: folded, twisted, plaited, moulded, etc.

Croissant dough

DIFFICULTY ♢

THE DAY BEFORE **Preparation:** 5 mins • **Fermentation:** 12 hrs

ON THE DAY **Freezing:** Variable, depending on the turns used

MAKES 580 G CROISSANT DOUGH

DÉTREMPE DOUGH

80 g water • 50 g milk • 125 g T45 flour • 125 g T55 flour • 5 g salt
• 18 g fresh compressed yeast • 30 g sugar • 25 g dry butter (see p.313)

TURNS

125 g cold dry butter (see p.313)

DÉTREMPE DOUGH (THE DAY BEFORE)

• Put the water, milk, flours, salt, yeast, sugar and butter into the bowl of a stand mixer. Mix for about 4 minutes on low speed until the dough is smooth. Increase the speed to make the dough fairly elastic. Form into a ball and wrap in cling film, then refrigerate for at least 12 hours.

TURNS (ON THE DAY)

• Roll out the dry butter in a folded sheet of baking parchment to form a square **(1) (2)**.

• Flour the work surface, then roll out the détrempe dough into a rectangle slightly larger than the butter **(3)**. Place the butter in the centre of the dough. Cut the edges of the dough **(4)** and put the two pieces of détrempe dough on the butter to enclose it.

• Using a rolling pin, make a diagonal cross to help the butter stay in place and press down the entire length **(5)**.

Note: it is important that the détempre dough and butter are of the same texture and are both cold, and to work quickly so that the butter does not soften.

Three methods are commonly used for turns in croissant dough:

- Three single turns
- One double turn + one single turn
- Two double turns

THREE SINGLE TURNS

• Roll out the dough into a 45 x 25 cm rectangle about 3.5 mm thick. Fold one-third of the dough over itself **(6)**, then fold the other third over (first single turn).

• Turn the dough 90 degrees **(7)**, then make a second single turn **(8) (9)**.

• Set aside for about 30 minutes in the freezer, then make a single turn.

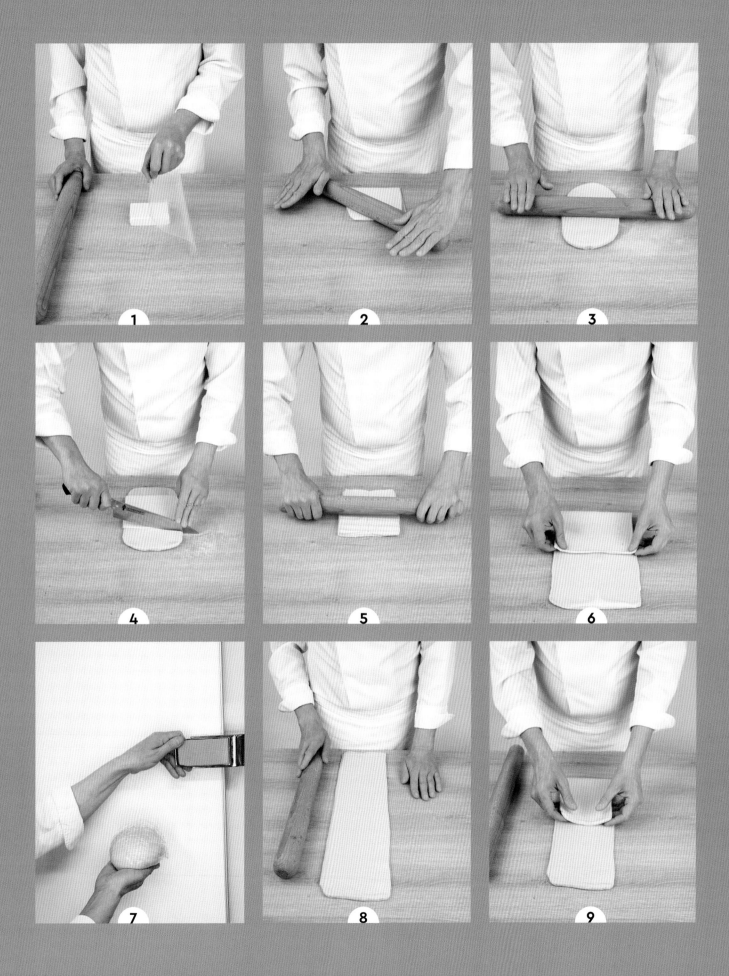

Croissant with three single turns

Croissant with one double turn + one single turn

Croissant with two double turns

ONE DOUBLE TURN + ONE SINGLE TURN

• Roll out the dough into a 50 x 16 cm rectangle about 3.5 mm thick **(10)**. Fold one-quarter of the dough over itself, then fold the remaining three-quarters over to meet the folded portion **(11)**. Fold the dough in half (first double turn) **(12)**.

• Turn the dough 90 degrees **(13)**, then make a single turn **(14)(15)**.

TWO DOUBLE TURNS

• Roll out the dough into a 50 x 16 cm rectangle about 3.5 mm thick **(16)**. Fold one-quarter of the dough over itself, then fold the remaining three-quarters **(17)** over to meet the folded portion. Then fold the dough in half (first double turn) **(18)**.

• Turn the dough 90 degrees, then turn to make a double turn.

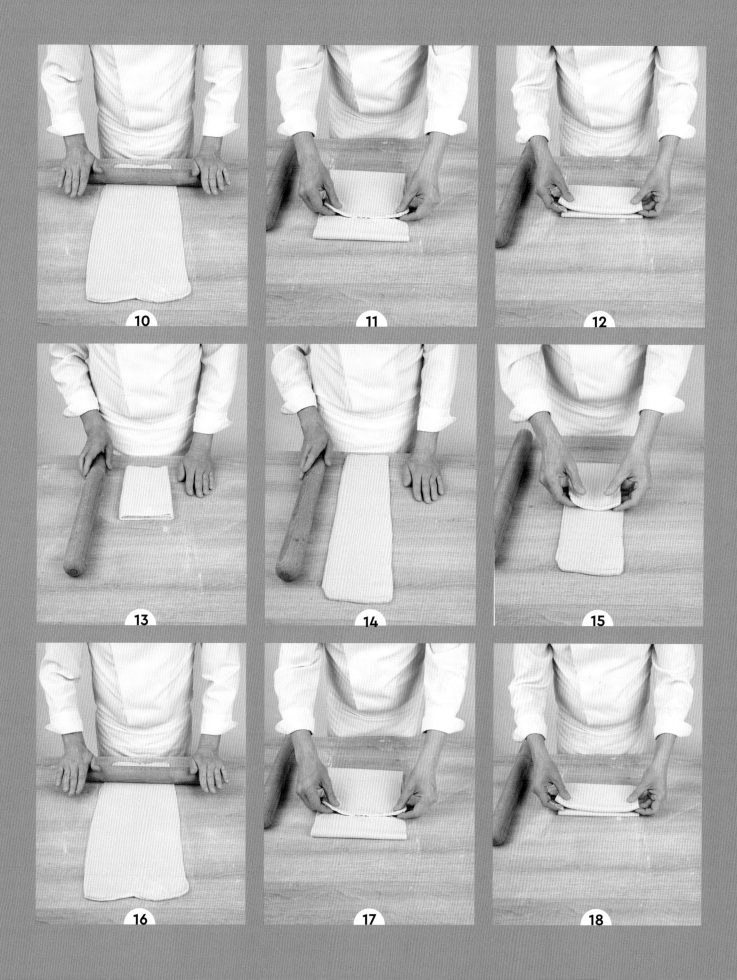

Puff pastry

DIFFICULTY ⌂

THE DAY BEFORE **Preparation:** 5 mins • **Chilling:** Variable, depending on the turns used

MAKES 560 G 4-TURN PUFF PASTRY

DÉTREMPE DOUGH
250 g T55 flour • 5 g salt • 100 g cold water • 25 g unsalted butter, melted

TURNS
180 g cold dry butter (see p.313)

DÉTREMPE DOUGH (THE DAY BEFORE)

- Put the flour, salt, water and butter into the bowl of a stand mixer fitted with the hook **(1) (2)**. Mix on low speed until the dough is smooth, without overworking it **(3)**.

- Shape into a ball, slit it crosswise in the centre **(4)**, wrap in cling film and refrigerate for at least 2 hours.

TURNS

- Roll out the dry butter in a folded sheet of baking parchment to form a square about 16 cm square.

- On a lightly floured work surface, using a rolling pin, roll the détrempe dough into a 24 cm-diameter disc. Place the butter in the centre so that the corners touch the outer edges of the détrempe dough. Pull the edges of the détrempe dough and fold towards the centre to enclose the butter like an envelope.

Two methlods are commonly used for turning a four-turn puff pastry:

- Four single turns
- Two double turns + one single turn

FOUR SINGLE TURNS (THE DAY BEFORE)

- Roll out the dough into a rectangle of about 40 x 16 cm **(5)**. Fold one-third of the dough over itself, then fold the other third over (first single turn) **(6)**. Cover with cling film and leave to rest for 20 minutes in the freezer.

- Take the dough out of the freezer and turn it 90 degrees, then make a second single turn.

- Repeat until dough has been given four single turns, then cover and refrigerate overnight.

TWO DOUBLE TURNS + ONE SINGLE TURN (THE DAY BEFORE)

- Roll out the dough into a rectangle of about 50 x 16 cm. Fold one-eighth of the dough over itself, then fold the remaining seven-eighths of the dough to meet the folded portion. Fold the dough in half (first double turn). Cover with cling film and leave to rest for 20 minutes in the freezer.

- Take the dough out of the freezer and turn it 90 degrees, then make a second double turn.

- Set aside for 20 minutes in the freezer, then take the dough out of the freezer, turn it 90 degrees and make a single turn.

- Cover with cling film and refrigerate for at least 24 hours.

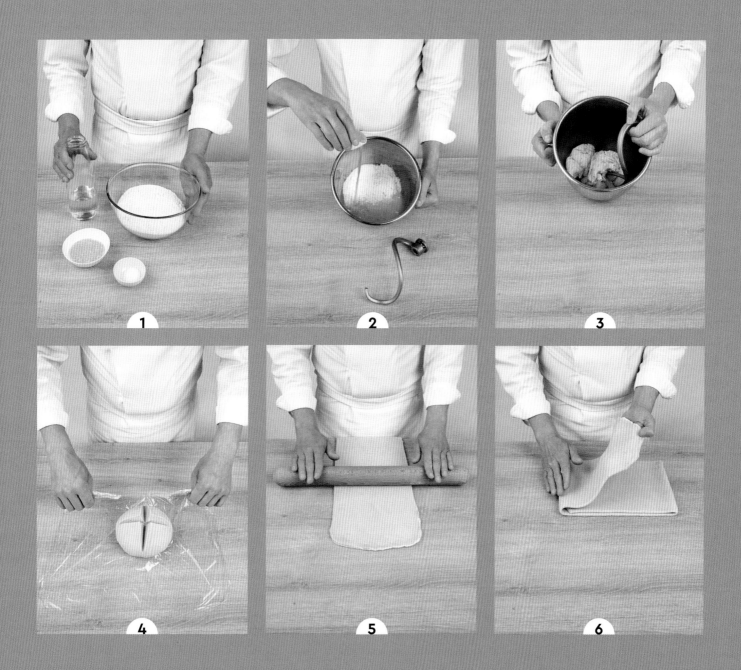

Nanterre brioche

DIFFICULTY ♢

THE DAY BEFORE Preparation: 5 mins • Fermentation: 12 hrs
ON THE DAY Preparation: 18 mins • Fermentation: 40 mins • **Chilling:** 1 hr
• **Proofing:** 1 hr 40 mins–1 hr 45 mins • **Baking:** 25 mins

MAKES 3 BRIOCHES

YEAST-BASED LEAVEN
1 g fresh compressed yeast • 93 g milk • 100 g T45 flour

KNEADING
67 g egg (1 large egg) • 58 g egg yolks (3 egg yolks) • 20 g fresh compressed yeast • 233 g T45 flour • 38 g sugar
• 12 g brown sugar • 7 g salt • 196 g cold unsalted butter

Room-temperature unsalted butter, for the loaf tins

EGG WASH
1 egg, beaten

YEAST-BASED LEAVEN (THE DAY BEFORE)

• Crumble the yeast on to the milk in a bowl and whisk together. Add the flour and mix. Cover with cling film and leave to rise for 12 hours at room temperature.

KNEADING (ON THE DAY)

• Put the yeast-based leaven, egg, egg yolks, yeast, flour, sugars and salt into the bowl of a stand mixer. Mix for 5 minutes on low speed, then knead for 8 minutes on high speed until the dough pulls away from the sides of the bowl. Add the butter, cut into small pieces, and knead for about 5 minutes on low speed until the dough comes away from the sides again and the butter is well incorporated.

• Take the dough out of the bowl, make two folds (rabats) and put into a covered container.

FIRST RISING AND FERMENTATION

• Leave to ferment for 40 minutes at room temperature, then refrigerate for 1 hour.

DIVIDING AND SHAPING

• Generously butter three 18 x 8 x 7 cm loaf tins.

• On a work surface, fold the dough, then divide it into 18 pieces of about 45 g. Pre-shape each dough into a ball, then cover with a dry cloth and leave to rest for 10–15 minutes. Reshape each dough piece tightly into balls, then place six balls in each tin with the seam underneath.

SECOND (FINAL) PROOFING

• Put the tins on to a 30 x 38 cm baking tray and leave to proof for 1 hour 30 minutes in a proving oven at 28°C (see p.54).

BAKING

• Preheat the fan-forced oven to 150°C.

• Carefully brush with egg wash without letting the wash run down the sides of the tins, then put into the centre of the oven and bake for about 25 minutes.

• Unmould and leave to cool on a wire rack.

Parisian brioche

DIFFICULTY ♙

Preparation: 15 mins • **Fermentation:** 1 hr 30 mins • **Proofing:** 2 hrs 20 mins • **Chilling:** 1 hr • **Baking:** 10–12 mins

MAKES 8 BRIOCHES

185 g T55 flour • 8 g fresh compressed yeast • 3 g salt • 18 g sugar
• 100 g eggs (2 eggs) • 90 g cold unsalted butter

Room-temperature unsalted butter, for the moulds

EGG WASH
1 egg, beaten

BRIOCHE DOUGH

• Put the flour, yeast, salt, sugar and eggs into the bowl of a stand mixer. Mix for 5 minutes on low speed, until the dough is soft and comes away from the sides of the bowl. Add the butter and knead for 10 minutes on high speed, until the dough is supple and smooth and comes away from the sides of the bowl again.

• Place on a work surface and form into a ball, lightly flour, then cover with a slightly damp cloth.

FIRST RISING AND FERMENTATION

• Leave to ferment for 1 hour 30 minutes at room temperature. At the end of fermentation, the dough should have doubled in volume.

• Fold (rabat), place in a container, cover and refrigerate for 1 hour.

DIVIDING AND SHAPING

• Flour the work surface, then divide the dough into eight pieces of about 35 g for the bases and eight others of about 15 g for the heads.

• Shape into round balls, cover with a dry cloth and leave to rest for 20 minutes on the work surface at room temperature.

• Butter eight 7–8 cm-diameter fluted brioche moulds.

• Form the small balls for the top into a pear shape. Using a finger, make a small 2 cm-diameter hole in the centre of the large balls for the base. Using scissors, make a 1 cm slit on the pointed part of each of the heads. Push the slit pointed part into the hole in a base and fold each slit part under the base.

SECOND (FINAL) PROOFING

• Put the brioche dough into the moulds, place them on a 30 x 38 cm baking tray and leave to proof for 2 hours in a proving oven at 28°C (see p. 54). The brioche doughs should have doubled in volume.

BAKING

• Using the fan-forced setting, preheat the oven to 180°C.

• Brush with egg wash, then place in the centre of the oven, lower the temperature to 160°C and bake for 10–12 minutes.

• Remove from the oven, unmould the brioches and leave to cool on a wire rack.

Bicolour folded brioche

DIFFICULTY ♔ ♔

THE DAY BEFORE Preparation: 12–15 mins • **Fermentation:** 30 mins • **Chilling:** 12 hrs
ON THE DAY Preparation: 40 mins • **Freezing:** 20–30 mins • **Proofing:** 2 hrs–2 hrs 30 mins • **Baking:** 42 mins

MAKES 2 BRIOCHES

PLAIN BRIOCHE DOUGH

80 g eggs (1½ eggs) • 40 g egg yolks (2 egg yolks) • 50 g milk • 125 g T45 flour • 125 g T55 flour
• 5 g salt • 20 g sugar • 10 g fresh compressed yeast • 75 g unsalted butter

Room-temperature unsalted butter, for the loaf tins

CHOCOLATE BRIOCHE DOUGH

22 g unsalted butter • 9 g icing sugar • 9 g unsweetened cocoa powder

TURNS

130 g cold dry butter (p.313)

CRISPY PRALINE

15 g dark chocolate • 65 g praline • 40 g crushed Gavottes® crêpes (wafers)

SYRUP

100 g water + 130 g sugar, brought to the boil

TIP

To roll out the crispy praline into a rectangle with straight sides, use a ruler or a large knife. Keep the praline in the refrigerator or freezer until ready to use, as it quickly comes to room temperature.

PLAIN BRIOCHE DOUGH (THE DAY BEFORE)

- Prepare the brioche dough without adding the vanilla (see p. 204).

CHOCOLATE BRIOCHE DOUGH (THE DAY BEFORE)

- Weigh out 100 g of plain brioche dough and put it into the bowl of a stand mixer fitted with a paddle. Add the butter, icing sugar and cocoa and mix on low speed (1). Put into a container, cover and refrigerate overnight.

TURNS (ON THE DAY)

- Roll out the dry butter in a folded sheet of baking parchment to form a rectangle.

- Roll out the plain brioche dough into a rectangle slightly larger than the butter rectangle, about 1 cm thick.

- Place the butter in the centre of the dough. Cut the edges of the dough and put the two pieces of dough on the butter to enclose it (2). Roll out to a thickness of about 3.5 mm. Make a double turn (3) (see p. 208). Turn the dough 90 degrees, then make a single turn (see p. 208). Lightly moisten the surface with water.

- Roll out the chocolate brioche dough to the same size as the plain dough and place it on top (4). Place on a tray covered with cling film and set aside in the freezer for 20–30 minutes.

- Roll out the bicoloured brioche dough into a 38 x 28 cm rectangle, about 4 mm thick (5). Using a cutter or knife and a ruler, score regular diagonal lines on the chocolate dough (6). Return to the freezer while you prepare the crispy praline.

CRISPY PRALINE

- In a bain-marie, melt the chocolate. Put the praline into a bowl, pour the melted chocolate over it and mix (7). Gently mix in the crushed Gavottes® crêpes.

- Spread thinly between two sheets of baking parchment to form a rectangle (8) and set aside in the refrigerator.

ASSEMBLY

- Place the bicoloured brioche dough gently on the work surface, chocolate side down. Remove the first sheet of baking parchment from the crispy praline, turn the praline over on to the dough, remove the second sheet of parchment and roll into a fairly tight sausage shape. Cut the sausage in half and place in two 19 x 9 x 7 cm buttered loaf tins (9).

- Leave to proof for 2 hours–2 hours 30 minutes in a proving oven at 25°C (see p. 54).

BAKING

- Using the fan-forced setting, preheat the oven to 200°C.

- Place in the centre of the oven, then lower the temperature to 140°C and bake for 40 minutes.

- After removing from the oven, brush with syrup and return to the oven for 2 minutes.

- Unmould and leave to cool on a wire rack.

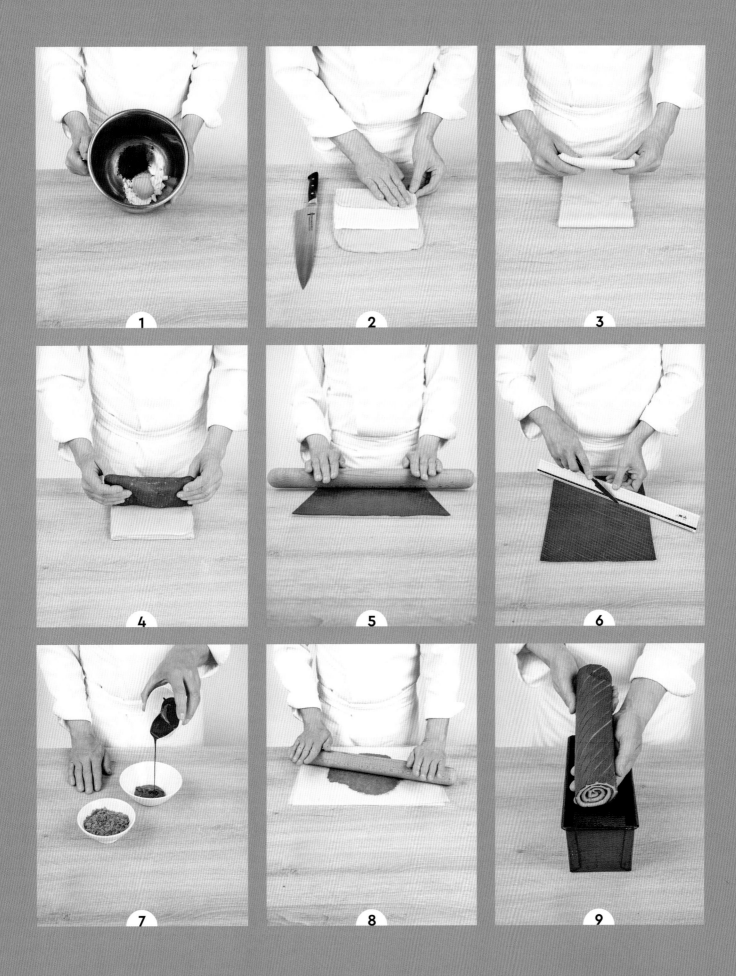

Brioche from Vendée

DIFFICULTY ♕

THE DAY BEFORE Preparation: 23 mins • **Fermentation:** 25 mins • **Chilling:** 12 hrs
ON THE DAY Preparation: 30 mins • **Proofing:** 50 mins–1 hr 15 mins • **Baking:** 25–30 mins

MAKES 2 BRIOCHES

211 g eggs (4 eggs) • 13 g fresh compressed yeast • 324 g T45 flour • 39 g sugar
• 7 g salt • 130 g cold unsalted butter

EGG WASH
1 egg, beaten

FINISH
Nibbed sugar (optional)

BRIOCHE DOUGH (THE DAY BEFORE)

- Put the eggs, yeast, flour, sugar and salt into the bowl of a stand mixer. Mix for 5 minutes on low speed, then knead for 8 minutes on high speed until the dough pulls away from the sides of the bowl.

- Add the butter, cut into small pieces, and knead for 10 minutes on low speed until the dough comes away from the sides of the bowl. Make a fold (rabat) and put into a container and cover.

FIRST RISING AND FERMENTATION

- Leave to ferment for 25 minutes at room temperature. Make a second fold and refrigerate overnight.

DIVIDING AND SHAPING (ON THE DAY)

- On a lightly floured work surface, flatten the brioche dough by hand to release the gas. Divide it into six pieces of about 120 g. Pre-shape into an elongated shape (see pp. 42–43), cover with a dry cloth and leave to rest for 10–15 minutes.

- One at a time, pick up a dough piece and tap to release the gas. Flatten, then shape tightly to elongate. Take one dough piece and roll by hand from the centre to the ends until you have a dough piece of about 30 cm long. Do the same with the other dough pieces.

- To plait together, align three dough pieces, then press the ends of the strands together to seal them. Take the left strand and pass it over the middle one, then the right one and pass it over the middle one, and so on **(1) (2)**. Continue until the dough is fully plaited, then press to seal the opposite ends and fold the seams under **(3)**. Repeat for the second brioche.

SECOND (FINAL) PROOFING

- Put the two brioches on to a 30 x 38 cm baking tray covered with baking parchment and brush with egg wash. Leave to proof for 40 minutes–1 hour in a proving oven at 28°C (see p. 54).

BAKING

- Using the fan-forced setting, preheat the oven to 170°C.

- Gently brush the surface of the plaits with egg wash a second time. Alternatively, sprinkle nibbed sugar on top.

- Place in the centre of the oven, then lower the temperature to 150°C and bake for 25–30 minutes.

- Remove from the oven and leave to cool on a wire rack.

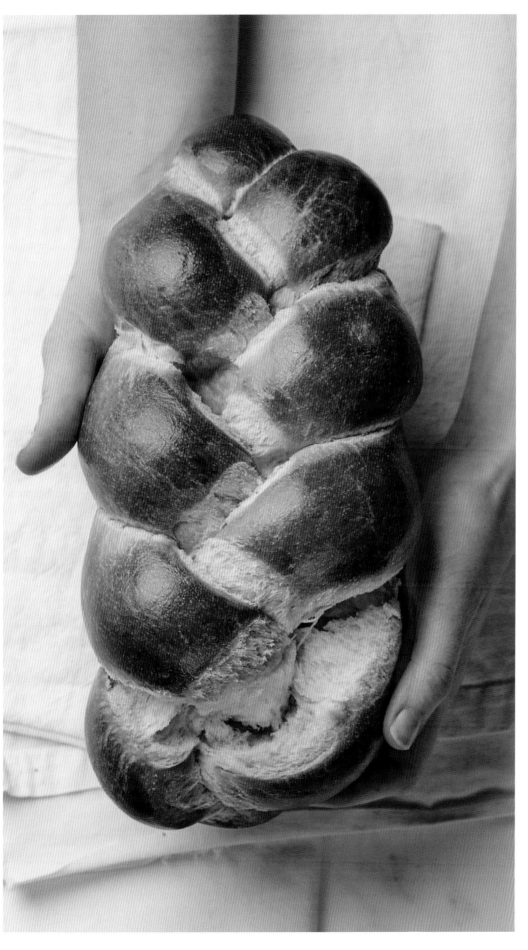

Milk bread rolls

DIFFICULTY ♙

Preparation: 15 mins • **Fermentation:** 30 mins
Proofing: 1 hr 45 mins • **Baking:** 12 mins

MAKES 8 MILK BREAD ROLLS

180 g water • 50 g egg (1 egg) • 20 g milk powder
• 320 g T45 flour • 10 g fresh compressed yeast • 7 g salt
• 30 g sugar • 65 g cold unsalted butter

EGG WASH
1 egg, beaten

KNEADING

• Put the water, egg, milk powder, flour, yeast, salt and sugar into the bowl of a stand mixer. Mix for 5 minutes on low speed until the flour absorbs the liquid and forms a sticky dough. Add the butter, cut into small pieces, and knead for 10 minutes on high speed until the dough is soft and smooth. Place the dough on a lightly floured work surface, form into a ball and cover with a damp cloth.

FIRST RISING AND FERMENTATION

• Leave to rise for 30 minutes at room temperature.

DIVIDING AND SHAPING

• Divide the dough into eight pieces of about 80 g. Form loosely into balls, cover with a damp cloth and leave to rest for 15 minutes at room temperature.

• Flour the work surface, form the dough balls into elongated shapes (see pp. 42–43), then shape them into 12 cm-long rolls. Put them on to a 30 x 38 cm baking tray covered with baking parchment.

SECOND (FINAL) PROOFING

• Leave to proof for 1 hour 30 minutes in a proving oven at 25°C (see p. 54) or until the dough pieces double in size.

BAKING

• Preheat the fan-forced oven to 180°C. Brush the pieces with egg wash and cut each one vertically and perpendicularly with scissors. Place in the oven, then lower the temperature to 160°C and bake for about 12 minutes.

• Remove from the oven and leave to cool on a wire rack.

Raspberry Danish

DIFFICULTY ♙

Preparation: 15 mins • **Fermentation:** 30 mins
Proofing: 1 hr 45 mins • **Baking:** 12 mins

MAKES 8 DANISH PASTRIES

680 g milk bread dough (see recipe opposite)
• Room-temperature unsalted butter, for the tartlet rings

SUGAR COATING
100 g room-temperature unsalted butter • 100 g sugar

EGG WASH
1 egg, beaten

DECORATION
2 punnets fresh raspberries
• 30 g pistachios, chopped

DIVIDING AND SHAPING

• Flour the work surface and divide the milk bread dough into eight pieces of about 80 g. Form loosely into balls, cover with a damp cloth and leave to rest for 15 minutes at room temperature.

• Flour the work surface, then roll the dough into 10 cm-diameter discs. Place in 10 cm-diameter buttered tartlet rings, on a 30 x 38 cm baking tray covered with baking parchment.

SECOND (FINAL) PROOFING

• Leave to proof for 1 hour 30 minutes in a proving oven at 25°C (see p. 54).

SUGAR COATING AND BAKING

• Using the fan-forced setting, preheat the oven to 180°C. Brush the discs with egg wash and press lightly in the centre to form a slight indentation.

• Cream the butter with the sugar. Fill a piping bag without a nozzle and pipe into the centre of the discs, 2 cm from the edge.

• Place in the oven, then lower the temperature to 160°C and bake for about 12 minutes.

• Remove from the oven, remove from the rings and leave to cool on a wire rack. Decorate with fresh raspberries and pistachios.

Saint-Genix brioche

DIFFICULTY 🎩

THE DAY BEFORE **Preparation:** 12–15 mins • **Fermentation:** 30 mins • **Chilling:** 12 hrs
ON THE DAY **Preparation:** 40 mins • **Fermentation:** 1 hr 30 mins • **Proofing:** 2 hrs • **Baking:** 35 mins

MAKES 3 BRIOCHES

BRIOCHE DOUGH
300 g eggs (6 eggs) • 250 g T45 flour • 250 g T55 flour • 10 g salt • 40 g sugar
• 25 g fresh compressed yeast • 250 g unsalted butter
....
340 g pink pralines

EGG WASH
1 egg + 1 egg yolk, beaten together

BRIOCHE DOUGH (THE DAY BEFORE)

• Prepare the brioche dough without the milk and vanilla (see p. 204).

FIRST RISING AND FERMENTATION (ON THE DAY)

• Leave the dough to ferment, under a damp cloth, for 30 minutes at room temperature.

• Flatten the dough by hand, then add half of the pralines. Make a fold (rabat), cover with a damp cloth and leave to ferment for 30 minutes at room temperature.

• Again, flatten the dough and add the remaining pralines. Make a fold (rabat), cover with a damp cloth and leave it to ferment for 30 minutes at room temperature.

DIVIDING AND SHAPING

• Divide the dough into three pieces of about 480 g. Form into balls and place on two 30 x 38 cm baking trays covered with baking parchment.

SECOND (FINAL) PROOFING

• Leave to proof for 2 hours in a proving oven at 28°C (see p. 54).

BAKING

• Using the fan-forced setting, preheat the oven to 160°C.

• Gently brush the three pieces with egg wash, then place in the oven, lower the temperature to 140°C and bake for 35 minutes.

Kouglof

DIFFICULTY ♙

This viennoiserie requires 4 days to establish a liquid leaven.

2 DAYS IN ADVANCE Maceration: 24 hrs
THE DAY BEFORE Preparation: 12–15 mins • Fermentation: 30 mins • Chilling: 12–24 hrs
ON THE DAY Proofing: 2 hrs • Baking: 50 mins

MAKES 3 KOUGLOFS

50 g liquid leaven

MACERATION
180 g sultanas • 30 g rum

DOUGH
90 g eggs (1½ eggs) • 70 g egg yolks (4 egg yolks) • 40 g milk • 290 g T45 flour
• 15 g fresh compressed yeast • 6 g salt • 70 g sugar • 250 g cold unsalted butter
....
Room-temperature unsalted butter, and whole almonds for the kouglof moulds

SYRUP
1 kg water + 500 g sugar, brought to the boil

FINISH
Clarified butter • Icing sugar

LIQUID LEAVEN (4 DAYS IN ADVANCE)

• Prepare a liquid leaven (see p. 35).

MACERATION (2 DAYS IN ADVANCE)

• Put the sultanas with the rum into a mixing bowl and leave to macerate for at least 24 hours.

KNEADING (THE DAY BEFORE)

• Put the eggs, egg yolks, milk and liquid leaven into the bowl of a stand mixer, then add the flour, yeast, salt and sugar. Knead like a brioche (see p. 204), adding the butter, cut into small pieces, when the dough comes away from the sides of the bowl. Add the sultanas at the end on low speed until they are well mixed into the dough.

FIRST RISING AND FERMENTATION

• Keeping the dough in the bowl, cover it with cling film and leave to ferment for 30 minutes.

• Transfer to a lightly floured work surface, then make a fold (rabat). Place the dough in a container, cover and refrigerate for 12–24 hours.

DIVIDING AND SHAPING (ON THE DAY)

• Generously butter three 13 cm-diameter kouglof moulds and place almonds in the base. Divide the dough into three pieces of about 360 g. Form into balls, pierce the centre of each dough and turn over with the seam on top into the moulds.

SECOND (FINAL) PROOFING

• Leave to proof for 2 hours in a proving oven at 25–28°C (see p. 54).

BAKING

• Using the fan-forced setting, preheat the oven to 180°C with a 30 x 38 cm baking tray in the centre. Place the moulds in the oven, lower the temperature to 145°C and bake for 50 minutes.

• Remove from the oven, unmould the kouglofs, dip them in the syrup, brush generously with melted clarified butter and place on a wire rack. Leave to cool, then sprinkle with icing sugar.

Babka

DIFFICULTY ♙

THE DAY BEFORE **Preparation:** 7–9 mins • **Chilling and Fermentation:** 12–24 hrs
ON THE DAY **Preparation:** 30 mins • **Proofing:** 1 hr 30 mins–2 hrs • **Baking:** 30 mins

MAKES 2 BABKAS

210 g water • 50 g egg (1 egg) • 500 g T55 flour • 60 g unsalted butter • 9 g salt • 40 g fresh compressed yeast
• 50 g sugar • 25 g milk powder • 2 g vanilla extract

FILLING

20 g unsalted butter • 120 g brown sugar • 11 g ground cinnamon • 10 g T55 flour

FINISH

1 beaten egg • 50 g water + 65 g sugar, brought to the boil

....

Room-temperature unsalted butter, for the loaf tins

A BRIOCHE FROM THE EAST

Originally from Eastern Europe, especially Poland, also known as *kranz* in Jewish cuisine, this plaited brioche evokes grandmothers' pleated skirts. It is made from a yeast-based pastry that can be filled in a thousand ways: chocolate, praline, dried fruit, nuts, blueberries and lemon or clementine jam.

KNEADING (THE DAY BEFORE)

- Put the water, beaten egg, flour, butter, salt, yeast, sugar, milk powder and vanilla into the bowl of a stand mixer. Mix for 2–3 minutes on low speed, then knead for 5–6 minutes on medium speed. Take the dough out of the bowl and form it into a tight ball. Put into a container, cover and leave to ferment 12–24 hours in the refrigerator.

FILLING (ON THE DAY)

- Using your fingertips, mix the butter, brown sugar, ground cinnamon and flour in a mixing bowl until it reaches a sandy consistency. Cover and refrigerate.

DIVIDING AND SHAPING

- On the floured work surface, using a rolling pin, roll the dough into a 50 x 30 cm rectangle about 4 mm thick **(1)**. Lightly moisten the surface with water, then sprinkle evenly with the filling **(2)**.

- Roll the dough on itself lengthways to obtain a 50 cm-long tight sausage shape. Using a large knife, cut the sausage in half lengthways **(3)**, then in half widthways to obtain four 25 cm-long pieces. Twist two pieces together **(4)**, then place in a buttered 25 x 8 x 8 cm loaf tin. Repeat with the remaining two pieces and place in a second buttered tin.

SECOND (FINAL) PROOFING

- Cover with a damp cloth and leave to proof for 1 hour 30 minutes–2 hours at room temperature.

BAKING

- Using the fan-forced setting, preheat the oven to 180°C.

- Brush with beaten egg, place the tins in the centre of the oven, lower the temperature to 150°C and bake for 30 minutes.

- As soon as they come out of the oven, brush the babkas with syrup, then leave to cool for 4–5 minutes in the tins before unmoulding and placing on a wire rack.

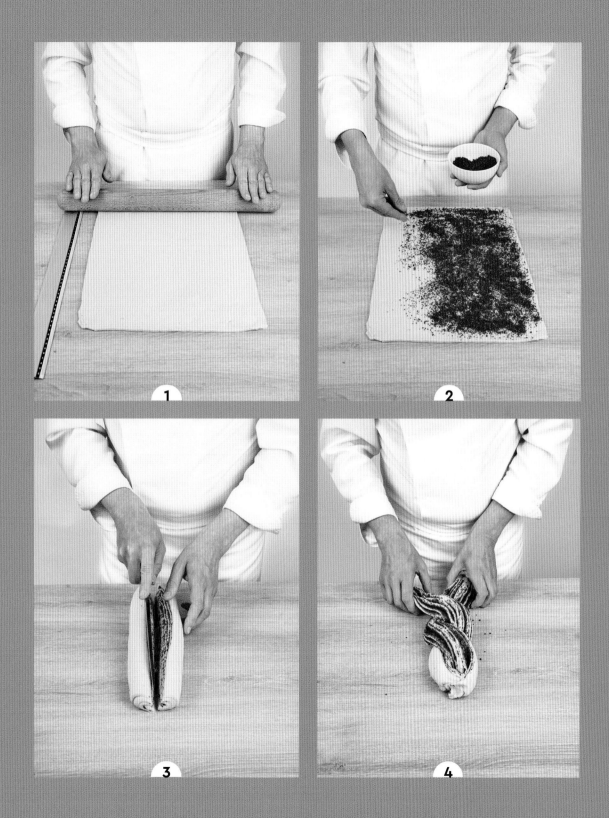

Stollen

DIFFICULTY ♔ ♔

Preparation: 40 mins • **Fermentation:** 2 hrs • **Proofing:** 1 hr 50 mins • **Baking:** 25 mins

MAKES 2 STOLLENS

LEAVEN
60 g milk • 18 g fresh compressed yeast • 80 g T45 flour • 22 g raw almond paste

KNEADING
50 g egg (1 egg) • 50 g milk • 170 g T45 flour • 4 g salt • 30 g sugar • 105 g cold unsalted butter

....

60 g candied orange peel, diced • 30 g candied lemon peel, diced • 30 g dried pears, diced • 60 g dried cranberries • 60 g whole almonds, blanched • 30 g pistachios, blanched • 120 g almond paste

FINISH
Unsalted butter, melted • Icing sugar

LEAVEN
- Put the milk, yeast, flour and almond paste into the bowl of a stand mixer. Mix for 3 minutes on low speed. Place in a bowl, cover with cling film and leave to ferment for 1 hour at room temperature. The dough should have doubled in volume.

KNEADING
- Return the leaven to the mixer bowl, then add the egg, milk, flour, salt and sugar. Mix for 4 minutes on low speed, then on high speed until the dough comes away from the sides of the bowl. Add the butter, cut into small pieces, and knead until the dough comes away from the sides of the bowl again.

- Add candied fruit, dried fruit and nuts on low speed until incorporated into the dough.

FIRST RISING AND FERMENTATION
- Put the dough into a container, cover and leave to ferment for 1 hour in the refrigerator.

DIVIDING AND SHAPING
- Divide the dough into two pieces of about 430 g each, form into balls, cover with a damp cloth and leave them to rest for 20 minutes.

- Form the almond paste into a 40 cm-long sausage shape and cut it in half.

- Form each dough piece into an elongated 25 cm-long shape (see pp. 42–43). Flatten them slightly, place an almond paste sausage in the centre of each one, then seal them inside the dough.

- Place them, seam side down, on a 30 x 38 cm baking tray covered in baking parchment.

SECOND (FINAL) PROOFING
- Leave to proof for 1 hour 30 minutes in a proving oven at 25°C (see p. 54).

BAKING
- Using the fan-forced setting, preheat the oven to 180°C. Place in the centre of the oven, lower the temperature to 150°C and bake for 25 minutes.

- After taking the stollens out of the oven, brush with melted butter and sprinkle with icing sugar.

Panettone

DIFFICULTY ♔ ♔

This viennoiserie requires 4 days to establish a stiff leaven.

THE DAY BEFORE Preparation: 15 mins • **Fermentation:** 12–16 hrs
ON THE DAY Preparation: 40 mins • **Fermentation:** 1 hr • **Proofing:** 5–6 hrs 45 mins
• **Baking:** 40 mins • **Drying:** 12 hrs

MAKES 2 PANETTONES

70 g stiff leaven

LEAVEN
80 g water at 23°C • 200 g T45 fine wheat flour • 110 g egg yolks (6 egg yolks) • 75 g sugar
• 100 g room-temperature unsalted butter

KNEADING
75 g T45 fine wheat flour • 10 g water • 18 g sugar • 25 g honey • 45 g unsalted butter
• ½ vanilla pod split and scraped • orange, lemon, mandarin zests • 36 g egg yolks (2 egg yolks)
• 6 g salt • 10 g water • 300 g glacé fruit, diced

MACARONADE
100 g egg whites (3 egg whites) • 35 g sugar • 100 g ground almonds
• 15 g T45 fine wheat flour • 20 g lemon juice • 3 g lemon zest

Icing sugar

STIFF LEAVEN (4 DAYS IN ADVANCE)

- Prepare a stiff leaven (see p. 36).

LEAVEN (THE DAY BEFORE)

- Put the water, stiff leaven, flour and one-third of the egg yolks into the bowl of a stand mixer. Mix for 8 minutes on high speed, then mix for 7 minutes with the remaining egg yolks, sugar and butter. Form into a ball and put into a large buttered container. Cover and leave to proof for 12–16 hours in a proving oven at 28°C (see p. 54). The dough should increase by 5 times its volume.

KNEADING AND FIRST RISING AND FERMENTATION (ON THE DAY)

- Remove the leaven from the proving oven 1 hour before using. Put the leaven into the bowl of a stand mixer and knead at a low speed until it comes away from the sides of the bowl. Add the flour and water, knead for 5 minutes on low speed, then add the remaining ingredients, one at a time, on low speed. Put the dough into a container and cover.

- Leave it to proof for 1 hour in a proving oven at 28°C (see p. 54).

DIVIDING AND SHAPING

- Divide the dough into two pieces of about 580 g, place on the work surface, cover with a damp cloth and leave to rest for 45 minutes. Form into balls and put them into two large 12 cm-high, 16 cm-diameter paper panettone moulds.

SECOND (FINAL) PROOFING

- Leave to proof for 4–6 hours in a proving oven at 28°C (see p. 54).

MACARONADE

- Mix the egg whites and sugar with a whisk. Pour in the ground almonds and flour and mix. Add the lemon juice and zest. Put into a piping bag without a nozzle, then pipe in a spiral pattern over the top of the doughs.

BAKING

- Preheat the fan-forced oven to 180°C. Dust each piece generously with icing sugar using a sieve. Leave to dry and dust again. Place in the base of the oven, lower the temperature to 145°C and bake for about 40 minutes.

- Remove from the oven, pierce the moulds with wooden skewers to suspend them upside down (to prevent them from collapsing) and leave to dry for 12 hours.

Caramelised pear tart

with candied pecans

DIFFICULTY ♡

THE DAY BEFORE Preparation: 12–15 mins • **Fermentation:** 30 mins • **Chilling:** 12 hrs
ON THE DAY Preparation: 20–30 mins • **Cooking:** 20 mins • **Proofing:** 1 hr 30 mins • **Baking:** 20–25 mins

MAKES 1 TART

600 g brioche dough

CARAMELISED PEARS WITH HONEY

100 g honey • 20 g crème fraîche • 500 g pears, peeled and cut into small cubes

CANDIED PECAN NUTS

60 g water • 80 g sugar • 100 g pecan nuts

FINISH

Icing sugar

BRIOCHE DOUGH (THE DAY BEFORE)

- Prepare the brioche dough (see p. 204).

DIVIDING AND SHAPING (ON THE DAY)

- Form the brioche dough into a ball, then using a rolling pin, roll it into a 26 cm-diameter disc. Place in a tart tin of the same size.

SECOND (FINAL) PROOFING

- Leave to proof for 1 hour 30 minutes in a proving oven at 25°C (see p. 54).

CARAMELISED PEARS WITH HONEY

- Put the honey into a frying pan over a medium heat and caramelise until it turns an amber colour. At the same time, heat the crème fraîche, then deglaze the caramelised honey with the hot crème fraîche. Add the pears and cook for a few minutes without allowing them to turn a purée. Transfer to a bowl and leave to cool to room temperature.

CANDIED PECAN NUTS

- Heat the water and sugar in a small saucepan to 120°C. Add the pecan nuts. Stir constantly with a plastic spatula until the pecan nuts are well candied. Transfer to a sheet of baking parchment and leave to cool.

BAKING

- Using the fan-forced setting, preheat the oven to 160°C.

- Fill the tart with the caramelised pears, leaving a 1 cm border, then place the candied pecan nuts on top. Dock the base with a fork, then put it into the centre of the oven, lower the temperature to 145°C and bake for 20–25 minutes.

- Remove from the oven and leave to cool on a wire rack. Sprinkle the rim with the icing sugar.

Bressane sugar and cream tart

DIFFICULTY 🍳

THE DAY BEFORE Preparation: 23 mins • **Fermentation:** 25 mins • **Chilling:** 12 hrs
ON THE DAY Proofing: 1 hr 45 mins • **Baking:** 15 mins

MAKES 4 TARTS

BRIOCHE DOUGH
100 g eggs (2 eggs) • 6 g fresh compressed yeast • 150 g T45 flour • 15 g sugar
• 3 g salt • 70 g cold unsalted butter

FILLING
80 g crème fraîche (30% fat) • 40 g unrefined raw sugar

EGG WASH
1 egg + 1 egg yolk, beaten together

BRIOCHE DOUGH (THE DAY BEFORE)

- Put the eggs, yeast, flour, sugar and salt into the bowl of a stand mixer. Mix for 5 minutes on low speed, then knead for 8 minutes on medium speed.

- Check the glutinous network, then add the butter, cut into small pieces. Knead for 10 minutes on low speed until the dough pulls away from the sides of the bowl.

- Remove the dough from the mixer bowl, cover with a dry cloth and leave to ferment for 25 minutes at room temperature.

- Make a fold (rabat), then place in a container, cover and refrigerate overnight.

DIVIDING AND SHAPING (ON THE DAY)

- Divide the dough into four pieces of about 85 g. Pre-shape each dough into a ball, cover with a dry cloth and leave to rest for 15 minutes. Using a rolling pin, roll the balls into 13 cm-diameter discs.

SECOND (FINAL) PROOFING

- Place the discs on two 30 x 38 cm baking trays covered with baking parchment. Brush with egg wash and leave to proof for 1 hour 30 minutes in a proving oven at 28°C (see p. 54).

FILLING

- Make five holes with a finger in each disc of dough, then use a small spoon or piping bag without a nozzle to fill each hole with the crème fraîche. Sprinkle with the unrefined raw sugar.

BAKING

- Using the fan-forced setting, preheat the oven to 180°C. Place in the oven, then lower the temperature to 160°C and bake for 15 minutes until the tarts are golden brown and the filling is melted.

- Remove from the oven and leave to cool on a wire rack.

Pompe aux grattons

DIFFICULTY ♙

THE DAY BEFORE Preparation: 12–15 mins • Fermentation: 30 mins • Chilling: 12–24 hrs
ON THE DAY Proofing: 2 hrs 20 mins • Baking: 35 mins

MAKES 1 POMPE AUX GRATTONS

BRIOCHE DOUGH

150 g eggs (3 eggs) • 125 g T45 flour • 125 g T55 flour • 4 g salt • 20 g sugar
• 10 g fresh compressed yeast • 75 g unsalted butter • 125 g pork grattons (scratchings)

EGG WASH

1 egg + 1 egg yolk, beaten together

BRIOCHE DOUGH (THE DAY BEFORE)

• Prepare the brioche dough without the milk and vanilla (see p. 204). At the end of the kneading process, add the pork grattons on a low speed until they are well mixed into the dough.

FIRST RISING AND FERMENTATION

• Put the dough into a container, cover and leave to ferment for 30 minutes at room temperature.

• Make a fold (rabat), then cover and refrigerate for 12–24 hours.

SHAPING (ON THE DAY)

• Shape the dough into a ball. Place on a 30 x 38 cm baking tray covered with baking parchment and cover with a damp cloth. Leave to rest for 20 minutes at room temperature.

• Pierce the centre of the ball and form it into a 25 cm-diameter wreath. Brush with egg wash.

SECOND (FINAL) PROOFING

• Leave to proof for 2 hours in a proving oven at 25°C (see p. 54).

BAKING

• Using the fan-forced setting, preheat the oven to 180°C.

• Gently brush the dough a second time with egg wash. Dip scissors into water and make sawtooth incisions on top, vertically and perpendicularly, all around the wreath. Place in the centre of the oven, lower the temperature to 150 °C and bake for 35 minutes.

• Remove from the oven and leave to cool on a wire rack.

Pastis landais

DIFFICULTY ♕

---

2 DAYS IN ADVANCE Preparation: 10 mins • **Fermentation:** 30 mins • **Chilling:** 12 hrs
THE DAY BEFORE Preparation: 15–17 mins • **Fermentation:** 25 mins • **Chilling:** 12 hrs
ON THE DAY Proofing: 1 hr 30 mins • **Baking:** 12–15 mins

MAKES 10 PASTIS LANDAIS

SYRUP
16 g water • 6 g salt • 50 g sugar • Zest of ½ lemon • Zest of ½ orange
• 14 g Grand Marnier® • 14 g rum • 14 g Cointreau® • 32 g orange blossom water

FERMENTED DOUGH
115 g fermented dough

KNEADING
140 g eggs (3 small eggs) • 257 g T45 flour • 77 g unsalted butter + extra for the moulds
• Sunflower oil for the container

EGG WASH AND FINISH
1 egg, beaten • Nibbed sugar

SYRUP (2 DAYS IN ADVANCE)

• Add the water, salt and sugar to a saucepan. Bring to a simmer, then add the lemon and orange zests, Grand Marnier®, rum, Cointreau® and orange blossom water. Bring to the boil, then transfer to a bowl. Leave to cool, cover with cling film and infuse overnight at room temperature.

FERMENTED DOUGH (2 DAYS IN ADVANCE)

• Prepare the fermented dough and refrigerate overnight (see p. 33).

KNEADING (THE DAY BEFORE)

• Put the eggs, fermented dough, cut into small pieces, the syrup, flour and butter into the bowl of a stand mixer. Mix for 5 minutes on low speed, then knead for 10–12 minutes on high speed until dough pulls away from the sides of the bowl.

• Place the dough on the work surface and make two folds (rabats), then place in an oiled container and cover with cling film.

FIRST RISING AND FERMENTATION

• Leave to ferment for 25 minutes at room temperature, then refrigerate overnight.

SHAPING (ON THE DAY)

• Divide the dough into ten pieces of about 70 g each. Form tight balls with each piece, then place in 10 buttered 7–8 cm-diameter fluted brioche moulds.

SECOND (FINAL) PROOFING

• Put the moulds on a 30 x 38 cm baking tray, then leave them to proof for 1 hour 30 minutes in a proving oven at 28°C (see p. 54).

BAKING

• Using the fan-forced setting, preheat the oven to 180°C.

• Gently brush with egg wash, without letting the egg wash go down the sides of the moulds. Sprinkle with nibbed sugar, then put into the centre of the oven, lower the temperature to 160°C and bake for 12–15 minutes.

• Remove from the oven, unmould and leave to cool on a wire rack.

Three Kings' brioche

DIFFICULTY ♙ ♙

THE DAY BEFORE Preparation: 20 mins • **Fermentation:** 1 hr 30 mins • **Chilling:** 12 hrs
ON THE DAY Preparation: 15 mins • **Proofing:** 2 hrs 20 mins • **Baking:** 20 mins

MAKES 2 BRIOCHES

LEAVEN
63 g T45 flour • 38 g full-fat milk • 3 g fresh compressed yeast

SYRUP
75 g butter • 63 g sugar • 25 g water • 13 g Cointreau® • 7 g vanilla extract

KNEADING
80 g eggs (1½ eggs) • 187 g T45 flour • 5 g fresh compressed yeast • 5 g salt • 100 g glacé fruit, diced

EGG WASH
1 egg + 1 egg yolk, beaten together

FINISH
2 porcelain figurines • Apricot glaze • Nibbed sugar • 115 g candied and glacé fruit

LEAVEN (THE DAY BEFORE)

- Using a silicone spatula, mix the flour with the milk and yeast in a bowl. Cover with cling film and and set aside for 1 hour at room temperature.

SYRUP

- Melt the butter in a small saucepan, then add sugar, water, Cointreau® and vanilla. Cover with cling film and set aside at room temperature.

KNEADING

- Place half the syrup (about 60 g), eggs, leaven, flour, yeast and salt into the bowl of a stand mixer. Mix for 4 minutes on low speed, then knead on high speed until the dough pulls away from the sides of the bowl. Add the remaining syrup for 'bassinage', then knead until the dough comes away from the sides of the bowl again. Add the glacé fruit on low speed to obtain a homogeneous mixture.

FIRST RISING AND FERMENTATION

- Place in a container, cover with cling film and leave to ferment for 30 minutes, then refrigerate overnight.

DIVIDING AND SHAPING (ON THE DAY)

- Divide the dough into two pieces of about 330 g, then shape each piece into a ball. Cover with a damp cloth and leave to rest for 20 minutes at room temperature.

- Pierce the centre of the ball by thumb to form a wreath 18 cm in diameter. Place the wreaths on two 30 x 38 cm baking trays covered with baking parchment.

SECOND (FINAL) PROOFING

- Leave to proof for about 2 hours in a proving oven at 25°C (see p. 54).

BAKING

- Using the fan-forced setting, preheat the oven to 145°C. Brush the wreaths with egg wash and bake for 20 minutes. Remove from the oven and leave to cool on a wire rack. Using the tip of a knife, pierce the base of the wreath and insert a porcelain figurine.

FINISH

- Warm the apricot glaze and use a brush to glaze the entire surface of the wreaths.

- Take a wreath in one hand and some nibbed sugar in the other. Place the sugar around the sides of each wreath, then arrange the candied and glacé fruit on the top.

Normandy surprise

DIFFICULTY ♙ ♙ ♙

THE DAY BEFORE Preparation: 12–15 mins • **Fermentation:** 30 mins • **Chilling:** 12–24 hrs
ON THE DAY Preparation: 40 mins • **Chilling:** 1 hr • **Proofing:** 3 hrs • **Baking:** 1 hr

EQUIPMENT

6 silicone cone moulds (4 cm in diameter), for the caramel inserts • 6 square moulds (6 x 6 cm) with a lid,
for the brioches • Cooking thermometer

MAKES 6 NORMANDY SURPRISE BRIOCHES

BRIOCHE DOUGH
270 g brioche dough

APPLE CHIPS
1 small apple • Icing sugar

CARAMEL
125 g sugar • 125 g single cream • 50 g unsalted butter • 1 vanilla pod, split and scraped
• ½ cinnamon stick • 2 g fleur de sel (fine sea salt)

POACHING SYRUP
500 g water • 100 g sugar • 1 vanilla pod, split and scraped • 1 cinnamon stick • 50 g Calvados

POACHED APPLES
6 small Royal Gala apples

....

Room-temperature unsalted butter, for the moulds

TIPS

The caramel inserts must be frozen well before being
pushed into the baked brioche. Make the syrup in
advance, even the day before, for a good infusion
of spices. It will add flavour to the apples during
poaching.

BRIOCHE DOUGH (THE DAY BEFORE)

- Prepare the brioche dough (see p. 204).

APPLE CHIPS (ON THE DAY)

- Preheat the oven to 90°C. Cut thin slices of apple with a mandolin. Put them on to a baking tray covered with baking parchment, sprinkle with icing sugar (1) and bake for about 45 minutes.

CARAMEL

- Add the sugar to a dry saucepan over a medium heat and cook until a nice amber colour is obtained. Heat the cream at the same time, then deglaze the caramel with the hot cream (2). Add the butter, vanilla seeds, cinnamon and fleur de sel. Cook to 112°C on the cooking thermometer. Pour 20 g of caramel into each cone mould and put into the freezer.

DIVIDING AND SHAPING

- Divide the brioche dough into six pieces of 45 g each, then shape into balls. Place on a baking tray covered with baking parchment, wrap in cling film and refrigerate for at least 1 hour.

POACHING SYRUP

- Place the water, sugar, vanilla pod and seeds, and cinnamon into a large saucepan. Bring to the boil, add the Calvados and set aside.

POACHED APPLES

- Peel and core the apples. Cut each apple into a 4 cm cube and place in the poaching syrup (3). Cover with baking parchment and a lid, then poach for 5 minutes. Remove the apples, drain on kitchen paper and leave to cool.

SHAPING

- Using a rolling pin, roll the dough into 10 cm-diameter discs, then wrap each apple cube in a disc (4) and seal like a purse. Place seam side down, into buttered moulds with a square of baking parchment at the base (5). Cover and place on a 30 x 38 cm baking tray.

SECOND (FINAL) PROOFING

- Leave the dough to proof for 3 hours in a proving oven at 28°C (see p. 54).

BAKING

- Using the fan-forced setting, preheat the oven to 160°C.

- Bake in the centre of the oven for 14 minutes.

- Remove from the oven, unmould on to a wire rack and leave to cool. Press a frozen caramel into the apple in the centre of each brioche (6). Sprinkle icing sugar around the edge and stick an apple chip on the top edge.

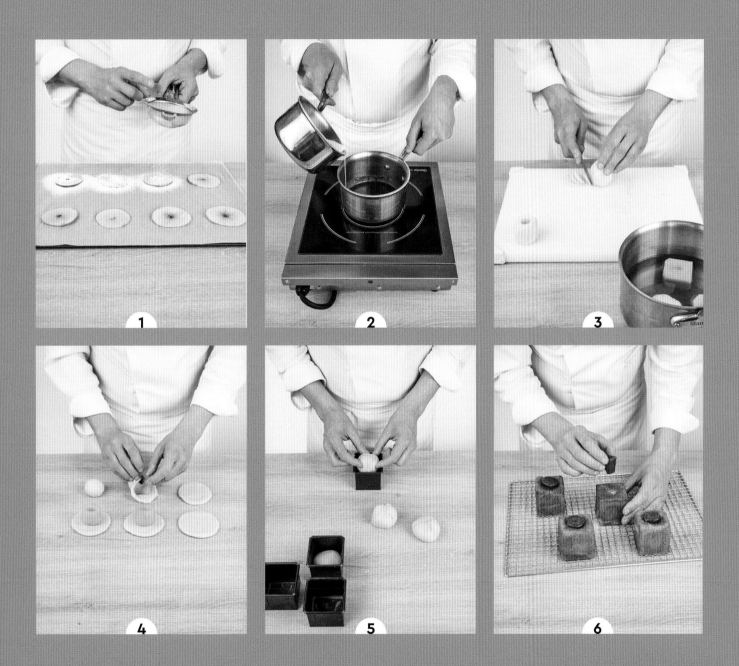

Raspberry choux buns

DIFFICULTY ♙ ♙ ♙

THE DAY BEFORE Preparation: about 35 mins • **Fermentation:** 30 mins • **Chilling:** 12–24 hrs
ON THE DAY Preparation: 20 mins • **Freezing:** 30 mins • **Proofing:** 2 hrs • **Baking:** 50 mins

EQUIPMENT

2 biscuit cutters (3 cm and 9 cm in diameter) • 6 silicone moulds (4 cm in diameter) • 6 tartlet rings (10 cm in diameter)

MAKES 6 CHOUX BUNS

PLAIN AND RED BRIOCHE DOUGH

650 g brioche dough • 1 knife tip of red food colouring

CRAQUELIN

10 g room-temperature unsalted butter • 1 pinch fleur de sel (fine sea salt) • 13 g unrefined raw sugar • 13 g T45 flour
• 1 pinch red food colouring

CHOUX PASTRY

62 g water • 1 pinch salt • 1 pinch sugar • 28 g butter • 35 g T45 flour • 60 g egg (1 large egg)

CHOCOLATE BROWNIE

38 g milk chocolate couverture • 38 g unsalted butter • 25 g egg (½ egg) • 42 g sugar • 15 g T45 flour

RASPBERRY CREAM

62 g single cream • 62 g raspberry purée • 25 g sugar • 25 g egg yolk (1 egg yolk) • 10 g cornflour
• ½ capful raspberry fruit brandy

EGG WASH

1 egg + 1 egg yolk, beaten together

SYRUP

100 g water + 130 g sugar, brought to the boil

PLAIN AND RED BRIOCHE DOUGHS (THE DAY BEFORE)

• Prepare the brioche dough (see p. 204).

• Before refrigerating the brioche dough, take 250 g and put into the bowl of a stand mixer fitted with a paddle and add the red food colouring. Mix to obtain a homogeneous colour. Form the dough into a ball **(1)**, wrap in cling film and refrigerate for 12–24 hours.

CRAQUELIN

• Mix the butter, cut into small pieces, salt, unrefined raw sugar, flour and food colouring in a bowl fitted with the paddle attachment until it forms a homogeneous dough. Shape into a ball, then roll out between two sheets of baking parchment to a thickness of about 2 mm and refrigerate **(2)**.

CHOUX PASTRY

• Bring the water, salt, sugar and butter to the boil in a saucepan. Remove from heat and add the flour. Mix with a silicone spatula to obtain a smooth and consistent dough. Return to the heat to dry out the dough while stirring.

• Leave to cool, then add the beaten egg, a little at a time, and mix well. The dough should have a good consistency and drop in a 'V' shape. Place in a piping bag fitted with a no. 10 plain nozzle. Refrigerate overnight. (It is possible to make the choux pastry on the day.)

ON THE DAY

• Using the fan-forced setting, preheat the oven to 200°C.

• Pipe 3 cm-diameter choux balls on a 30 x 38 cm baking tray covered with baking parchment. Cut out six craquelin discs of the same diameter as the choux balls and cover each choux **(3)**. Bake in the oven for 30 minutes. Leave to cool on a wire rack.

CHOCOLATE BROWNIE

• Using the fan-forced setting, preheat the oven to 170°C.

• Melt the chocolate and butter over a bain-marie. Using a whisk, lightly whisk the egg with the sugar, then add the flour. Mix the two preparations together and place 20 g into each silicone mould **(4)**. Bake in the oven for 8 minutes.

RASPBERRY CREAM

• Bring the cream and raspberry purée to the boil in a saucepan. Separately, whisk the sugar with the egg yolk, then add the cornflour. Pour in one-third of the hot mixture and mix. Transfer back to the pan and cook until thickened. Remove from the heat and add the raspberry fruit brandy. Put into a bowl, cover with cling film in contact with the cream and refrigerate.

SHAPING

• Divide the 400 g of plain brioche dough into two pieces, one of 250 g and the other of 150 g. Roll out both the plain and red 250 g pieces to a thickness of 2 mm into two rectangles of the same dimensions. Moisten the plain rectangle and place the red rectangle on top **(5)**. Freeze for 15 minutes on a baking tray, then roll out again to about 3 mm thick. Return to the freezer for a further 15 minutes.

• Cut the bicoloured dough into 54 discs with a 3 cm-diameter biscuit cutter **(6)**. Refrigerate on a 30 x 38 cm baking tray covered with cling film.

• Roll out the 150 g plain brioche dough to a thickness of 1.5 mm and dock with a fork. Place on a baking tray in the freezer until hardened, then cut out six discs with a 9 cm-diameter biscuit cutter. Place on a 30 x 38 cm baking tray covered with baking parchment. Put buttered tartlet rings around each piece. Lightly moisten the surface with water, then place nine 3 cm-diameter bicoloured discs around the edge of each one, overlapping them **(7)**.

SECOND (FINAL) PROOFING

• Leave to proof for about 2 hours in a proving oven at 25°C (see p. 54).

BAKING

• Using the fan-forced setting, preheat the oven to 145°C.

• Remove the baking tray, then press a brownie firmly into the centre of each ring **(8)**.

• Smooth the raspberry cream with a whisk, put into a piping bag fitted with a plain no. 8 nozzle and fill six choux buns. Place a choux bun on each brownie **(9)**. Brush the pieces with egg wash (without washing the choux) and bake for 12 minutes.

• Remove from the oven, remove the rings and brush with the syrup. Return to the oven for a few seconds to dry the syrup, then leave on a wire rack.

Choco-coco

THE DAY BEFORE Preparation: 12–15 mins • **Fermentation:** 30 mins • **Chilling:** 12–24 hrs

ON THE DAY Preparation: 40 mins • **Fermentation:** 1 hr • **Proofing:** 1 hr 30 mins • **Baking:** 17 mins

EQUIPMENT

6 silicone insert moulds (6 cm in diameter) • 6 silicone frieze stencils (30.5 cm long) • 6 tartlet rings (10 cm in diameter)

MAKES 6 CHOCO-COCOS

BRIOCHE DOUGH

270 g brioche dough

COCONUT CREAM

140 g coconut purée • 60 g coconut paste • 16 g cornflour • 18 g Malibu®

CIGARETTE BATTER

25 g room-temperature unsalted butter • 25 g icing sugar • 25 g egg white (1 small egg white) • 10 g unsweetened cocoa powder • 25 g T55 flour

COCONUT CRUMBLE

30 g T55 flour • 25 g unsalted butter • 25 g unrefined cane sugar • 25 g desiccated coconut

EGG WASH

1 egg + 1 egg yolk, beaten together

CHOCOLATE GLAZE

65 g single cream • 11 g honey • 65 g dark couverture chocolate (64% cocoa) • 11 g unsalted butter

DECORATION

Gold leaf (optional)

BRIOCHE DOUGH (THE DAY BEFORE)

- Prepare the brioche dough (see p. 204).

COCONUT CREAM (ON THE DAY)

- Bring the coconut purée and paste to a simmer in a small saucepan. Mix 1 tablespoon of water with the cornflour. Add the mixture to the hot liquid and bring to the boil while whisking. Add the Malibu® and mix. Transfer to a piping bag without a nozzle and fill the silicone insert moulds **(1)**. Place in the freezer for 1 hour or until hardened.

CIGARETTE BATTER

- Cream the butter and icing sugar in a bowl. Add the egg white, cocoa and flour, and mix with a silicone spatula to obtain a smooth dough. Using a small palette knife, fill the frieze stencils **(2)** and refrigerate.

DIVIDING AND SHAPING

- Cut the brioche dough into six pieces of 45 g each, shape into balls, place on a 30 x 38 cm baking tray covered with baking parchment **(3)** and refrigerate for about 1 hour.

- Using a rolling pin, roll the balls into 9 cm-diameter discs.

- Put the tartlet rings on a 30 x 38 cm baking tray covered in baking parchment. Line with the cold friezes, with the pattern towards the inside of the rings, then place the brioche discs in the centre **(4)**.

SECOND (FINAL) PROOFING

- Leave to proof for 1 hour 30 minutes in a proving oven at 25°C (see p. 54).

COCONUT CRUMBLE

- Place the flour, butter, unrefined cane sugar and desiccated coconut in the bowl of a stand mixer fitted with the paddle attachment **(5)** mix to a sandy consistency. Cover with cling film and set aside in the refrigerator until ready to use.

BAKING

- Using the fan-forced setting, preheat the oven to 160°C.

- Brush the moulded pieces with egg wash and sprinkle with the coconut crumble. Press the frozen coconut cream insert firmly into the centre **(6) (7)**. Place in the oven, then lower the temperature to 145°C and bake for 17 minutes.

- Turn out of the moulds and carefully remove the frieze stencils. Put on to a wire rack.

CHOCOLATE GLAZE

- Bring the cream and honey to a simmer. Pour over the chocolate, then add butter, cut into small pieces, and stir **(8)** until smooth. Weigh a second time to make sure there is 150 g of glaze. Add more cream if necessary.

- Fill the centre of each brioche with 25 g of chocolate glaze **(9)**.

DECORATION

- Decorate with gold leaf if desired.

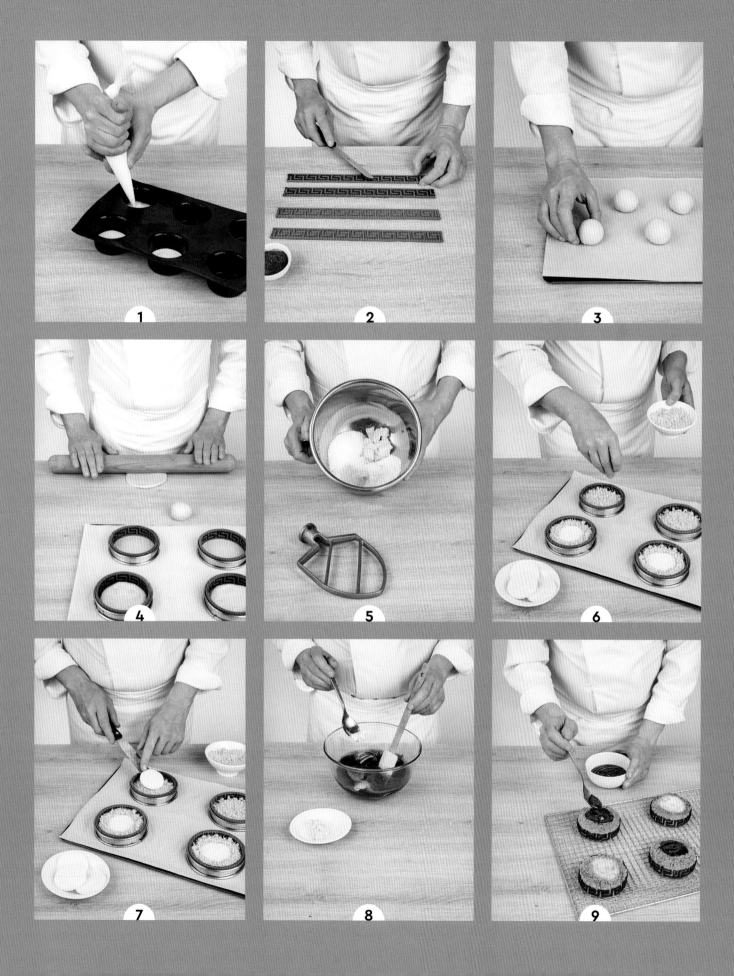

Croissant

DIFFICULTY ♙ ♙

THE DAY BEFORE Preparation: 5 mins • Fermentation: 12 hrs
ON THE DAY Preparation: 20 mins • Proofing: 2–3 hrs • Baking: 18 mins

MAKES 6 CROISSANTS

CROISSANT DOUGH
580 g croissant dough, using turns of your choice

EGG WASH
1 egg + 1 egg yolk, beaten together

SPECIAL BUTTER FOR TURNS (TOURAGE)

In France, a special dry butter, or tourage butter, is often used in pastry making and bakery. Composed of at least 84% fat, it is firmer than conventional butter, is easier to use in hot places and has an exceptional plasticity that facilitates stretching dough pieces. It is mainly used to make puff pastry and viennoiseries.

CROISSANT DOUGH (THE DAY BEFORE)

• Prepare the croissant dough (see p. 206).

DIVIDING AND SHAPING

• On a lightly floured work surface, use a rolling pin to roll the dough into a 35 x 28 cm rectangle about 3.5 mm thick **(1)**.

• Cut out six triangles, 9 cm wide and 26 cm high **(2)(3)**, then roll them up from the base **(4)(5)**.

SECOND (FINAL) PROOFING

• Place the croissants on a 30 x 38 cm baking tray covered in baking parchment. Brush with egg wash **(6)** and leave to proof for 2–3 hours in a proving oven at 25°C (see p. 54) or at room temperature covered with a dry cloth until doubled in size **(7)**.

BAKING

• Using the fan-forced setting, preheat the oven to 180°C. Gently brush with egg wash a second time **(8)**, then place in the centre of the oven, lower the temperature to 165°C and bake for 18 minutes **(9)**.

• Remove from the oven and place the croissants on a wire rack.

Note: save the croissant dough trimmings. Lay them flat, wrap in cling film and place in the freezer. They can be used in other recipes such as Apple Tatin baker's style (see p. 296) or Almond-hazelnut mini cakes (see p. 298). They can be kept for about 15 days.

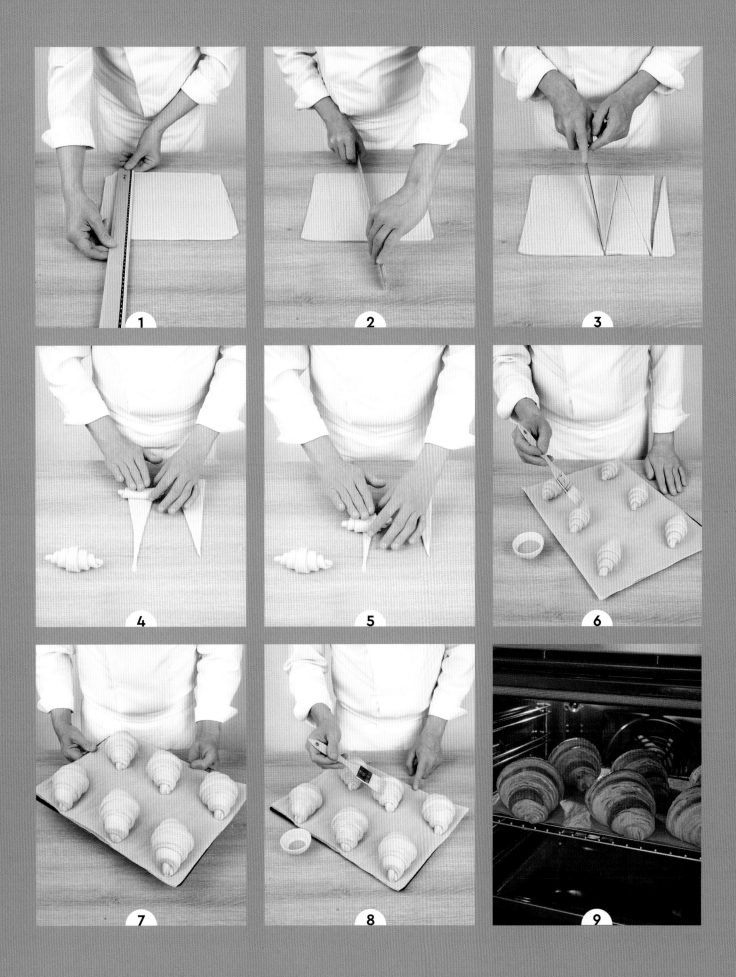

Pain au chocolat

DIFFICULTY ♙

THE DAY BEFORE **Preparation:** 15 mins • **Fermentation:** 12 hrs
ON THE DAY **Preparation:** 20 mins • **Proofing:** 2–3 hrs • **Baking:** 18 mins

MAKES 6 PAINS AU CHOCOLAT

CROISSANT DOUGH
450 g croissant dough • 12 chocolate bars

EGG WASH
1 egg + 1 egg yolk, beaten together

CROISSANT DOUGH (THE DAY BEFORE)

• Prepare the croissant dough, making two double turns (see p. 206 and p. 208).

DIVIDING AND SHAPING (ON THE DAY)

• Flour the work surface, then using a rolling pin, roll the dough into a 35 x 28 cm rectangle about 3.5 mm thick.

• Cut out six rectangles of 13 x 8 cm. Place two chocolate bars on each rectangle and roll them up.

SECOND (FINAL) PROOFING

• Place the pains au chocolat on a 30 x 38 cm baking tray covered with baking parchment. Brush with egg wash, then leave to proof for 2–3 hours in a proving oven at 25°C (see p. 54) or at room temperature covered with a dry cloth until doubled in size.

BAKING

• Using the fan-forced setting, preheat the oven to 180°C.

• Gently brush with egg wash a second time, then put into the centre of the oven, lower the temperature to 165°C and bake for 18 minutes.

• Remove from the oven and transfer to a wire rack.

> **Note:** save the croissant dough trimmings. Lay them flat, wrap in cling film and place in the freezer. They can be used in other recipes such as Apple Tatin baker's style (see p. 296) or Almond-hazelnut mini cakes (see p. 298). They can be kept for about 15 days.

Pain au gianduja
with hazelnuts

DIFFICULTY ♙ ♙

THE DAY BEFORE **Preparation:** 15 mins • **Fermentation:** 12 hrs
ON THE DAY **Preparation:** 45 mins • **Chilling:** 1 hr • **Proofing:** 2–3 hrs • **Baking:** 18 mins

MAKES 6 PAINS AU GIANDUJA

PLAIN CROISSANT DOUGH
450 g croissant dough

CHOCOLATE DOUGH
110 g croissant détrempe dough (see p. 206) • 9 g icing sugar • 9 g unsweetened cocoa powder • 22 g dry butter (see p. 313)

CRISPY GIANDUJA INSERT
15 g milk chocolate • 60 g gianduja • 25 g hazelnuts, chopped • 40 g crushed Gavottes® crêpes (wafers)

SYRUP
100 g water + 130 g sugar, brought to the boil

AN ITALIAN-STYLE DELICACY

Invented in the 19th century, this recipe is named after Gioan d'la douja (John with the mug), a colourful character from the Commedia dell'arte. Gianduja is composed of chocolate and at least 30% hazelnut paste. The traditional recipe is made with Piedmont hazelnuts.

CROISSANT DOUGH (THE DAY BEFORE)

- Prepare croissant dough, making two double turns (see p. 206 and p. 208).

CHOCOLATE DOUGH (ON THE DAY)

- Put the croissant détrempe dough, icing sugar, cocoa and butter into the bowl of a stand mixer. Mix on low speed until a homogeneous dough forms. Shape into a 15 cm-square, cover with cling film and refrigerate until hardened (about 1 hour).

CRISPY GIANDUJA INSERT

- Melt the chocolate with the gianduja over a bain-marie. Add the hazelnuts to a mixing bowl, then add the melted chocolate. Using a silicone spatula, mix in the crushed Gavottes® crêpes. Put the preparation on the work surface and form into a sausage shape 1 cm in diameter. Wrap in cling film and refrigerate until firm, then cut into six 8 cm-long pieces.

ASSEMBLING

- Roll out the croissant dough into a 15 cm-square, then, using a brush, lightly moisten the surface with water.

- Place the chocolate dough on top. Roll out into a 35 x 28 cm rectangle about 3.5 mm thick. Using a cutter or small knife and a ruler, score regular diagonal lines on the chocolate dough (1). Refrigerate until hardened, then gently turn the dough out on to the work surface, chocolate side down.

- Cut into six 13 x 8 cm rectangles (2). Place a crispy gianduja insert on each rectangle (3), then roll them up (4) and place on a 30 x 38 cm baking tray covered with baking parchment.

SECOND (FINAL) PROOFING

- Leave to proof for 2–3 hours in a proving oven at 25°C (see p. 54).

BAKING

- Using the fan-forced setting, preheat the oven to 180°C.

- Place in the centre of the oven, lower the temperature to 165°C and bake for 18 minutes.

- Remove from the oven, transfer to the wire rack and brush with the syrup.

Pain aux raisins

DIFFICULTY ⌂

THE DAY BEFORE Preparation: 15 mins • **Fermentation:** 12 hrs
ON THE DAY Preparation: 30 mins • **Chilling:** 1hr • **Proofing:** 2 hrs • **Baking:** 19 mins

MAKES 6 PAINS AUX RAISINS

580 g croissant dough

....

100 g sultanas, soaked in 40 g rum the day before

PASTRY CREAM
20 g egg yolk (1 egg yolk) • 20 g sugar • 10 g custard powder
• ½ vanilla pod, split and scraped • 100 g milk

SYRUP
100 g water + 130 g sugar, brought to the boil

CROISSANT DOUGH (THE DAY BEFORE)

• Prepare the croissant dough, making two double turns (see p. 206 and p. 208).

PASTRY CREAM (ON THE DAY)

• Whisk the egg yolk with the sugar in a bowl, then add the custard powder and vanilla seeds. Bring the milk to the boil in a saucepan, then pour half of it over the previous mixture and mix.

• Return the mixture to the saucepan with the remaining milk and bring to the boil over medium heat, whisking constantly. Boil for about 30 seconds, then pour into a bowl, cover with cling film in contact with the pastry cream and refrigerate until cool.

SHAPING AND SECOND (FINAL) PROOFING

• Using a rolling pin, roll the croissant dough into a 60 x 20 cm rectangle, 2 mm thick. Lightly crush the base edge with your fingertips to stabilise the dough, then moisten 1 cm around the edges with water.

• Using a silicone spatula, spread the pastry cream over the dough, leaving the moist edge free. Sprinkle with the macerated sultanas, then roll from the long side into a tight roll from the top to the base edge.

• Refrigerate to firm up before cutting the length into 6 pieces. Place on a 30 x 38 cm baking tray covered with baking parchment and place a 10 cm-diameter buttered tartlet ring around each one.

• Leave to proof for 2 hours in a proving oven at 28°C (see p. 54) or until the pieces double in size.

BAKING

• Using the fan-forced setting, preheat the oven to 180°C. Place in the centre of the oven, then lower the temperature to 165°C and bake for 18 minutes.

• Remove from the oven and raise the temperature to 220°C, remove the tartlet rings and brush the pains aux raisins with syrup. Return to the oven for about 1 minute.

• Remove from the oven and transfer to a wire rack.

....

Rolled praline-pecan nut buns

VARIATION

• Prepare a praline pastry cream with 20 g egg yolk, 20 g sugar, 10 g custard powder, the seeds from ½ a split and scraped vanilla pod, 90 g milk and 10 g crème fraîche. At the end of the baking time, add 40 g praline. Replace the sultanas with 100 g coarsely chopped pecan nuts.

Kouign-amann

DIFFICULTY ♙

THE DAY BEFORE OR 2 DAYS BEFORE Preparation: 10 mins • **Fermentation:** 30 mins • **Chilling:** 12–48 hrs
ON THE DAY Freezing: 20 mins • **Proofing:** 2 hrs 30 mins • **Baking:** 30 mins
• **Basic temperature:** 54

MAKES 6 KOUIGN-AMANNS

120 g water • 200 g 'French tradition' flour • 20 g salt • 8 g fresh compressed yeast

TURNS
150 g dry butter (see p.313) • 180 g sugar + extra for the cake tins

---

KNEADING (THE DAY BEFORE OR 2 DAYS BEFORE)

• Put the water, flour, salt and yeast into the bowl of a stand mixer. Mix for 4 minutes on low speed, then knead for 6 minutes on medium speed. After kneading, the temperature of the dough should be 23–25°C.

FIRST RISING AND FERMENTATION

• Remove the dough from the bowl, place in a container, cover and leave to ferment for 30 minutes at room temperature. Fold (rabat), cover and refrigerate for 12–48 hours.

TURNS (ON THE DAY)

• Roll the butter out in a folded sheet of baking parchment (see p. 206) to form a square.

• Roll out the dough into a rectangle slightly larger than the butter. Place the butter in the centre of the dough. Cut the edges of the dough and put the two pieces of détrempe dough on top of the butter to enclose it. Roll out to a thickness of about 3.5 mm. Make a single turn (see p. 206), then cover the dough and freeze for 20 minutes.

• Place the dough on the lightly floured work surface. Sprinkle the surface with half of the sugar for the turns, then make a second single turn. Cover with a dry cloth and leave to rest for about 30 minutes on the work surface.

• Sprinkle with the remaining sugar, then make a third single turn. Cover again with a dry cloth and leave to rest for about 30 minutes.

SHAPING

• Roll out the dough to 4 mm thick and cut out six 10 cm-squares. Fold the corners towards the centre. Put the dough pieces into six 10 cm-diameter sloped-sided cake tins, sprinkle with sugar and place on a 30 x 38 cm baking tray.

SECOND (FINAL) PROOFING

• Leave to proof for 1 hour 30 minutes in a proving oven at 28°C (see p.54).

BAKING

• Using the fan-forced setting, preheat the oven to 180°C, then place in the centre of the oven and bake for 10 minutes. Lower the temperature to 170 °C and bake for 10 minutes. Lower the temperature to 160 °C and bake for a further 10 minutes.

• Remove from the oven, unmould and leave to cool on a wire rack.

Note: this recipe can be made with croissant dough. To do this, replace the bread dough in the recipe with 350 g of croissant dough and proceed in the same way.

Crisp pineapple

DIFFICULTY ✿ ✿ ✿

THE DAY BEFORE Preparation: 10 mins • **Chilling:** 12 hrs

ON THE DAY Preparation: 30 mins • **Freezing:** 1 hr 30 mins • **Proofing:** 1 hr 30 mins • **Baking:** 32 mins

EQUIPMENT

6 tartlet rings (10 cm in diameter) • 1 biscuit cutter (8 cm in diameter) • 6 silicone insert moulds (6 cm in diameter)
• 6 silicone half-sphere moulds (3 cm in diameter)

MAKES 6 TARTLETS

CROISSANT DOUGH

DÉTREMPE DOUGH

300 g T45 flour • 6 g salt • 12 g fresh compressed yeast • 42 g sugar
• 30 g unsalted butter • 96 g water • 60 g milk

TURNS
180 g cold dry butter (see p.313)

PINEAPPLE COMPOTE

35 g sugar • 25 g unsalted butter • 1 vanilla pod, split and scraped • 200 g pineapple, cut into cubes
• 4 g custard powder • 8 g pineapple juice • 7 g rum • 3 g Malibu®

....

3 slices pineapple, cut in half horizontally

COCONUT CREAM

56 g coconut purée • 24 g coconut paste • 6 g cornflour • 7 g of Malibu®

SYRUP

100 g water + 130 g sugar, brought to the boil

DECORATION

Zest of 1 lime

....

Sunflower oil for the tartlet rings

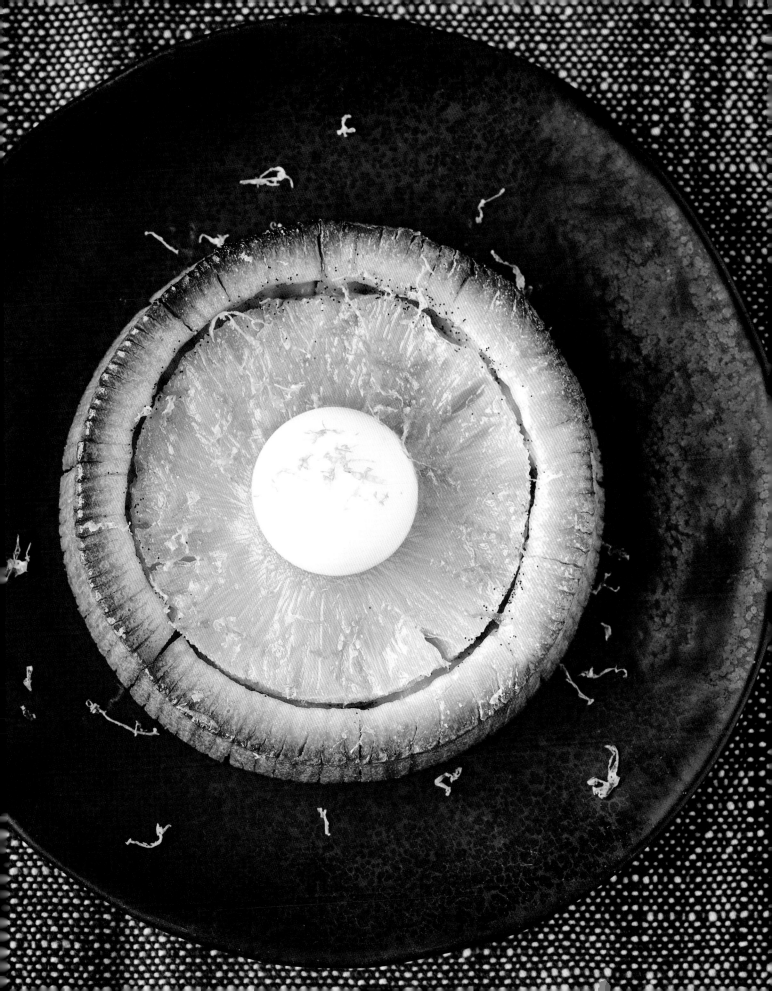

DÉTREMPE DOUGH (THE DAY BEFORE)

- Put the flour, salt, yeast, sugar, butter, water and milk into the bowl of a stand mixer. Mix for 5 minutes on low speed, then knead for 5 minutes on medium speed. Shape into a ball, then cover with cling film and refrigerate for at least 12 hours.

TURNS (ON THE DAY)

- Roll out the détrempe dough to a thickness of 1.5 cm and make a double turn and then a single turn with the butter (see p. 208). Cover and freeze for 30 minutes.

- Place the dough with the fold towards you. Mark vertical strips 2 cm wide, then cut and separate them **(1)**. Using a brush, moisten each strip with cold water. Turn the strips upright and place them side by side so that the layers are visible. Press the strips so that they stick together **(2)**. Place on a baking tray covered with baking parchment and put into the freezer for 20 minutes.

- Return the dough to the work surface, with the layers placed vertically in front of you. Roll out the dough to 3.5 mm thick and freeze for 20 minutes.

- Cut 2 cm-wide strips in the opposite direction of the layers **(3)**. Use six strips to line the inside of the oiled tartlet rings **(4)**. Adjust with remaining strips to fill in the gaps in each ring and make sure the dough is tight all the way around the sides.

- Gather up the trimmings from the dough used to line the rings and lay them out flat together. Roll out to a thickness of 1.5 mm and dock with a fork **(5)**. Set the dough aside on a baking tray covered with baking parchment and freeze for 20 minutes.

- Cut out six discs with a biscuit cutter and place them in the bottom of the tartlet rings. Leave to proof for a maximum of 1 hour 30 minutes in a proving oven at 28°C (see p. 54).

PINEAPPLE COMPOTE

- Make a dry caramel with the sugar in a saucepan, then add the butter, cut into small pieces, the vanilla seeds and the pineapple cubes. Dilute the custard powder in the pineapple juice, then add to the pan to bind the mixture. Add the rum and Malibu®.

- Spoon 30 g of compote into each silicone insert mould **(6)** and place in the freezer until hardened.

COCONUT CREAM

- Bring the coconut purée and paste to a simmer in a small saucepan. Mix 1 tablespoon of water with the cornflour. Pour the mixture into the hot liquid and bring to the boil while whisking. Add the Malibu® and mix well. Use a small spoon to fill six silicone half-sphere moulds **(7)**. Place in the freezer until hardened.

PINEAPPLE COMPOTE INSERTS

- Place a pineapple compote insert into each croissant dough ring **(8)**, then add a pineapple slice (15 g) **(9)**. Cover with a silicon mat and two baking trays.

BAKING

- Using the fan-forced setting, preheat the oven to 180°C. Place in the centre of the oven, then lower the temperature to 165°C and bake for 25 minutes. Raise the temperature to 180 °C and bake for a further 5 minutes. Remove the baking trays, silicon mat and tartlet rings, brush with the syrup and return to the oven for 2 minutes. Leave to cool on a wire rack.

FINISH

- Place a half-sphere of coconut cream in the centre of each viennoiserie and sprinkle with freshly grated lime zest.

Vanilla flan

DIFFICULTY ⌂ ⌂ ⌂

THE DAY BEFORE Preparation: 15 mins • **Fermentation:** 12 hrs

ON THE DAY Preparation: 30 mins • **Freezing:** 2 hrs • **Proofing:** 1 hr–1 hr 30 mins • **Baking:** 20 mins

EQUIPMENT
4 slope-sided cake tins (10 cm in diameter) • 1 biscuit cutter (9 cm in diameter)

MAKES 4 FLANS

CROISSANT DOUGH
530 g croissant dough • Sunflower oil, for the cake tins

VANILLA CREAM
50 g egg yolks (about 3 egg yolks) • 60 g sugar • 25 g custard powder • 1 vanilla pod, split and scraped • 160 g full-fat milk • 160 g single cream

EGG WASH
1 egg yolk, beaten

CROISSANT DOUGH (THE DAY BEFORE)

• Prepare the croissant dough, making one double turn and one single turn (see p. 206 and p. 208).

PREPARATION (ON THE DAY)

For the first three steps, you can refer to photographs 1–3 on page 281.

• Place the dough with the fold towards you. Mark vertical strips 2 cm wide, then cut and separate them. Using a brush, moisten each strip with cold water. Turn the strips upright and place them side by side so that the layers are visible. Press the strips so that they stick together. Place on a baking tray covered with baking parchment and put into the freezer for 20 minutes.

• Return the dough to the work surface, with the layers placed vertically in front of you. Roll out the dough to a 3.5 mm thickness and place in the freezer for 20 minutes.

• Cut 3 cm-wide strips in the opposite direction of the layers. Use four strips to line the inside of the oiled cake tins. Adjust with remaining strips to fill in the gap in each tin and make sure the dough is tight all the way around the sides.

• Roll out the trimmings to a thickness of 2 mm and dock with a fork. Place in the freezer for 20 minutes, then cut out discs with a biscuit cutter. Place the discs in the base of the tins, sealing the edges to the dough strip.

SECOND (FINAL) PROOFING

• Leave to proof for 1 hour–1 hour 30 minutes in a proving oven at 28°C (see p. 54). Place in the freezer for 1 hour or until hardened.

VANILLA CREAM

• Whisk the egg yolks with the sugar in a bowl, then add the custard powder and vanilla seeds. Bring the milk and cream to the boil in a saucepan. Pour half of it over the previous preparation and mix.

• Return the mixture to the saucepan with the remaining milk and cream and bring to the boil over medium heat, whisking constantly. Boil for about 30 seconds.

BAKING

• Using the fan-forced setting, preheat the oven to 200°C.

• Place the tins on a 30 x 38 cm baking tray, then fill while still frozen with the hot vanilla cream. Brush the hot cream with egg wash, then place into the centre of the oven, lower the temperature to 165°C and bake for 20 minutes.

• Remove from the oven, unmould and place on a wire rack.

Chocolate dome

with a caramel centre

DIFFICULTY ✿ ✿ ✿

THE DAY BEFORE **Preparation:** 5 mins • **Fermentation:** 12 hrs
ON THE DAY **Preparation:** 1 hr • **Freezing:** about 4 hrs • **Proofing:** 3 hrs • **Baking:** 35 mins

EQUIPMENT

6 half-sphere silicone moulds (3 cm in diameter), for the caramel
• 6 half-sphere silicone moulds (5 cm in diameter) for the mi-cuits • 1 biscuit cutter (7 cm in diameter)
• 6 half-sphere silicone moulds (7 cm in diameter), for the swirled strips
• Cooking thermometer

MAKES 6 CHOCOLATE DOMES

CROISSANT DOMES

450 g croissant détrempe • 125 g dry butter (see p.313)

CARAMEL

60 g sugar • 60 g single cream • 9 g unsalted butter

CHOCOLATE MI-CUIT

47 g dark chocolate • 25 g unsalted butter • 47 g egg (1 small egg) • 75 g sugar • 20 g T55 flour

CHOCOLATE SHORTBREAD

27 g unsalted butter • 66 g T65 flour • 1 g salt • 32 g icing sugar • 5 g ground almonds • 5 g unsweetened cocoa powder
• 17 g egg (½ small egg)

CARAMEL POWDER

100 g sugar

FINISH

Dark chocolate, melted, for sticking

....

Room-temperature unsalted butter, for the silicone mat and baking tray

CROISSANT DÉTREMPE DOUGH (THE DAY BEFORE)

- Prepare the croissant détrempe dough (see p. 206).

TURNS AND SHAPING (ON THE DAY)

- Make one double turn and one single turn with the croissant détrempe dough and a 12 cm-square of butter (see p. 208). Make sure the dough is no more than 14 cm square at the end of making the turns. Cover and freeze for 20 minutes.

- Place the dough with the fold towards you. Lightly flour the work surface, then roll out firstly to 35 cm. Return to the freezer for 20 minutes.

- Continue rolling until the dough reaches 65 cm in length. Using a large knife, cut eight strips 60 cm long and 8 mm wide. Set aside the trimmings. Roll each strip on itself into a swirl and lay flat on a buttered silicone mat **(1)**.

SECOND (FINAL) PROOFING

- Leave the swirled strips to proof for 3 hours in a proving oven at 28°C (see p. 54).

SHAPING (CONTINUED)

- Roll out the croissant dough trimmings to 1.5 mm thick. Dock with a fork and set aside on a baking tray for at least 2 hours in the freezer.

CARAMEL

- In a small saucepan, moisten the sugar with a little water and heat to 180-190°C (check the temperature on a cooking thermometer). Pour in the heated cream and cook to 118°C. Add the butter and smooth the caramel with a silicone spatula. Fill six half-sphere moulds and place for at least 2 hours in the freezer.

CHOCOLATE MI-CUIT

- In a bowl, melt the chocolate and butter over a bain-marie. Whisk the egg and sugar. Incorporate the chocolate and melted butter, then the flour. Fill six half-sphere moulds **(2)**, then press a frozen caramel insert into the centre **(3)**. Set aside in the freezer until ready to use.

CHOCOLATE SHORTBREAD

- Mix the butter, flour, salt, icing sugar, ground almonds, cocoa powder and egg in the bowl of a stand mixer fitted with the paddle attachment.

- Using the fan-forced setting, preheat the oven to 160°C.

- On the work surface, roll out the chocolate shortbread dough between two sheets of baking parchment to a thickness of 2 mm, then cut out six discs with a biscuit cutter **(4)**. Place the discs on a baking tray covered with baking parchment, then place in the centre of the oven and bake for 10 minutes.

- Remove from the oven and transfer to a wire rack.

CARAMEL POWDER

- Cook the sugar in a saucepan until it turns an amber colour, then pour on to a baking tray covered with baking parchment. Leave to cool, then blend in a food processor to a fine powder **(5)**.

BAKING

- Using the fan-forced setting, preheat the oven to 170°C. Place the swirled croissant dough strips in the half-sphere moulds on a 30 x 38 cm baking tray **(6)**. Add a chocolate mi-cuit and caramel fondant insert to each. Cut out six 7 cm-diameter discs from the croissant dough trimmings.

- Moisten the edges of the domes with water, then place the discs on the moulds to seal them **(7)**. Cover with a sheet of baking parchment and a 30 x 38 cm baking tray, place in the centre of the oven and bake for 20 minutes.

- Remove from the oven and raise the temperature to 180°C. Carefully turn the domes right side up on to the baking tray and sprinkle with the caramel powder **(8)**. Return to the oven for 5 minutes.

- Remove from the oven and transfer to a wire rack.

FINISH

- Use dots of melted chocolate to stick the dome to the chocolate shortbread **(9)**.

Raspberry-lemon flower

DIFFICULTY ♔ ♔ ♔

THE DAY BEFORE **Preparation:** 15 mins • **Chilling and freezing:** 12–24 hrs • **Cooking:** 10 mins
ON THE DAY **Preparation:** 30 mins • **Freezing:** about 1 hr 30 mins • **Proofing:** 1 hr 30 mins • **Baking:** 20–23 mins

EQUIPMENT

6 silicone inserts (6 cm in diameter), for the raspberry compote • 1 flower-shaped biscuit cutter (3 cm in diameter)
• 6 silicone half-sphere moulds (3 cm in diameter), for the flowers and lemon jelly
• 2 biscuit cutters (3 cm and 10 cm in diameter), for the croissant dough • 6 tartlet rings (10 cm in diameter)

MAKES 6 RASPBERRY-LEMON

FLOWERS
450 g croissant détrempe dough • 125 g dry butter (see p.313)

RED DOUGH
100 g T45 fine wheat flour • 50 g beetroot juice • 10 g unsalted butter • 4 g fresh compressed yeast
• 15 g sugar • 2 g salt

RASPBERRY COMPOTE
115 g frozen raspberries • 30 g sugar • 3 g pectin NH nappage

LEMON JELLY
60 g sweet lemon juice • 20 g water • 20 g sugar • 3 g pectin NH nappage

SYRUP
125 g water + 125 g sugar, brought to the boil
....
Timut pepper (optional)

ADVICE

Be careful not to exceed the baking temperature, otherwise the dough's red colour will darken. Don't cut the red dough too deeply, or the petals will split in half.

CROISSANT DÉTREMPE DOUGH (THE DAY BEFORE)

- Prepare the croissant détrempe dough (see p. 206).

RED DOUGH

- Put the flour, beetroot juice, butter, yeast, sugar and salt into the bowl of a stand mixer. Mix for 5 minutes on low speed, then knead for 5 minutes on medium speed. Form a ball, cover with cling film and refrigerate for 12–24 hours.

RASPBERRY COMPOTE

- Put the raspberries into a saucepan and simmer. Mix the sugar and pectin and add them to the pan. Cook, stirring, over a low heat for 3 minutes, then place 20 g into each silicone insert mould and freeze.

- Spread the remaining compote on a sheet, freeze, then cut out 6 flowers with a biscuit cutter. Place in six half-sphere moulds and harden in the freezer **(1)**.

LEMON JELLY

- Bring the lemon juice and water to a simmer in a small saucepan. Mix the sugar and pectin, add to the pan and bring to a simmer over a low heat, stirring. Pour over each raspberry compote flower, then return to the freezer.

TURNS AND SHAPING (ON THE DAY)

- Dust the work surface with flour. Make one double turn and one single turn with the croissant dough and a 12 cm-square of butter (see p. 208). Make sure the dough forms a 14 cm-square at the end of making the turns.

- Roll out the red dough into a 15 cm-square. Place the red dough on the croissant dough moistened with water. Cover with cling film and freeze for 15 minutes.

- Roll out the dough into a 30 x 28 cm rectangle with a thickness of 3 mm **(2)**. Using a cutter or small knife and a ruler, score regular diagonal lines on the red side, then freeze until hardened.

- Cut out 48 3 cm-diameter discs with a biscuit cutter **(3)**. Put into the freezer until hardened. Roll out the remaining dough to a thickness of 1.5 mm, then dock with a fork and freeze until hardened.

- Using the biscuit cutter, cut out six 10 cm-diameter discs and place in the tartlet rings on a 30 x 38 cm baking tray covered with baking parchment. Place six to eight of the 3 cm-diameter discs in the base of each ring, overlapping them slightly.

SECOND (FINAL) PROOFING

- Leave to proof for 1 hour 30 minutes in a proving oven at 25°C (see p. 54).

BAKING

- Using the fan-forced setting, preheat the oven to 145°C.

- Place a frozen raspberry compote insert in the centre of the dough **(4)**, then place in the centre of the oven and bake for 20 minutes. Remove the tartlet rings, then return to the oven for 3 minutes if necessary.

- Remove from the oven, brush with the syrup and leave to cool, then add a raspberry-lemon half-sphere in the centre. Add a grinding of Timut pepper if desired.

Plaited wreath
with mango and passion fruit

DIFFICULTY ♤ ♤ ♤

THE DAY BEFORE **Preparation:** 15 mins • **Fermentation:** 12 hrs
ON THE DAY **Preparation:** 45 mins • **Freezing:** 30 mins • **Proofing:** 1 hr–1 hr 30 mins • **Cooking:** 10 mins
• **Baking:** 18 mins

EQUIPMENT
6 tartlet rings (10 cm in diameter) • 6 silicone insert moulds (6 cm in diameter)

MAKES 6 WREATHS

CROISSANT DOUGH
580 g croissant dough

EGG WASH
1 egg + 1 egg yolk, beaten together

....

Room-temperature unsalted butter, for the tartlet rings

MANGO-PASSION FRUIT CREAM
63 g single cream • 32 g passion fruit purée • 30 g mango purée
• 25 g egg yolk (1 egg yolk) • 25 g sugar • 10 g cornflour • ½ capful of Malibu®

MANGO-PASSION FRUIT GLAZE
38 g passion fruit purée • 86 g mango purée • 34 g sugar • 5 g pectin NH nappage

A VERY FINE PLAIT

For the best results ensure the dough strips are thin, cool and tightly plaited. Do not exceed 40 cm in length, in which case you will have to shorten them and the laminated effect will not be clean on part of the wreath.

CROISSANT DOUGH (THE DAY BEFORE)

• Prepare the croissant dough, making two double turns (see p. 206 and 208).

ON THE DAY

• Roll out the croissant dough to 35 x 20 cm. Place on a baking tray covered with baking parchment and freeze until slightly hardened. Roll the dough out into a 45 x 20 cm rectangle to a thickness of 3.5 mm.

• Using a large knife, cut 18 strips to 40 cm long and 1 cm wide, then make six plaits of three strips each **(1)**.

• Roll out the dough trimmings to a 1.5 mm of thickness, dock with a fork and return to the freezer until hardened. Cut out six 9 cm-diameter discs and place on a 30 x 38 cm baking tray covered with baking parchment.

• Place a plait around the edge of each disc, taking care to moisten the discs with water. Brush with egg wash, then place buttered tartlet rings around each piece and leave to proof for 1 hour–1 hour 30 minutes in a proving oven at 28°C (see p. 54).

MANGO-PASSION FRUIT CREAM

• Put the cream, passion fruit purée and mango purée into a saucepan and bring to the boil. At the same time, whisk the egg yolk with the sugar in a mixing bowl, then add the cornflour and mix.

• Pour some of the hot liquid over the previous mixture, stir, then pour it back into the pan off the heat. Stir and return the cream to the heat until it boils.

• At the end of cooking, add the Malibu® and mix.

• Using a spoon or piping bag, fill each insert mould with 25 g of cream **(2)**. Tap the moulds against the work surface to even out the cream, then put into freezer until hardened.

BAKING

• Using the fan-forced setting, preheat the oven to 180°C.

• Brush the wreaths a second time with egg wash and press a frozen mango-passion cream insert into the centre of each one **(3)**. Place in the centre of the oven, lower the temperature to 165°C and bake for 18 minutes.

• Remove from the oven, remove the tartlet rings and leave to cool on a wire rack.

MANGO-PASSION GLAZE

• Put the passion fruit purée and mango purée into a saucepan and bring to the boil. Mix the sugar and pectin and add to the pan. Mix well and bring to the boil, then pour while still hot into a pipette or small sauce boat **(4)**. Top each wreath with 20 g of glaze. Allow the glaze to gel before eating.

Apple Tatin
baker's style

DIFFICULTY ♙

Preparation: 10 mins • **Proofing:** 1 hr 30 mins • **Baking:** 40 mins

MAKES 6 APPLE TATINS

420 g croissant dough trimmings, stored flat
• Room-temperature unsalted butter + sugar, for the tins

FILLING
120 g unsalted butter • 3 Granny Smith apples

MOULD PREPARATION

• Butter and line six 10 cm-diameter sloped-sided cake tins with the butter and sugar and place on a 30 x 38 cm baking tray.

FILLING

• Cut the butter into thin slices and place 20 g in each tin. Peel and core the apples, then cut them in half horizontally. Put half an apple into each tin.

BAKING

• Using the fan-forced setting, preheat the oven to 200°C, place in the centre of the oven and bake for 20 minutes. Leave to cool in the tins.

• Place the croissant dough cut into 3.5 mm squares on top. Leave to proof for 1 hour 30 minutes at room temperature.

• Using the fan-forced setting, preheat the oven to 165°C, place in the centre of the oven and bake for 20 minutes.

• Remove from the oven, cover with baking parchment and press down with a baking tray to compact them. Remove the baking tray, then turn out each apple tatin from the tin.

Almond-hazelnut
mini cakes

DIFFICULTY ♙

Preparation: 20 mins • **Proofing:** 2 hrs
Baking: 20 mins

MAKES 4 MINI CAKES

160 g croissant dough trimmings, stored flat
• Room-temperature unsalted butter, for the moulds

ALMOND CREAM
35 g room-temperature unsalted butter • 35 g icing sugar
• 35 g ground almonds • 35 g egg (½ large egg)
....
35 g roasted hazelnuts, roughly chopped

FINISH
Icing sugar

FILLING THE MOULDS

• Cut the croissant dough trimmings into 1 cm-squares and place them in four buttered 11 x 4 cm rectangular moulds. Leave to proof for about 1 hour in a proving oven at 25°C (see p. 54).

ALMOND CREAM

• Combine the butter and icing sugar, then whisk well to obtain a homogeneous mixture. Add the ground almonds, then the egg and mix again. Pour the cream into a piping bag without a nozzle.

ASSEMBLY AND BAKING

• Pipe the almond cream on to the croissant dough and leave to proof for about 1 hour. Sprinkle with the roasted and roughly chopped hazelnuts.

• Using the fan-forced setting, preheat the oven to 165°C, place the moulds in the centre of the oven and bake for 20 minutes. Unmould and leave to cool on a wire rack. Sprinkle with icing sugar.

Lime-meringue
mini cakes

DIFFICULTY ♙

Preparation: 20 mins • **Proofing:** 2 hrs
Baking: 20 mins

MAKES 4 MINI CAKES

160 g of croissant dough trimmings, stored flat
• Room-temperature unsalted butter, for the moulds

LEMON ALMOND CREAM
35 g room-temperature unsalted butter • 35 g icing sugar
• 35 g ground almonds • 27 g egg (½ egg) • 8 g lemon juice
• Zest of 1 lime

ITALIAN MERINGUE
100 g sugar • 40 g water • 50 g egg whites
(2 small egg whites)

FINISH
Zest of 1 lime

ASSEMBLING

• Follow the recipe of the almond-hazelnut mini cakes (see opposite). Make the lemon almond cream by adding the lemon juice and lime zest after the egg. Place in a piping bag without a nozzle. Fill the moulds and leave to proof for about 1 hour.

BAKING

• Using the fan-forced setting, preheat the oven to 165°C, place the moulds in the centre of the oven and bake for 20 minutes. Remove from the oven, unmould and leave to cool on a wire rack.

ITALIAN MERINGUE

• Heat the sugar and water to 119°C in a saucepan. Put the egg whites into a mixing bowl and whisk until frothy. Pour in the hot syrup and whisk until cool. Transfer to a piping bag fitted with a star nozzle.

FINISH

• Pipe a zigzag of Italian meringue on to each cake. Run a chef's blowtorch over the meringue to colour, then sprinkle with freshly grated lime zest.

Three Kings' cake

with frangipane

DIFFICULTY ♙ ♙

---

2 DAYS IN ADVANCE **Preparation:** 5 mins • **Chilling:** Overnight
THE DAY BEFORE **Preparation:** 45 mins • **Chilling:** 12 hrs
ON THE DAY **Preparation:** 15 mins • **Baking:** 41 mins

MAKES 1 CAKE

PUFF PASTRY

560 g puff pastry

FRANGIPANE

PASTRY CREAM

20 g egg yolk (1 egg yolk) • 20 g sugar • 10 g custard powder
• ½ vanilla pod, split and scraped • 100 g milk

ALMOND CREAM

50 g unsalted butter • 50 g icing sugar • 50 g ground almonds • 50 g egg (1 small egg) • 6 g dark rum

....

1 porcelain figurine

EGG WASH

1 egg + 1 egg yolk, beaten together

SYRUP

100 g water + 130 g sugar, brought to the boil

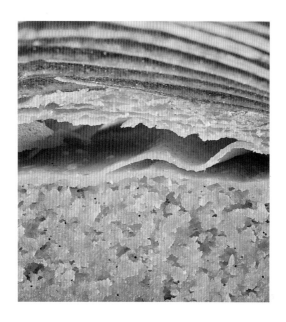

PUFF PASTRY (2 DAYS IN ADVANCE)

• Prepare the puff pastry, making four single turns (see p. 212).

PREPARATION (THE DAY BEFORE)

• Make a fifth single turn with the puff pastry dough, then roll out into a 23 x 45 cm rectangle to a thickness of 2 mm. Cut the dough in half and place on two baking trays lined with baking parchment. Refrigerate until hardened (about 1 hour).

> **Note:** the puff pastry trimmings can be kept, layered flat and not rolled, to make sacristains (see p. 308), for example.

PASTRY CREAM

• Whisk the egg yolk with the sugar in a bowl, then add the custard powder and vanilla seeds. Bring the milk to the boil in a saucepan, then pour half over the previous mixture and mix.

• Return the mixture to the saucepan with the remaining milk and bring to the boil over a medium heat, whisking constantly. Boil for about 30 seconds, then pour into a bowl, cover with cling film in contact with the pastry cream and refrigerate.

ALMOND CREAM

• Cream the butter and icing sugar in a bowl. Add the ground almonds, egg and rum, then whisk briskly to emulsify.

FRANGIPANE

• Whisk together 60 g of pastry cream with 200 g of almond cream in a bowl until smooth. Transfer to a piping bag fitted with a no. 10 nozzle.

ASSEMBLING

• Place the puff pastry on a work surface and cut out two 21 cm-diameter discs **(1)**. Place one disc on a baking tray covered with baking parchment, then, using a brush, lightly moisten the edge with water. Mark a small 16 cm-diameter indentation in the centre, then pipe the frangipane in a spiral pattern inside this outline **(2)**. Add the porcelain figurine. Seal with the remaining disc, sealing the edges together well. Brush with egg wash and refrigerate overnight.

FINISH (ON THE DAY)

• Take the cake out of the refrigerator. Using an 18 cm-diameter pastry circle and a cutter, cut away the excess dough, then with a knife, crimp the edges of the dough. Brush a second time with egg wash, then score the surface of the cake from the centre in an arc to the edge **(3)**.

BAKING

• Using the fan-forced setting, preheat the oven to 180°C. Bake in the centre of the oven for 40 minutes **(4)**.

• Remove the cake from the oven and raise the temperature to 220°C. Brush the cake with syrup and return it to the oven for 1 minute.

• Remove from the oven and transfer to a wire rack.

French Apple turnover (chausson aux pommes)

DIFFICULTY ♢

THE DAY BEFORE **Preparation:** 5 mins • **Chilling:** Overnight
ON THE DAY **Preparation:** 45 mins • **Chilling:** 4 hrs • **Baking:** 30 mins

MAKES 5 TURNOVERS

PUFF PASTRY
560 g puff pastry

APPLE COMPOTE
30 g unrefined cane sugar • 35 g unsalted butter • 2 pinches fleur de sel (fine sea salt)
• 450 g Granny Smith apples, cut into small cubes
• 1 vanilla pod, split and scraped

EGG WASH
1 egg + 1 egg yolk, beaten together

SYRUP
100 g water + 130 g sugar, brought to the boil

AN APPLE MADE FOR COOKING

The Granny Smith is a tart, low-sugar apple that holds up well to cooking. It will allow you to produce a semi-liquid compote with pieces that provide more texture in the mouth.

PUFF PASTRY (THE DAY BEFORE)

- Prepare the puff pastry, making four single turns (see p. 212).

SHAPING (ON THE DAY)

- Make a fifth single turn with the puff pastry dough, then roll out into a 30 x 38 cm rectangle about 2 mm thick. Place on a 30 x 38 cm baking tray covered with baking parchment and refrigerate for 1 hour.

- Cut out five pieces using a 17 x 12.5 cm-oval fluted cutter **(1)**. Place them back on the baking tray and refrigerate until hardened (about 1 hour).

> **Note:** the puff pastry trimmings can be kept, layered flat and not rolled, to make sacristains (see p. 308), for example.

APPLE COMPOTE

- Put the unrefined cane sugar into a saucepan over a medium heat and dry cook until amber in colour. Add the butter and fleur de sel, then add the apples and vanilla pod with its seeds. Stir and cook over low heat, keeping pieces of apple.

- After cooking, place in a covered bowl and refrigerate. Before use, remove the vanilla pod.

ASSEMBLING

- Put the turnover dough ovals on to a work surface, place the rolling pin in the centre of each oval, then lengthen them a little. Moisten the edge of one half of the dough with water and fill one half of each oval with 65 g of compote, leaving a border of about 2 cm **(2) (3)**.

- Close the turnovers and pinch the edges with your fingers, then turn them over and place on a 30 x 38 cm baking tray covered with baking parchment. Brush with egg wash and refrigerate for at least 2 hours before baking.

- Brush the turnovers a second time with egg wash. Using a small knife, score lines on the surface **(4)**, then pierce in one or two places to allow steam to escape during cooking.

BAKING

- Using the fan-forced setting preheat the oven to 180°C. Bake in the centre of the oven for 30 minutes.

- Remove from the oven and raise the temperature to 220°C. Brush the turnovers with syrup for a shiny finish and return to the oven for about 30 seconds. Remove from the oven and transfer to a wire rack.

Sacristain

DIFFICULTY ♔

Preparation: 15 mins • **Baking:** 30 mins

MAKES 10 SACRISTAINS

Puff pastry trimmings (see p.302) • Sugar

CUTTING AND SHAPING

• Place puff pastry trimmings – taking care they are flat and not rolled into a ball to retain the dough's layers – on a work surface. Using a rolling pin, roll the dough into a rectangle 20 cm long and 4 mm thick. Sprinkle sugar on one side, then cut 2 cm-wide strips and twist each piece. Place on a 30 x 38 cm baking tray covered with baking parchment, lightly pressing the ends on the parchment to stabilise them.

BAKING

• Using the fan-forced setting, preheat the oven to 180°C. Bake in the centre of the oven for 10 minutes, then lower the temperature to 165°C and bake for a further 20 minutes.

....

VARIATION NO. 1

Chopped almonds and nibbed sugar

• Roll out the dough, then sprinkle with chopped almonds on one side. Embed them into the dough with a rolling pin, then turn the dough over. Sprinkle and encrust the other side with nibbed sugar. Cut strips and twist.

VARIATION NO. 2

Royal icing

• In a bowl, whisk 125 g icing sugar with 30 g egg white (1 egg white), then add 8 g lemon juice. Using a brush, brush a thin layer of royal icing on one side. Cut strips and twist.

VARIATION NO. 3

Grated cheese and Espelette pepper

• Sprinkle a thin layer of grated cheese mixed with Espelette pepper on one side. Cut the strips and twist.

GLOSSARY

ADDING FLOUR

During kneading or mixing, extra flour is added to make the dough firmer. See also MIXING.

AUTOLYSE

A technique that involves mixing the water and flour of a recipe, then leaving to sit for 30 minutes to several hours before adding the remaining ingredients. The hydration of the flour triggers the activity of the enzymes it contains and initiates the formation of the glutinous network, reducing the final kneading time.

BAISURE

A mark left on the crust where one loaf has touched another during baking.

BAKER'S CLOTH

A linen cloth (or tea towel) on which the dough rises during fermentation.

BAKING

Action and manner of cooking a food.

BAKING POWDER

Rising agent composed of bicarbonate of soda and cream of tartar that gives no odour or flavour to the dough. It reacts only in the oven, unlike fresh compressed yeast.

BALL

To turn a dough piece on itself to loosen the gluten and form a smooth ball that traps the carbon dioxide in the dough.

BANNETON

A small wicker basket covered with a linen cloth, where the dough rises during the final proofing.

BASIC LEAVEN

Basic leaven with maximum microbial activity, used to prepare the leaven chef or final leaven.

'BASSINAGE'

Adding a small amount of liquid (usually water) to a dough, in order to soften the gluten at the end of kneading if the hydration is insufficient.

BÂTARD

An initial pre-shaping form, and also the semi-long oval shape that falls between a ball and a baguette.

BATCH

A quantity of shaped doughs that are baked together in the oven.

BENDING

Said of bread that deforms during baking into an arc or curve.

BIND

Thicken or solidify with a thickener (starch or pectin, cream or fruit compote).

BREAKING OPEN (JET)

During baking, the detachment or opening of the blade slashes that have been made to the top of the crust. See also SLASH/SCORE.

CARAMELISE

1. To cook sugar until it turns amber in colour for various preparations.

2. To obtain a colour on the crust at the end of cooking through the Maillard reaction of a food brought to high temperature. (Carbohydrate molecules and amino acids then react to create a very complex flavour and odour.)

COLLAPSING SIDES

Deformation of a bread baked in a mould, with the sides of the bread hollowing out.

CONFIT

Food that is saturated with one of the following ingredients: vinegar (vegetables), sugar (fruit), alcohol (fruit), fat (poultry). The process used for cooking or preservation.

CRUST

Outer part of the bread after baking.

CRUSTING

1. Action of voluntarily exposing a dough piece to the open air to obtain a dry film on the surface.

2. The outer part of the bread dough before baking that has dried out after excessive contact with dry air.

CUT

1. To slice, divide into pieces.

2. Using a pair of scissors, a knife or a biscuit cutter to cut out specific shapes in preparation.

DARK HARD CRUST

Said of a crust that has strongly coloured at the beginning of baking.

DÉTREMPE DOUGH

Preparation of a basic dough requiring turns comprising a mixture of flour, water and salt and/or fresh compressed yeast. Used for croissant, puff pastry, bread or brioche dough.

DEVELOP

When talking about a dough, the increase in volume during fermentation and baking.

DICE

Small regular cubes.

DILUTE

To mix a substance (e.g. fresh compressed yeast or cornflour) in a liquid.

DIVISION/DIVIDING

Operation consisting of separating a dough into several pieces, most often according to a determined weight.

DRY BUTTER/BUTTER FOR TURNS

A French variety of butter (beurre sec/beurre de tourage) with a higher fat content and more elastic than classic butter. It also contains less water (between 5 and 8% depending on the quality of the butter). Its melting point is higher. It is used for puff pastry and laminated yeast-based doughs (e.g. croissant and brioche or laminated breads).

DUST
Lightly flour a work surface in contact with the dough to prevent sticking.

EGG WASH
The preparation (beaten whole egg or yolk, possibly with added water and salt) brushed on dough before cooking.

ELONGATE
To lenghten and give a dough piece its final shape before final proofing.

ENCASE
To enclose dry butter in a detrémpe dough (e.g. croissant, puff pastry, bread or brioche) before making turns to obtain a flaky (layered) effect.

FERMENTATION
Period during which the starches are degraded into sugar, then in a second time, transformation of sugars into alcohol molecules and carbon dioxide by the action of zymases (enzymes of yeast) and heat.

FERMENTED DOUGH
A dough which after kneading, is fermented for several hours, and is integrated into a subsequent kneading to give strength. It improves the taste and helps to preserve the product.

FIRST RISING AND FERMENTATION
Period corresponding to the fermentation, taking place after the kneading and between the shaping and baking. See also SECOND (FINAL) PROOFING.

FOLD
To fold one surface of dough over another (for a fold [rabat], turns in a puff pastry or laminated leavened dough).

FOLD (RABAT)
Stretch and fold a dough on itself to release the gas in it in order to give it strength and to restart the fermentation process. This technique is performed during the first rising and fermentation period.

FOLDING
To fold a dough over butter to incorporate it (e.g. puff pastry, croissant dough).

FORCE (STRENGTH)
Association of the three mechanical properties of a dough: flexibility, tenacity, elasticity. Too much force gives an excess of elasticity; a lack of force causes an excess of extensibility, a lack of elastic resistance.

GIVE STRENGTH
To provide elasticity to a hand-kneaded dough by forcing the gluten to work.

GLAZE
A mixture of ingredients with a syrupy consistency, savoury or sweet, used to coat a food in pastry, confectionery or cuisine.

GLUTEN
Protein part of flour, insoluble in water.

'GRIGNE'
The baker's signature, the result after baking of the incision made on the dough with a baker's blade before putting it into the oven. See also SCARIFICATION, SLASH/SCORE.

HOLD
Term used to characterise the maintenance of the dough or the dough piece during fermentation.

HYDRATION
Amount of water absorbed by the flour during kneading.

IMBIBE
To wet or soak a food with syrup, alcohol or liqueur in order to flavour it and make it moist.

INCORPORATE
Gradually add one ingredient to another, mixing them gently.

INFUSE
Put an aromatic ingredient into a simmering liquid and leave it to stand so that the flavour diffuses in it (e.g. tea).

JELLY
Fruit juice or purée to which a thickener (e.g. pectin or gelatine) is added for an insert or to glaze cakes or entrements.

KNEAD
To work a dough by hand or by machine so as to develop the glutinous network by cutting, stretching, folding and incorporating air to obtain a homogeneous mixture.

KNIFE TIP
Measure corresponding to what can be held on the tip of a knife (e.g. knife tip of vanilla powder).

LEAVEN
Fermentation started with a more whole grain flour (containing part of the husks) and a liquid, without adding fresh compressed yeast. The leaven is refreshed over several days to feed the micro-organisms present in the flour (lactic bacteria, wild yeast).

LEAVEN CHEF (FINAL LEAVEN)
Through a succession of refreshments, the quantity of leaven is gradually increased from a basic leaven.

LINE
To line the base and sides of a mould or other container with dough.

LUSTRE
To make a preparation shiny at the end of cooking by brushing it with syrup or butter.

MACERATE

To let a food (often fresh, dried or candied fruit) soak for some time in a liquid to flavour or soften it.

MAKE A WELL

Dry ingredients arranged in a circular shape to place other ingredients in the centre to make a dough.

MIXING

The ingredients are mixed either by hand or in the bowl at low speed. This is the first step of the kneading process.

MIXTURE

Several elements mixed together that make up the final recipe, which usually includes eggs (e.g. soufflé mixture).

MOISTEN

Humidify with liquid.

MOULD

To fill a tin or other mould with a mixture or dough before baking.

OOZE

When some of the water or butter seeps out, referring to a dough that has been over-kneaded and overheated.

OPEN/POROUS

Said of a dough with small holes on the surface.

PANIFICATION

Different stages of bread-making.

PÂTON (PIECE OF DOUGH)

Piece of uncooked dough (e.g. puff pastry, bread dough) obtained after dividing it from the main bulk of dough.

PIPE

Using a piping bag, to pipe a preparation on a baking tray at regular intervals or on a food preparation in a decorative way.

POACH

To cook in a simmering liquid.

POOLISH

A fermented liquid dough made from an equal mixture of flour and water to which fresh compressed yeast is added.

POURING WATER (COULER)

Addition of water to the dough to hydrate it.

PRE-FERMENT

First period of fermentation to create a leaven or starter to help accelerate the fermentation process.

PRE-SHAPING

The step of shaping the dough into a slightly elongated or ball shape. Preparing it for the final shaping.

PROOF (RISE)

To leave a dough (e.g. brioche, bread or croissant dough) to develop and grow in a warm and humid environment.

REFRESH

To renew and enrich the composition that nourishes and gives vitality to a leaven by adding water and flour. To avoid excess acidity, it may be necessary to add sugar in the form of honey or to provide lactic ferments in the form of yoghurt or other dairy products.

RELEASE GAS (DEGAS)

To make the carbonic gas contained in a dough escape by pressing it by hand. This process often occurs during shaping.

'RESSUAGE' (STEAM ESCAPE)

The period after the bread is baked, during which it loses some of its water in the form of steam. Final essential step of the bread-making process.

REST

The time in which dough pieces, after having been pre-shaped, are left to facilitate their final shaping.

ROLL OUT

Using a rolling pin, to roll a dough to the desired thickness and size.

RUB IN

To rub fat into flour to distribute it evenly. It has to be stopped as soon as it looks like fine breadcrumbs.

SCARIFICATION

Incisions made on the top of the dough before baking. See also 'GRIGNE', SLASH/SCORE.

SEAM

The place where the folds of the dough are joined during pre-shaping and final shaping.

SEAM SIDE DOWN (TOURNE À CLAIR)

The seam is left underneath after shaping and during second (final) proofing.

SEAM SIDE UP (TOURNE À GRIS)

Placing the dough piece with the seam on top after shaping and during the second (final) proofing.

SECOND (FINAL) PROOFING

The last stage of fermentation between shaping and baking, ideally carried out between 22 and 25°C in a sufficiently humid environment and protected from the air. See also FIRST RISING AND FERMENTATION.

SHAPE

To give the dough its final shape.

SIFT OR SIEVE

To shake or pass (press) through a sieve.

SLACK

Defect of a dough that loses its strength and relaxes.

SLASH/SCORE

To make one or more incisions with a baker's blade into the dough just before putting it into the oven to remove the carbonic gas during the baking process. See also 'GRIGNE', SCARIFICATION.

SMOOTHING

Action at the end of kneading that homogenises a dough by incorporating air and stretching it. It can be translated into a turn in a mixer to optimise the glutinous network. A firm dough will smooth out more quickly than a soft one.

SPREAD

To place a layer of cream or other filling on a preparation or food.

STALE

Said of a food such as bread that has hardened from ageing in dry air. Which is no longer fresh (bread).

STALING

Modification of the structure of the bread caused by the evaporation of water.

STEAM

Water injected into the oven, which is transformed into water vapour. It delays the formation of the bread's crust and favours its final development as well as its shine.

STENCIL

Support used to reproduce a pattern on a product before or after baking.

STICK/GLUE

To moisten a surface with water to join two doughs together. To adhere baked goods to a support (e.g. party bread) with a sticky dough.

STRETCHING AND FOLDING

Action of incorporating air into a dough during kneading.

TIGHTEN

Roll the dough on itself, exerting more or less pressure to remove as much carbon dioxide as possible during shaping.

TOLERANCE

The ability of a dough or dough piece to withstand a lack or excess of fermentation without damage.

TORN

The crust is no longer smooth or has visible cracks. It is a dough piece that has grown too much and lacks extensibility or has an excess of strength.

TRIMMINGS

Leftover pieces of dough.

TURN/MAKE TURNS/TOURAGE

Action of incorporating butter into a dough by several foldings, which results in a superposition of the two to create layers.

TWIST

To intertwine two pieces of dough together (e.g. babka) or a dough turned on itself (e.g. Sacristain).

UNMOULD

To remove a culinary preparation from the mould in which it has been placed to give it a particular shape.

WHISK

To beat with a whisk (e.g. egg whites or cream).

WORK (DOUGH)

Kneading, stirring, mixing.

YEAST/FRESH COMPRESSED YEAST

A single-celled microscopic fungus (*Saccharomyces cerevisiae*) derived from molasses, which comes from the fermentation of sugar beetroot. Mixed with water and flour, the yeast causes a fermentation that releases carbon dioxide.

YEAST-BASED STARTER

Bread-making method during kneading that introduces a small quantity of pre-fermented dough using fresh compressed yeast. Most often used in viennoiseries.

ZEST

To remove the outer, coloured skin of a citrus fruit (orange, lemon). The zest can be incorporated into a preparation to flavour it, or can be candied.

ALPHABETICAL INDEX OF RECIPES

Almond-hazelnut mini cakes 298

Apple Tatin baker's style 296

Babka 232

Bagel with salmon and seaweed
   butter 182

Baguette using fermented dough 62

Baguette using poolish 64

Batbout 166

Beaucaire bread 148

Beaujolais bread with
   Rosette de Lyon sausage 116

Bicolour folded brioche 218

Borodinsky bread 176

Bressane sugar and cream tart 242

Brioche dough 204

Brioche from Vendée 222

Buckwheat loaf 84

Caramelised pear tart with
   candied pecans 240

Challah 170

Choco-coco 258

Chocolate dome with
   a caramel centre 284

Ciabatta 160

Cider bread with apples 100

Cocktail brioche 198

Corn bread (broa) 178

Country-style bread
   (cold bulk fermentation)
   using liquid leaven 78

Crisp pineapple 278

Croissant 262

Croissant dough 206

Croque-monsieur with ham,
   buckwheat butter
   and Mornay sauce 184

Ekmek 162

Fermented dough 33

Festive rolls 90

Focaccia 158

Fougasse with olives 146

French apple turnover
   (chausson aux pommes) 304

'French tradition' baguette
   (cold bulk fermentation)
   using liquid leaven 70

'French tradition' baguette
   (cold bulk fermentation) without
   pre-fermentation 68

'French tradition' baguette
   using stiff leaven 66

Gluten-free bread with grains 118

Hand of Nice 152

Harlequin bread 110

Festive rolls 90

Kouglof 230

Kouign-amann 276

Lime-meringue mini cakes 298

Liquid leaven 35

Lodève bread 138

Milk bread baguette 74

Milk bread baguette with
   white chocolate 74

Milk bread rolls 226

Nanterre brioche 214

Natural leaven 34

Nutritional bread with mixed grains 80

Neapolitan pizza 186

Normandy surprise 250

Orange muffins 200

Pain au chocolat 266

Pain au gianduja with hazelnuts 270

Pain aux raisins 274

Pain perdu quiche Lorraine 190

Panettone 238

Parisian brioche 216

Party bread 94

Pastis landais 246

Pitta 164

Plaited wreath with mango
   and passion fruit 292

Pompe aux grattons 244

Poolish 32

Potato tourte 188

Provençal laminated bread 102

Puff pastry 212

Pulse and grain bread 104

Raspberry choux buns 254

Raspberry Danish 226

Raspberry-lemon flower 288

Rolled praline-pecan nut buns 274

Rye bread with pink pralines 114

Rye loaf 132

Sacristain 308

Saint-Genix brioche 228

Savoury tartlets with bacon and
   Béchamel sauce 184

Short rye loaves with raisins 114

Smoked duck magret sandwich
   with goat's cream cheese,
   pear and honey 194

Special bread for foie gras 108

Special buffet milk rolls 124

Spelt bread using liquid leaven 88

Spent grain muffins 200

Spinach-goat's cheese bars with
   dried apricots, pumpkin seeds
   and rosemary 122

Steamed bao buns 168

Stiff leaven 36

Stollen 236

Sübrot bread 140

T110 Stoneground bread
   using stiff leaven 76

Three Kings' brioche 248

Three Kings' cake with frangipane 300

Traditional Normandy bread 136

Vanilla flan 282

Vegetarian open sandwich with
   avocado, horseradish, celery
   and Granny Smith apple 196

Vegetarian toast with red cabbage,
   carrot, cauliflower and currants 192

Vollkornbrot 174

White baguette without
   pre-fermentation 60

Whole wheat bread using stiff
   leaven 82

Yeast-based leaven 33

ACKNOWLEDGEMENTS

The publication of this book would not have been possible without the professionalism, the close guidance and the enthusiasm of the management teams. Thanks to Leanne Mallard and the Chefs Olivier Boudot, Frédéric Hoël, Vincent Somoza and Gauthier Denis. Thanks to the photographers Delphine Constantini and Juliette Turrini, and to the stylist Mélanie Martin. Thanks to Kaye Baudinette, Isaure Cointreau and Carrie Lee Brown of the administrative team.

Special thanks to Isabelle Jeuge-Maynart and Ghislaine Stora of Larousse Editions and their entire team, Émilie Franc, Géraldine Lamy, Ewa Lochet, Laurence Alvado, Élise Lejeune, Aurore Élie, Clémentine Tanguy and Emmanuel Chaspoul.

Le Cordon Bleu and Larousse would like to thank the teams working with Le Cordon Bleu Chefs around the world, located in nearly 20 countries and more than 30 institutes, who have made this book possible thanks to their expertise and creativity.

We would like to express our gratitude to:

Le Cordon Bleu **Paris** and the Chefs Eric Briffard MOF, Patrick Caals, Williams Caussimon, Philippe Clergue, Alexandra Didier, Olivier Guyon, René Kerdranvat, Franck Poupard, Christian Moine, Guillaume Siegler, Fabrice Danniel, Laurent Bichon, Frédéric Deshayes, Corentin Droulin, Oliver Mahut, Emanuele Martelli, Soyoun Park, Frédéric Hoël and Gauthier Denis;

Le Cordon Bleu **London** and the Chefs Emil Minev, Loïc Malfait, Éric Bédiat, Jamal Bendghoughi, Anthony Boyd, David Duverger, Reginald Ioos, Colin Westal, Colin Barnett, Ian Waghorn, Julie Walsh, Graeme Bartholomew, Matthew Hodgett, Nicolas Houchet, Dominique Moudart, Jerome Pendaries, Nicholas Patterson and Stéphane Gliniewicz;

Le Cordon Bleu **Madrid** and the Chefs Erwan Poudoulec, Yann Barraud, David Millet, Carlos Collado, Diego Muñoz, Natalia Vázquez, David Vela, Clement Raybaud, Amandine Finger, Sonia Andrés and Amanda Rodrigues;

Le Cordon Bleu **Istanbul** and the Chefs Erich Ruppen, Marc Pauquet, Alican Saygı, Andreas Erni, Paul Métay and Luca De Astis;

Le Cordon Bleu **Lebanon** and the Chefs Olivier Pallut and Philippe Wavrin;

Le Cordon Bleu **Japan** and the Chef Gilles Company;

Le Cordon Bleu **Korea** and the Chefs Sebastien de Massard, Georges Ringeisen, Pierre Legendre, Alain Michel Caminade and Christophe Mazeaud;

Le Cordon Bleu **Thailand** and the Chefs Rodolphe Onno, David Gee, Patrick Fournes, Pruek Sumpantaworaboot, Frédéric Legras, Marc Razurel, Thomas Albert, Niruch Chotwatchara, Wilairat Kornnoppaklao, Rapeepat Boriboon, Atikhun Tantrakool, Damien Lien and Chan Fai;

Le Cordon Bleu **Shanghai** and the Chefs Phillippe Groult MOF, Régis Février, Jérôme Rohard, Yannick Tirbois, Benjamin Fantini, Alexander Stephan, Loic Goubiou, Arnaud Souchet and Jean-Francois Favy;

Le Cordon Bleu **Taiwan** and the Chefs Jose Cau, Sébastien Graslan and Florian Guillemenot;

Le Cordon Bleu **Malaysia** and the Chefs Stéphane Frelon, Thierry Lerallu, Sylvain Dubreau, Sarju Ranavaya and Lai Wil Son;

Le Cordon Bleu **Australia** directed by Chef Tom Milligan.

Le Cordon Bleu **New Zealand** and the Chefs Sébastien Lambert, Francis Motta, Vincent Boudet, Evan Michelson and Elaine Young;

Le Cordon Bleu **Ottawa** and the Chefs Thierry Le Baut, Aurélien Legué, Yannick Anton, Yann Le Coz and Nicolas Belorgey;

Le Cordon Bleu **Mexico** and the Chefs Aldo Omar Morales, Denis Delaval, Carlos Santos, Carlos Barrera, Edmundo Martínez and Richard Lecoq;

Le Cordon Bleu **Peru** and the Chefs Gregor Funcke, Bruno Arias, Javier Ampuero, Torsten Enders, Pierre Marchand, Luis Muñoz, Sandro Reghellin, Facundo Serra, Christophe Leroy, Angel Cárdenas, Samuel Moreau, Milenka Olarte, Daniel Punchin, Martín Tufró and Gabriela Zoia;

Le Cordon Bleu **São Paulo** and the Chefs Patrick Martin, Renata Braune, Michel Darque, Alain Uzan, Fabio Battistella, Flavio Santoro, Juliete Soulé, Salvador Ariel Lettieri and Paulo Soares;

Le Cordon Bleu **Rio de Janeiro** and the Chefs Yann Kamps, Nicolas Chevelon, Mbark Guerfi, Philippe Brye, Marcus Sales, Pablo Peralta, Philippe Lanie, Gleysa Brito, Jonas Ferreira, Thiago de Oliveira, Bruno Coutinho and Charline Fonseca;

as well as the Le Cordon Bleu **Chile** and Le Cordon Bleu **India** teams.

Le Cordon Bleu would also like to thank Electrolux for their equipment (www.electrolux.fr).

This English language edition published in 2022 by
Grub Street
4 Rainham Close
London
SW11 6SS

Email: food@grubstreet.co.uk
Web: www.grubstreet.co.uk
Twitter: @grub_street
Facebook: Grub Street Publishing

Reprinted 2022

Copyright © Larousse 2021
Copyright for the text © Le Cordon Bleu International 2021
Published originally in French as *L'École de la Boulangerie*
Cover : Clémentine Tanguy
Recipe photography and presentation:
Delphine Constantini, assisted by Pauline Guerrier
Recipe styling : Mélanie Martin
Step-by-step photographs : Juliette Turrini
Photographs on pages 7, 13, 17, 18, 19, 20 © Le Cordon Bleu
Photographs on pages 33, 34, 52, 53, 196, 204 © Shutterstock
A CIP catalogue record for this book is available from the British Library

ISBN 978-1-911667-42-1

Printed and bound by Finidr